EDUCATION

ASSUMPTIONS
VERSUS HISTORY

EDUCATION

ASSUMPTIONS VERSUS HISTORY

□ COLLECTED PAPERS □

THOMAS SOWELL

HOOVER INSTITUTION PRESS

STANFORD UNIVERSITY STANFORD, CALIFORNIA

www.hoover.org

Hoover Institution Press Publication No. 311
Hoover Institution at Leland Stanford Junior University,
Stanford, California 94305-6003

First printing 1986
23 22 21 20 19 18 17 16   13 12 11 10 9 8 7 6

Manufactured in the United States of America

The paper used in this publication meets the minimum requirements of the American National Standard for Information Sciences—Permanence of Paper for Printed Library Materials, ANSI/NISO Z39.48-1992. ⊚

Library of Congress Cataloging-in-Publication Data
Sowell, Thomas, 1930–
Education: assumptions versus history.
Includes index.
1. Afro-Americans—Education—United States—History—20th century.
2. Discrimination in education—United States—History—20th century.
3. College integration—United States—History—20th century.
I. Title.   LC2801.S64 1986   370.19'34'0973   85-18131

ISBN-13: 978-0-8179-8112-9
Cover design by P. Kelley Baker

To Lorraine

Contents

Preface

Education, in the broadest sense, is each generation's legacy to the next. How well the next generation is prepared to carry on after us determines the fate of the nation, and of the civilization it represents, far more than the officials and events that command the headlines of the day. Formal schooling is only part of that education, but for most people it is the fundamental part. How well the meaning and logic of words and numbers are mastered determines how wide the doors of the mind are opened to the world of knowledge and ideas from around the world and across the centuries. It is not simply what education teaches us directly, but how well it prepares us to learn ourselves that is the ultimate measure of its value.

How well has American education measured up to its high responsibilities in our generation? Far too many indicators say: not well enough. Declining test scores are only the most obvious symptom. It has become a cliché that "Johnny can't read." Those who teach, especially at the college level, have also learned that, too often, Johnny can't think. Sometimes he doesn't seem to understand what thinking is, but says instead, "I feel" this or that. Whether such feelings are true or false, they are not thinking.

Education has not all been failure, however. The successes must be studied if we are to have any constructive ideas as to what needs to be done. Above all, we need to look at *evidence* as to what has and has not worked. We cannot simply "feel" that this or that should be done.

The central theme of the essays that follow is that we cannot educate on the basis of assumptions, but must test even our most cherished beliefs against the facts of the past and the present. Heterogeneous as these writings are—ranging from essays to scholarly studies to testimony and interchanges with congressmen—their repeated theme is the extent to which the various "innovations" and buzzwords of education have ignored evidence on their validity or—more often—lack of validity.

The writings reprinted here span more than a decade, and some of the data go back several decades. History may have seemed "irrelevant" to some in the heady days of educational (and social) reforms in the 1960s. But now the 1960s are history, and much of the 1970s is a record of which of these sweeping ideas would stand the test of time. Many would not—and we need to understand why. Because some who wrote of education two decades ago saw no need then to look back at history, it has become especially urgent that we now look back at what they did, and at what the results were.

The range of subjects covered reaches from the elementary school to the university, and from the educational insights of Thorstein Veblen to the contemporary controversy over "affirmative action."

Not everything that we said a decade ago can be repeated unchanged without a second thought. Yet, on the whole, it has been a pleasant surprise to discover how much of it I would say again today with the same conviction, and sometimes with even more evidence. Here and there minor stylistic changes have been made for the sake of clarity, but I have avoided becoming wiser with hindsight or even changing money amounts now outdated by inflation and skyrocketing tuition costs. The reader can note the dates of these essays and multiply by two or ten, as the case may be. The principles are still the same.

A debt of gratitude is owed the various publications that have allowed me to reprint writings that first appeared in their pages. Their respective names appear with each article. I thank them all.

While my feelings are quite strong on some of the issues raised in these pages, I believe even more strongly that the process of subjecting educational questions to empirical analysis is more important than the particular conclusions reached. If I can get others to think in those terms, that will be much more important than whether or not their policy conclusions agree with mine.

Race and IQ

Despite the bitter controversies over how to explain low IQs among blacks, no one has asked whether there was really anything to explain. Is there anything peculiar about either the level or the pattern of black IQs?

Extensive IQ data are available on white ethnic minorities around the time of World War I and in the 1920s. The U.S. Army conducted massive mental tests during World War I and considerable IQ data were gathered by civilian researchers during the years of controversy preceding the passage of restrictive immigration laws in the mid-1920s. To fill in the picture since the 1920s, a nationwide sample of more than 70,000 school records was collected by a research project which I directed at the Urban Institute. The various data sources all led to the same conclusion: The European immigrant IQs then were virtually identical to black IQs now. What is encouraging is that the low-IQ immigrant groups of the past now have IQs at or above the U.S. average.

Surveys in the 1920s of mental-test studies of immigrants from southern and eastern Europe, such as Italians, Poles, and Greeks, showed their average IQs to be in the 80s, occasionally in the 70s. Data on Jewish-Americans were harder to find because the early researchers, during the controversies over immigration laws, focused on nationality groups. However, the U.S. Army tests showed soldiers of Polish and Russian ancestry scoring consistently at or near the bottom of the list of

European ethnic groups, and it was known then that half or more of the Polish and Russian immigrants were Jews. This prompted a leading psychologist of that era, Carl Brigham (originator of the College Board Scholastic Aptitude Test), to declare that the Army tests tended to "disprove the popular belief that the Jew is highly intelligent." His observation was at best premature. Over the years, more than a fourth of all American Nobel Prize winners have been Jewish, even though Jews make up only about 3 percent of the United States population.

The Germans, the Irish, and other northern and western Europeans who had immigrated generations earlier than the southern and eastern Europeans had IQs around the American national average. The IQ differences between the older and the newer immigrant groups were widely noted at the time—and almost invariably attributed to genetic differences, rather than to the great difference in their number of years of exposure to American culture.

My surveys found that the IQs of later-arriving groups—Polish, Jewish, and Italian—rose over the decades until today they equal or exceed the national average. This historical pattern is not confined to minorities of European ancestry. Chinese- and Japanese-Americans also had lower-than-average IQs in earlier surveys, but today both exceed the U.S. average in IQ as well as in other socioeconomic indicators.

The average IQs of Italian-Americans and Polish-Americans have risen by 20 to 25 points from the time of the surveys conducted around World War I to the surveys conducted in the 1970s. This rise is greater than the current IQ difference—about 15 points—between blacks and whites.

Various other studies have shown IQs in the 80s for white groups in isolated communities in the United States, in socially isolated canalboat communities in England, and among inhabitants of the Hebrides Islands off Scotland.

The IQs of Mexican-Americans and Puerto Ricans remain in the 80s, though both groups are recorded as predominantly white in the Census. Both Latin groups continue not only to suffer socioeconomic disadvantages, but, in addition, have a relatively slow assimilation of American culture. One indication of this is that most members of both groups report Spanish as the language spoken in the home—and those who do not have much higher incomes. Moreover, both groups have substantial movement back and forth between the United States and their Latin homelands. This also tends to retard assimilation of American culture.

Comparison of any minority with the national average can be very misleading unless one realizes that this "national average" is itself a product of widely varying averages for different groups, whether racial, regional, or economic. Moreover, a group that has a rise in its absolute economic condition should not be expected to raise its IQ unless it has also risen relative to the position of the general population. Black and Hispanic minorities have had no substantial relative socioeconomic rise before the present generation. It should be some time before dramatic IQ changes can be expected, but there are already some indications that this is likely. For example, black orphans raised in white families have an average IQ of 106 according to a recent study by Professor Sandra Scarr of the University of Minnesota. In addition, several all-black schools I have studied have consistently equaled or exceeded national norms on mental tests. One such school, in Washington, D.C., had an average IQ of 111 in 1939—15 years before the Supreme Court and the sociologists declared that separate schools are inherently inferior. That school happens to be within walking distance of the Supreme Court, which virtually declared its existence impossible.

Professor Arthur Jensen claims that what is peculiar about low black performance on mental tests is that it is lowest on *abstract* material— that is, material not dependent on specific cultural information and therefore not explainable by "cultural deprivation." Powerful as this evidence might seem at first, a glance at the history of other low-IQ groups at various times and places shows a very similar pattern of poor performance on the abstract portions of mental tests.

In 1917, a study of various immigrant groups on Ellis Island found that they were particularly deficient on the abstract sections of mental tests. Four years earlier, the noted psychologist H. H. Goddard had summarized his experience there by saying flatly: "These people cannot deal with abstractions." Similar results were found for white children in isolated mountain communities, among rural working-class children in England, and even among Chinese-Americans during their early years in this country. The case of Chinese-Americans is striking because recent studies show them doing their best on the abstract portions of mental tests, and they are prominent among American scientists and mathematicians.

Another way in which patterns found in black mental-test scores differ from the national average is that black females consistently score higher on mental tests than do black males. This has been true for decades and for a variety of mental tests. By contrast, among high-IQ individuals in the general population, the sexes are almost equally represented (with a slight male advantage), but the persistent female advantage among blacks becomes even more pronounced at the higher IQ levels. Studies of black children with IQs of 120 and above have found from three to five times as many girls as boys at these levels. Since blacks of both sexes have the same genetic background, there is obviously some unexplained influence here. But before trying to explain this apparent peculiarity, it should first be determined whether it really is a peculiarity of blacks.

There are few data available on differences in mental-test performance between the sexes during the immigrant era. But Jewish mental test scores during that period showed females generally scoring higher than males. In England, working-class girls score higher in mental tests than do working-class boys, even though there is no such difference among the higher classes, which have higher IQs. My own data for Mexican-Americans and Puerto Ricans—whose IQs still range in the 80s—show a small but persistent higher IQ among females.

There is considerable evidence of greater resistance to environmental influences among females from all races and classes. Infant mortality, for instance, is always higher among boys than girls in every social class and in every culture. Epidemics kill a higher proportion of men than women. The death rate among survivors of the nuclear blasts at Hiroshima and Nagasaki was higher among men than women. Indeed, this pattern extends not only across the human race but among mammals in general.

If differences in mental-test performance between the sexes are simply part of the general, biological pattern of greater female resistance to environmental forces, it has weighty implications. It is an important piece of evidence that a low IQ is an environmental phenomenon, which is why males are more affected by it. No alternative theory seems to explain why this difference should be peculiar to low-IQ groups. Among black orphans raised in white families, no such pattern was found. Higher female performance is no more racial than the average IQ level of blacks.

Those who want quick and simple answers often act as if mental tests must either measure innate intelligence or else such tests are "irrelevant" or "biased" against the culturally deprived. But if tests are viewed not as quasi-magic panaceas but as limited tools for limited purposes, they can be judged by how well or how badly they serve various specific purposes, compared to other ways of serving those same purposes. In short, tests cannot be measured against perfection but only against alternative methods of detecting talent and predicting performance in an academic setting, on the job, or elsewhere.

Every school or college has its examples of students who scored low on mental tests but performed well in their academic work, as well as examples of high-scoring students who simply never produced up to expectations, or even up to prevailing norms. This merely establishes the imperfection of mental tests. The real issue revolves around the available alternatives.

There are instances where a shrewd and involved teacher can hand-pick a talented or hard-driving student who will succeed despite low mental test scores. This only shows that a sufficiently large input of human judgment, insight, and intimate knowledge of the individual can substitute for test results and even do a better job. But the question is how rare are such Solomon-like people, and can we confidently pick them out any better than we can sort out the students? In a similar way, there may also be shrewd and insightful people who could judge guilt and innocence better than our elaborate criminal justice system. But in both instances, we rely on certain systematic processes instead because, in general, these processes produce better results than the arbitrary judgments of individuals. Moreover, in both instances the systematic procedures are supplemented by human judgments.

What about bias against the poor, the black, or the culturally-deprived? In one sense, that bias is admitted by virtually everyone, including Professor Arthur Jensen, who has conducted research to document it. A detailed study of IQ test questions would also suggest cultural bias. Tests that ask, "Who wrote 'Faust'?" or use words like "hither" and "ingenuous" are clearly testing information more readily available to middle-class children than to lower-class children.

Some critics regard class bias as invalidating IQ and other mental tests for all selection or prediction purposes. But the hard evidence shows that mental tests do predict the future academic success of students from a lower-class background as accurately as they predict the success of students from middle- or upper-class backgrounds. Although this might seem, at first, to contradict the evidence on cultural bias, in reality two very different things are measured here. The evidence on cultural bias deals with some measure of mental capacity at a given time, but prediction involves future performance over some span of years, and performance in this sense involves much more than raw brainpower: It involves self-discipline, attitudes, and a store of knowledge, among other things. To say that all measured differences besides differences in raw brainpower are "biases" is to ignore the important role of many other traits which may not be randomly distributed across social or ethnic lines. As someone has said: "Tests are not unfair. Life is unfair, and tests measure the results."

Tests are not meant to predict what would happen in a vacuum, but what will happen in the real world. The tragedy is when test results are used by people who blindly regard them as measures of innate potential, or who use them to justify providing inferior education to children from

disadvantaged backgrounds. If biased people use mental tests to discrim-
inate, eliminating the test will not eliminate the bias. Objective tests at
least put some limits on their bias. Tests can be used to open up opportunities as well as to close them. Historically, standardized tests first
opened up many of the top colleges in America to bright youngsters from
lower-class backgrounds who had previously been passed over by traditional methods of selection. Alfred Binet, the originator of intelligence
tests, used them to rescue individuals wrongly incarcerated as mentally
incompetent.

Tests are not immune to misuse any more than any of the other
features or artifacts of human life. Tests do not need to be held in superstitious awe, but neither do they need to be banned in superstitious fear.

Patterns of
Black Excellence

The history of the advancement of black Americans is almost a labora-tory study of human achievement, for it extends back to slavery and was accomplished in the face of the strongest opposition confronting any American racial or ethnic group. Yet this mass advancement is little discussed and seldom researched, except for lionizing some individuals or compiling a record of *political* milestones. But the story of how millions of people developed from the depths of slavery—acquired work skills, personal discipline, human ideals, and the whole complex of knowledge and values required for achievement in a modern society—is a largely untold story. A glance at the mass of human misery around the world shows that such development is by no means an automatic pro-cess. Yet how it was accomplished remains a matter of little concern—in contrast to the unflagging interest in social pathology.

One small, but important, part of the advancement of black Ameri-cans has been educational achievement. Here, as in other areas, the pathology is well known and extensively documented, while the healthy or outstanding functioning is almost totally unknown and unstudied. Yet educational excellence has been achieved by black Americans.[1] Current speculative discussions of the "prerequisites" for the quality education of black children proceed as if educational excellence were

Reprinted from *The Public Interest*, No. 43 (Spring 1976), pp. 26–58. ©1976 by National Affairs, Inc.

only a remote possibility, to be reached by futuristic experimental methods—indeed, as if black children were a special breed who could be "reached" only on special wavelengths. When quality education for black youngsters is seen, instead, as something that has *already* been achieved—that happened decades ago—then an attempt to understand the ingredients of such education can be made on the basis of that experience, rather than as a search for exotic revelations. The problem is to assess the nature of black excellence, its sources, and its wider implications for contemporary education and for social policy in general.

There are a number of successful black schools in various cities that exemplify this educational excellence—for the purposes of this study, six high schools and two elementary schools were selected. The high schools were chosen from a list, compiled by the late Horace Mann Bond, which shows those black high schools whose alumni included the most doctorates during the period from 1957 through 1962. The two elementary schools were added because of their outstanding performance by other indices. Some of the schools were once outstanding but are no longer, while others are currently academically successful. The schools were researched not only in terms of such "hard" data as test scores but also in terms of such intangibles as atmosphere and school/community relations, as these could be either observed or reconstructed from documents and from interviews with alumni, former teachers, and others. On the basis of this research, several questions were raised:

1. Is black "success" largely an individual phenomenon—simply "cream rising to the top"—or are the successes produced in such isolated concentrations as to suggest powerful forces at work in special social or institutional settings? Strong and clear patterns would indicate that there are things that can be done through social policy to create or enhance the prospect of individual development.

2. Does the environment for successful black education have to be a special "black" environment—either culturally, or in terms of the race of the principals and teachers, or in terms of the particular teaching methods used? Are such conventional indices as test scores more or less relevant to black students? For example, do these top black schools have average IQ scores higher than the average (around 85) for black youngsters in the country as a whole? Are their IQ scores as high as white schools of comparable performance by other criteria?

3. How much of the academic success of these schools can be explained as a product of the "middle-class" origins of their students?

Have most of the children taught in these schools been the sons and daughters of doctors and lawyers, or have they represented a cross section of the black community?

4. How important was the surrounding community as an influence on the quality of education in these schools? Did this influence come through involvement in school decision-making or through moral support in other ways?

5. How many of the assumed "prerequisites" of quality education actually existed in these outstanding schools? Did they have good facilities, an adequate budget, innovative programs, internal harmony, etc.?

6. What kind of individual was shaped by these institutions? More bluntly, was the black excellence of the past an accommodationist or "Uncle Tom" success molded by meek or cautious educators, or the product of bold individuals with high personal and racial pride?

Although these questions will be treated in the course of this article, the first question is perhaps the easiest to answer immediately. Black successes—whether measured by academic degrees or by career achievement—have not occurred randomly among the millions of black people scattered across the United States, as might be expected if individual natural ability were the major factor. On the contrary, a very few institutions in a few urban centers with a special history have produced a disproportionate share of black pioneers and high achievers. In Horace Mann Bond's study, 5 percent of the high schools produced 21 percent of the later Ph.D.'s.[2] Four of the six high schools studied here—McDonough 35 High School, in New Orleans; Frederick Douglass High School, in Baltimore; Dunbar High School, in Washington, D.C.; and Booker T. Washington High School, in Atlanta—produced a long list of black breakthroughs, including the first black state superintendent of schools (Wilson Riles, from McDonough 35), the first black Supreme Court justice (Thurgood Marshall, from Frederick Douglass), the first black general (Benjamin O. Davis, Sr., from Dunbar), the first black Cabinet member (Robert C. Weaver, from Dunbar), the discoverer of blood plasma (Charles R. Drew, from Dunbar), a Nobel Prize winner (Martin Luther King, Jr., from Booker T. Washington), and the only black senator in this century (Edward W. Brooke, from Dunbar). From the same four schools, this list can be extended down to many regional and local "firsts," as well as such national "firsts" as the first black federal judge (William H. Hastie, from Dunbar), the first black professor at a major university (Allison Davis, from Dunbar, at the University of

Chicago), and others. All of this from just four schools suggests some systematic social process at work, rather than anything as geographically random as outstanding individual ability—though these particular individuals had to be personally outstanding, besides being the products of special conditions.

The locations of these four schools are suggestive: Washington, D.C., Baltimore, New Orleans, and Atlanta. Baltimore, New Orleans, and Washington were the three largest communities of "free persons of color" in the Southern or border states in 1850.[3] None of these schools goes back to 1850, and some of them are relatively new, but the communities in which they developed had long traditions among the old families, and historical head starts have enduring consequences in many contexts. New Orleans had the most prosperous and culturally advanced community of "free persons of color" and the largest number of high schools on H. M. Bond's list—all three of which are still outstanding high schools today.

THE SCHOOLS

Atlanta: Booker T. Washington High School

When Booker T. Washington High School was founded in 1924, it was the first public high school for Negroes in Atlanta and in the state of Georgia, and one of the first in the nation. However, the black community of Atlanta had had both primary and secondary education for its children long before that. In 1869, the American Mission Society— which greatly influenced quality education for Southern blacks— established in Atlanta several "colleges" and "universities," whose initial enrollments were actually concentrated in elementary and secondary study, with only a few real college students.[4] The first principal of Booker T. Washington High School was, in fact, a man who had been in charge of the high school program at Morris Brown College.

Professor Charles Lincoln Harper was principal of Booker T. Washington for its first nineteen years, and a major influence on the shaping of the institution. By all accounts, he was a man of great courage, ability, and capacity for hard work. Far from being middle-class in origin, he came from a black farm family living on a white-owned plantation. As a child, he attended the only available school, which was ten miles away and which held classes only three months of the year. Somehow Harper managed to educate himself and go on to college, and later to do graduate work at the University of Chicago and Columbia. In addition to becoming a principal, Harper was a civil rights activist at a time when economic retaliation, lynchings, and Ku Klux Klan violence were an ever-present threat. The times were such that many blacks gave money to the NAACP *anonymously* through Harper, who bore the onus of converting it into checks to mail to the NAACP headquarters in New York. Thurgood Marshall said that Harper "stood out head and shoulders above many others because of his complete lack of fear of physical or economic repercussions."[5]

As principal, it was common for Harper to work Saturdays, and to spend part of his summer vacation taking promising students to various colleges and universities, trying to gain admission or scholarships for them. A contemporary described him as a man of "utter sincerity" who "lives on the job." Though he was a man who drove himself, with teachers he was "affable" and "easy to approach," and he showed "vast stores of patience" with students. A man of modest means—he owned only one suit—he nevertheless gave small sums of money to poor children in his school when they needed it. Yet for all his dedication to black people, he was not uncritical of black institutions. As late as 1950, he said, "There is not a single first-class, accredited college in the state for the education of Negro students."[6] To say that must have required considerable courage in Atlanta, home of Morehouse, Spelman, and Morris Brown colleges, and of many proud alumni.

The cohesion of the Atlanta black community and the political sophistication of its leaders were directly responsible for the building of Booker T. Washington High School. A public high school for Negroes was unprecedented in the state of Georgia, and some members of the all-white school board considered it an outrageous demand. Black voters enforced their demand by turning out in sufficient numbers—in the heyday of the Ku Klux Klan—repeatedly to defeat school bond issues until it was agreed that the high school would be built. But the board of education did not go one step beyond its grudging agreement: The school building alone was built on bare land. Harper conducted a fund-raising campaign in the community to provide landscaping and to build a statue of the school's namesake in front of the entrance. The board of education's tightfistedness continued to be a problem for the school for decades. Classes were large in the early years: 45 to 50 pupils per class was not unusual. The students received hand-me-down textbooks discarded after years of use in white schools.

Extra efforts by Harper, the staff, and the community overcame these obstacles. The community contributed money for the building of an athletic stadium and helped support school athletics out of their own pockets. The board of education provided no money at all for athletic uniforms, or for athletes to travel. However, the coach obtained uniforms from a local sports store and drove the teams in his own car with gas supplied free by a gas station in the community. The team ate hot dogs donated by a black drugstore. On their own time, teachers drove students to cultural events during the spring vacation. The teachers of this era also maintained closets full of secondhand clothing and shoes for needy pupils—all brought to school in paper bags so that no one would ever know whose old clothes he was wearing.

The atmosphere in the school during this era was a blend of support, encouragement, and rigid standards. One alumnus described it as a "happy school" with "hard taskmasters." Of one teacher it was said: "She did not tolerate sloppy work any more than a Marine sergeant tolerates a coward on a battlefield." Another teacher "threw homework at you like you were in college instead of the sixth grade." Those who did not learn on the first try in school stayed after school for as many days as it took to learn. Yet the students found the teachers inspiring rather than oppressive. A sense of individual worth and pride of achievement were constantly sought. "You couldn't go wrong," an alumnus said. "The teachers wouldn't let you."

Racial and political awareness were part of the early curriculum, but traditional subjects—including Latin—dominated. Racial pride was developed by example as well as by words. Many teachers refused the indignity of riding in the back of segregated buses, which meant that some of them had to walk, during years when cars were rare.

In its 50 years of existence, Booker T. Washington has had only five principals: C. L. Harper for 17 years (1924–1941), C. N. Cornell for 20 years (1941–1961), J. Y. Moreland for 8 years (1961–1969) before being promoted to area superintendent, and A. A. Dawson for four years (1968–1973), also before being promoted to area superintendent. The present principal, Robert L. Collins, Jr., assumed the post in 1973. He is a graduate of the school, and his daughter is the third generation of his family to attend.

The school has undergone some metamorphoses in the half-century of its existence. It is no longer the only black high school in the city, and the neighborhood in which it is located is run down—both factors tending to lower academic performance—while there are such offsetting tendencies as better financial support and better physical equipment. The available records do not go back far enough to permit comparison with the performance of the early years, but the current academic performance of Booker T. Washington is far from that of an elite school. On a variety of tests, its students scored significantly below the national average, and below the average of other Atlanta high schools. The demeanor of its students also seems much more in keeping with that of a typical urban ghetto school than a school with a distinguished past. Black Atlantans seemed defensive about discussing these changes, though one characterized the school as "a little thuggish" today. It is not unusual for a school which loses its monopoly of black high school students and is located in a declining neighborhood to have difficulties maintaining standards. Other schools in this study have suffered similar fates. But the justifiable pride of Atlantans in the school's past makes it difficult to trace the process by which the present uninspiring situation came about. Certainly it is clear that the present financial resources and political clout—a black superintendent of schools and a black mayor of the city—are no substitute for the human resources that enabled earlier generations to overcome heavy handicaps.

Interestingly enough, the current principal is not as defensive as other Atlantans inside or outside the school system. While he will not openly concede a decline in academic performance, he freely acknowledges a number of factors which make it a harder job to get good performance from students of a given level of ability. Chief among these is less parental support and cooperation: Parents may be more "involved" in school decisions today, but they are less cooperative than in earlier decades. In particular, parents are less willing to take the side of the schoolteacher or principal who wants an able student to take more demanding courses, instead of following the path of least resistance. Even when the parents understand the long-run educational need, they are often not willing to risk immediate problems in relations with their children. Discipline problems are also more numerous and more difficult, and there are fewer methods available for dealing with them. Corporal punishment was still permissible in the mid-1940s, when Collins was a student, but it is no longer an option. Moreover, whatever discipline is imposed is less likely to have parental support or reinforcement, and more likely to provoke parental indignation. Still, Collins works at it—twelve hours or more a day. It is too early to tell if he can turn the situation around, especially since the general problem extends well beyond Atlanta, is not limited to black schools, and has had a varying impact on schools across the country.

Atlanta: St. Paul of the Cross

A very different school in many ways is St. Paul of the Cross. Its openness was the first of many contrasts. Records just received from a testing organization were taken straight from the envelope and spread out on the table for my inspection. This confidence was based on years of solid performance.

A sample of IQ scores for this Catholic elementary school shows them consistently at or above the national norm of 100—which is to say, significantly above the national average of about 85 for other black children. This school came to our attention as a result of an earlier research project surveying IQ scores. The mean IQ of the St. Paul student body for the years surveyed (1960–1972) ranged from 99 to 107.

St. Paul is located in a middle-class black suburban area of Atlanta, but its students are drawn from various parts of the city. Of all the schools in this study for which we were able to obtain the data, St. Paul has the highest proportion of white-collar and professional occupations among its students' parents. For the period 1960–1972, 40 percent of the parents were either white-collar or professional. Our breakdown shows 33 percent white-collar and 7 percent professional, but that is based on counting schoolteachers in the white-collar category, and the two categories are presented together simply to avoid needless (and endless) debate over where the line should be drawn. For the other schools in this study, this internal breakdown is of little significance, since the two categories together usually add up to no more than 10 percent. But although St. Paul has a substantial proportion of white-collar and professional parents for a black school, it is still not predominantly middle-class in the usual sense of having children whose parents are doctors, engineers, or professors, or are in similar occupations.

Quiet, calm, and orderliness prevail in St. Paul's modern building, even during the changing of class. Yet the students do not seem either repressed or apprehensive. There was talking during the change of classes, but no yelling or fighting. Corporal punishment is one of the disciplinary options, but it is seldom used. Discipline is usually maintained through individual discussions between the teachers—half nuns and half laity—and the children. For example, a little boy who had spilled his soda in the hall without cleaning it up was told that the cleaning woman works hard to keep the school nice, and it was suggested that he apologize to her for making her job harder—but all this was done very gently without burdening him with guilt. This calm, low-key approach is made possible by small classes (about 30), small student body (about 200), and an automatically self-selective admissions process, since hard-core troublemakers are unlikely to apply for admission to a private school.

Instruction is highly individualized. Instead of the classic picture of the teacher standing in front of the class lecturing, the more usual scene in the classroom at St. Paul was a teacher very much engaged with an individual student or a small group, while the other members of the class worked intently on their respective assignments. This individualized approach extended even to allowing students to go to the library on their own. The child's self-confidence is built up in subtle ways. However, there was no single teaching method or formula imposed from above. The usual bureaucratic paperwork was absent at St. Paul. Records were well kept and complete, but not cluttered with trivia. Administrators had time to circulate through the school and get to know the students, rather than being stuck at their desks behind piles of paper. Morale is high enough to attract lay teachers at lower salaries than they receive elsewhere.

St. Paul has had only four principals in its 21-year history. Three of these were nuns of the Sisters of St. Joseph, and the other was a black layman appointed in the 1960s at the height of the emphasis on "blackness." However, the initiative for a black lay principal came from whites in the religious order, rather than from either the black community or black parents. The current principal is a white nun.

The children are encouraged to take pride in their black heritage, but the curriculum is heavily oriented toward the basics of education—especially reading. There is also religious instruction, but the student body is about 70 percent *non-Catholic*, though it was initially predominantly Catholic. Black non-Catholic students in Catholic schools are common in cities around the country, as black parents seek the education, the discipline, and the sheer physical safety which the public schools often cannot offer. The tuition is modest—about $450 per year for non-Catholics and $360 for Catholics—and the school runs a deficit, which is made up from general church funds.

Though quite different from Booker T. Washington High School in many ways, St. Paul has one problem in common with it: Some parents think that the school is *too* intellectually challenging for their children. Interestingly, this view is more common among those parents who are public school teachers.

Baltimore: Frederick Douglass High School

As of 1850, the 25,000 "free persons of color" in Baltimore were the largest number in any city in the United States, so it is not surprising that Baltimore's high school for black children was among the earliest founded, in 1892. Like many other black schools throughout the United States, Frederick Douglass High School survived for decades with inadequate financial support, was located in a succession of hand-me-down buildings that whites had discarded, and was stocked with old textbooks used for years before by white students, refinished desks from white schools, secondhand sports equipment, and so on. Douglass was for many years the only black high school in Baltimore. The school contained academic, vocational, commercial, and "general" programs. Because the surrounding communities had no high schools for Negro children, black students from outside Baltimore also came to Douglass—some legitimately, through stiff tests given to outsiders, and many others by the simple expedient of giving false addresses in Baltimore, often the addresses of relatives or friends.

Although pupils from Baltimore faced no tests for admission, there was a self-selection factor at work. Those without sufficient interest or skills would have dropped out before high school, in an era when students left school at earlier ages and when substandard students repeated grades, instead of today's automatic promotion. In short, while Frederick Douglass in its early decades was formally an all-inclusive black high school serving Baltimore and vicinity, in practice there were automatic selection factors which screened out the wholly uninterested or negative student. These were not high academic admission standards, such as elite private schools imposed, but even this wholly informal screening was sufficient to keep the school free of "discipline problems."

The teachers included men and women trained at the leading colleges and universities in the country. An alumnus of the 1930s recalls that his principal, Mason Hawkins, had a Ph.D. from the University of Pennsylvania and his teachers included individuals with degrees from Harvard, Brown, Smith, and Cornell. They were trained in content rather than educational "methods"—and their teaching styles approximated those of rigorous colleges: discussions rather than lectures, reading lists rather than day-by-day assignments, papers rather than exclusive reliance on "objective" tests. But there was no single teaching method imposed from above. The teachers often put in extra time, without pay, especially to work with promising students from low socioeconomic backgrounds.

Students were given pride in their achievements as individuals, but no mystique of "blackness." Negro history week was observed, and there was an elective course in black history, but it was not a prominent element in the curriculum. Although formal guidance counseling was minimal, the individual teachers actively counseled students on their own. But the teachers' concern for the students took the form of getting them to meet standards, not of bringing the standards down to their level of preparation. In reminiscing about her 40 years as teacher and administrator at Douglass High School, former principal Mrs. Edna Campbell said of her students, "Even though you are pushing for them, and dying inside for them, you have to let them know that they have to produce."

The interest of the teachers in the students was reciprocated by the interest of the parents in supporting the teachers and the school. "The school could do no wrong" in the eyes of the parents, according to alumni. Parental involvement was of this supportive nature rather than an actual involvement in school decision-making. "Parent power" or "community control" were unheard-of concepts then.

Most of the whites in Baltimore were relatively unaware of Frederick Douglass High School—they did not know or care whether it was good or bad—and this indifference extended to the board of education as well. Under the dual school system in the era of racial segregation, the lack of interest in black schools by the all-white board of education allowed wide latitude to black subordinates to run the black part of the system, so long as no problems became visible. "Benign neglect" is perhaps the most charitable characterization of this policy. In short, Douglass High School's achievements were not a result of white input, at either the administrative or the teaching levels.

Color differences within the black community were significant in the school as well. Light-skinned alumni tended to minimize this factor, but darker-skinned alumni sometimes still carry bitter memories. One man, now an official of the Baltimore school system, recalls being maneuvered out of the honor of being class valedictorian at Douglass, in favor of a lighter-skinned student from a socially prominent family.

Like several of the schools studied, Douglass' days of glory are past. A decline began with the building of other black high schools in Baltimore and became precipitous in the wake of the Supreme Court's desegregation decision in 1954. While the mean IQ in the academic program at Douglass ranged from 93 to 105 for the 20 years before the 1954 decision, it fell immediately below 90 in 1955 and remained in the 80s from February 1955 through February 1958. This reflected the exodus of more capable students to white high schools. A concerted effort was made to reverse this trend in the 1960s, especially from 1965 to 1973, when Mrs. Edna Campbell was the principal. Our sampling of test scores for this period indicates some success. IQ scores went back into the 90s from 1965 through 1971, the last year for which we have a sample of 20 or more scores.

Today, in its decline, Frederick Douglass High School has better physical facilities, some integration of the faculty, and more parental input into the decision-making process, as well as a Baltimore school system dominated by black officials. There is little evidence that this compensates for what it has lost. Indeed, some knowledgeable people in Baltimore believe that it is precisely the growth of "student rights" and "parent power" that is responsible for declining discipline in schools. There certainly was evidence of such discipline problems at Douglass. A researcher collecting data for this study had her purse snatched in the school building itself, and some weeks earlier there had been a shooting there. This was a far cry from the school that had once been second in the nation in black Ph.D.'s among its alumni, and the only black school to produce a Supreme Court justice.

New Orleans: McDonough 35 High School

New Orleans has had a unique role in the history of American race relations, and so it is not surprising that the city has had not one, but three outstanding black high schools on Horace Mann Bond's list—and all three are *still* outstanding. Long before the Civil War, the free Negro community in New Orleans had rights, privileges, and economic success well in advance of its counterpart in any other American city. By 1850, "free persons of color" owned $13 million worth of taxable property in New Orleans, a remarkable sum at nineteenth-century price levels and a significant portion of the total taxable property in the city.

The pattern of race relations in New Orleans had been established before the city became a part of the United States as a result of the Louisiana Purchase in 1803, and it was—and largely remained—the pattern common to Latin America rather than the pattern of Anglo-Saxon slave societies in the Western Hemisphere. For example, the "free colored" population of Latin America had a far wider range of occupations open to them than did American Negroes, and they often dominated the skilled artisan trades in Latin countries—simply because there were just not enough whites. The French, Spanish, and Portuguese who colonized the Western Hemisphere did not bring women, families, or a working class with them to the extent that the Anglo-Saxons did, and so were both economically and sexually more dependent upon the indigenous populations and those of African descent. This dependency led to a greater relaxation of racism in practice, even though the Latins subscribed in principle to the same "white supremacy" doctrines as the Anglo-Saxons.

New Orleans, as a former French (and Spanish) colony, reflected the Latin pattern in the skills of "free persons of color," few of whom were laborers, many of whom were small businessmen, some of whom were wealthy, and a few of whom were even commercial slave owners. New Orleans also reflected the multicolored caste system characteristic of

Latin American countries in contrast to the stark black/white dichotomy of Anglo-Saxon nations. The celebrated "quadroon balls" of antebellum New Orleans were but one aspect of this system.

Segments of the "free colored" population of New Orleans had been giving their children quality education (sometimes including college abroad) for more than a century before the first black public high school was founded in 1916. This school—McDonough 35 High School—was for many years the only public high school for New Orleans Negroes, but it was preceded by, and accompanied by, private black secondary schools, including Catholic schools—again, reflecting the Latin influence. Two Catholic high schools—St. Augustine and Xavier Preparatory—and McDonough 35 make up today's three outstanding black high schools in New Orleans.

So many schools in New Orleans are named for philanthropist John McDonough that numbers are added to distinguish them. McDonough 35 High School is outstanding among these. It has had only four principals in its nearly 50-year history. The first principal, John W. Hoffman, was a well-traveled man with a cosmopolitan outlook. The second principal, Lucien V. Alexis, was a graduate of Phillips Exeter Academy (1914) and Harvard (1918), and was an "iron-fisted" ex–army officer. The third principal, Mack J. Spears, was a more diplomatic man with considerable political savvy—which proved to be decisive in saving the school from the physical or educational extinction which came upon other outstanding black high schools during the time when "integration" was regarded as an educational panacea. The current principal, Clifford J. Francis, is a quiet, thoughtful man who accepts overtime work as a normal part of his job. He runs a smoothly operating, high-quality school which, for the first time, has a good physical plant and a good, racially integrated staff.

When McDonough 35 was opened in 1917, it was housed in a building built in the 1880s. As late as 1954, this building was heated by potbellied stoves, with the students keeping the fires going by carrying coal. When a hurricane passed through New Orleans in 1965, the ancient building simply collapsed. At this point, the all-white board of education decided to disband the school and assign its pupils to other schools in New Orleans. But, unlike other outstanding black schools which were destroyed by white officials who were unaware of their quality, McDonough 35 fought back. Principal Mack Spears organized community support to save the school, lobbied congressmen, and ultimately obtained the use of an abandoned federal courthouse to house the institution until a new school building could be constructed.

The institution he saved was one which was an inspiration to its students, as well as a leading producer of later black Ph.D.'s. By chance, I happened to encounter Wilson Riles, the California state superintendent of schools, the day after my first visit to McDonough 35, and the very mention of the school's name caused his face to light up and provoked a flood of warm memories of his student days there. He credited the school with taking him and other black youngsters from an economically and culturally limited background, and giving them both the education and the self-confidence to advance in later life. Mack Spears, a student and later a principal at McDonough 35, told a very similar story. Spears was the son of a poor farmer, but he remembers vividly how his teachers promoted the idea of the worth of the individual—how they always called the boys "Mister" and the girls "Miss," emotionally important titles denied even adult Negroes throughout the South at that time.

Although the school had few counselors in its earlier days, the teachers acted as counselors, and as instructors and role models. But with all the psychological strengthening that was an integral part of the educational process, there was no parochial "blackness" in McDonough 35. Cultural expansion was the goal. Questions about "black English" in McDonough 35 brought a "hell no " from Spears. The current principal more gently observed that this was a recent and minor matter, of interest to only a few young white teachers.

Like some other outstanding black high schools, McDonough 35 suffered a decline in quality as other black high schools were built in the same city and as neighborhood changes left it in a less desirable part of town. At one point in the 1950s, there was a controversy over the right of its teachers to carry guns for self-protection. The academic deterioration of this period matched the deterioration in social conditions and morale. The median IQ of the school population in the mid-1950s was in the low 80s; but, under the new policies introduced when Spears became principal in 1954, IQs began to rise, to a peak of 99 in the 1965–66 school year, and they have remained in the mid-to-upper 90s since then. Unfortunately, there are no IQ data available for the earlier period of the school's academic excellence—the period during which the Ph.D.'s studied by H. M. Bond would have been high school students there. The present IQ scores—at about the national average and therefore significantly above the average for black students—must be interpreted in the context of a city where private Catholic schools attract large numbers of both white and black students with higher educational aspirations and achievements. McDonough 35 median IQs have consistently been above the city-wide average for public school students—white and black—for the past decade.

The policies introduced in the mid-1950s which reversed

McDonough 35's decline included keeping neighborhood derelicts out of the school, ability-grouping or "tracking" to deal with the variation in student capabilities and interests, and a widening of school boundaries beyond the immediate neighborhood. Spears, a former football player, was perfect for keeping the derelicts out of the school—for even though he spoke softly, the big stick was implicit in his very presence. Instead of explaining away low test scores by "cultural deprivation" or dismissing them as "irrelevant," Spears used those scores to demonstrate to parents and to the black community the full depth of the problem and to get support for educational change, including ability-grouping to deal with the wide range of scores and a self-selection admissions system to supersede neighborhood boundaries.

All was not harmony in McDonough 35, even in its heyday. The internal class differences within the black community—which revolved around color differences going back to the era of slavery—were more pronounced in New Orleans, just as intragroup color differences in Latin cultures generally exceeded those in Anglo-Saxon cultures. However, light-skinned Negroes were *not* noticeably overrepresented among students, faculty, or administrators. And darker Negroes, such as Riles and Spears, were nevertheless accepted by the school even though the larger community was divided socially along internal color lines.

Whites were, at best, a negligible factor in the development of McDonough 35 High School. According to former principal Spears, the all-white board of education "did not give a damn—and we took *advantage* of that to build academic excellence."

New Orleans: St. Augustine High School

St. Augustine High School is a school for boys founded in 1951 by the Josephite Fathers. Its first principal was a young white priest, Father Matthew O'Rourke, with neither experience nor training in education. Keenly aware of these gaps in his preparation, Father O'Rourke began a crash program, taking education courses at a local university—but found them "empty" and "a big zero." He and the other similarly inexperienced young priests and laymen on the faculty proceeded by trial and error—and dedication.

One of the first issues to arise came with the introduction of corporal punishment. In an era of growing racial sensitivities, some white priests outside the school were disturbed by the thought of white men (even in priestly garb) beating black youths. But Father O'Rourke and the other priests felt no guilt—the Josephite Order had been founded in the nineteenth century to serve blacks—and viewed the problem in purely pragmatic terms. Their options were to allow disruptive students to undo their work with others, to save the school by expelling such students, or to attempt to save both the students and the school by an occasional paddling. They elected to try the last. Despite the misgivings of some outside priests, the black parents backed the teachers completely, and the system worked. It has remained a feature of St. Augustine to the present—strongly believed in, but infrequently used. The student/ teacher relations in St. Augustine are more relaxed and warm than in most public schools, where corporal punishment is usually forbidden by law.

The school was neither wedded to tradition nor seeking to be in the vanguard of "innovation." It did whatever worked educationally, and abandoned what did not. The wide range of student preparation led to ability-grouping, and to the jettisoning of the traditional English courses for the least-prepared students in favor of an emphasis on reading, at virtually any cost. *Time* magazine was found to be an effective vocabulary tool for many students, and hundreds of St. Augustine students subscribed, at the urging of their teachers. A special summer course featured speed reading, with assignments of a novel per week, including reports.

The teachers' inexperience and lack of familiarity with educational fashions paid off handsomely. The first Southern Negro student to win a National Merit Scholarship came from St. Augustine. So did the first Presidential Scholar of any race from the state of Louisiana in 1964, and ten years later, St. Augustine had produced 20 percent of all the Presidential Scholars in the history of the state. In the National Achievement Scholarship program for black students, St. Augustine has produced more finalists and semifinalists than any other school in the nation. In 1964—*before* the big college drive to enroll black students—St. Augustine's students won more than $100,000 in college scholarship money. This is all the more remarkable since the total enrollment is less than 700.

The pattern of IQ scores over time at St. Augustine shows a generally upward movement, beginning at a level very similar to the average for black students and reaching a level at or above that for the United States population as a whole. In its early years, St. Augustine had mean IQs as low as 86, but during the period from 1964 through 1972, IQs were just over 100 for every year except one.

The reasons for the rising IQs at St. Augustine cannot be easily determined. Father O'Rourke is reluctant to claim credit for the school itself. But in recalling his years as principal, he cited a number of instances where students with potential, but without cultural development, had improved after extra attention—improved not only on achievement tests, but also on IQ tests, "though that's not supposed to happen." Test scores were never used as a rigid admissions cutoff at St. Augustine. Our sample includes individual IQs in the 60s, as well as many others more than twice that high.

Father O'Rourke was succeeded as principal in 1960 by Father Robert H. Grant, one of the other young priests teaching at St. Augustine. Where Father O'Rourke had been universally liked, Father Grant tended to have both enthusiasts and detractors. Under Father Grant's administration, a heavy emphasis on academic achievement and tighter discipline brought Merit and Presidential scholars, school-wide IQs averaging over 100—and murmurs of discontent in the community. The discontented usually were *not* parents of students at St. Augustine. The rise of racial militancy raised questions about a white principal of a black school and brought demands for a "black" orientation of the curriculum. In retrospect, Father Grant describes his administration as "benignly autocratic" and himself as "blunt." "We didn't spend much time hassling, debating, or dialoguing." The teachers and principal had their meetings, but once an agreement had been reached, they did not "waste time" with "parent power" or "student rights," but relied instead on parental trust and on student achievement as a vindication of that trust. He met the demands for "black studies" by establishing an elective course on the subject— meeting at a time that was otherwise available as a study period. Only six students enrolled, out of more than 600 students in the school.

Although Father Grant fought a legal battle to integrate Louisiana's high school athletics, and was sympathetic to the civil rights movement in general, he was also opposed to the introduction of "extraneous elements, issues, and concerns" into the school itself. Keenly aware of both the students' cultural disadvantages and the need to overcome them, he felt that "we absolutely could not do the two things well," though both were important. It was a matter of time and priorities: "Don't consume my time with extraneous issues and then expect me to have enough time left over to dedicate myself to a strong academic program where I will turn out strong, intelligent, competent kids."

In 1969, Father Grant accepted a post in Switzerland and was replaced by a black lay principal—just what the doctor ordered politically, but apparently not administratively or educationally. He was replaced after a few years. The current principal, Leo A. Johnson, is also a black layman and, in addition, the first alumnus of St. Augustine to head the school. His term began in 1974, and it is too early to assess his impact on the school.

Teaching methods at St. Augustine are traditional, and both its academic and behavioral standards are strict. Students must wear "a dress shirt with a collar," and the shirttail "must be worn inside the trousers at all times." The general atmosphere at St. Augustine is relaxed, but serious. Its halls are quiet, and its students are attentive and engrossed in what they are doing, as are the teachers. Yet it is not a wholly bookish place. Its athletic teams have won many local championships in football, basketball, and baseball. At lunchtime, the students were as noisy as any other high school students, and the boys in the lunchroom were visibly appreciative of a shapely young woman who was part of our research team. One of the real accomplishments of St. Augustine has been to give education a masculine image so that black youths need not consider intellectual activity "sissy."

The achievements of St. Augustine cannot be explained by the usual dismissal phrase, "middle-class." Although it is a private school, its modest tuition ($645 per year) does not require affluence, and about 15 percent of the students pay no tuition at all, while others pay reduced tuition because of their parents' low income. The school runs a chronic deficit despite the low pay scale for those teachers who are clergy. Despite the color/caste history of New Orleans, the students at St. Augustine are physically indistinguishable from the students at any other black high school. Their demeanor and their work are *very* different, but their skin color is the same.

Our statistical tabulation of parents' occupations covers only the years from 1951 through 1957, but in each year during that span more than half of the known parental occupations were in the "unskilled and semiskilled" category, and the parents with professional or white-collar jobs added up to less than one-tenth as many. While the students are seldom from the lowest poverty level, there is only occasionally the son of a doctor. Many come from families where the father is a bricklayer, carpenter, or other artisan, and has only a modest educational background. They are not middle-class in income, career security, culture, or lifestyle. Many are ambitious for their children and send them to school with attitudes that allow the education to "take." But such attitudes are not a monopoly of the middle class, despite sociological stereotyping. If such attitudes were in fact a monopoly of the middle class, neither blacks nor other ethnic minorities could ever have risen.

New Orleans: Xavier Prep

Xavier Prep is an all-girl Catholic school run by the Sisters of the Blessed Sacrament. It was founded in 1915 and was coeducational until 1970. It had eighteen graduating seniors in 1918, and the enrollment increased to about 500 in 1940. It has about 350 students today, after the male students were phased out in the 1960s. Even when it was coeducational, it had more female than male students. One of the reasons for the difficulty of maintaining a masculine image for education among black youths is that throughout the country and down through the years, Negro girls have outperformed Negro boys by a wide margin on grades, tests, and virtually every measure of intellectual ability. Studies of high-IQ black students have consistently found the girls outnumbering the boys by from two-to-one to more than five-to-one.

Over 90 percent of the graduates of Xavier Prep go on to college. Until the 1960s, almost all went to Xavier University in New Orleans, run by the same order of nuns. Today about 60 percent of the graduates go to either Xavier University, Loyola, or Tulane—all in New Orleans—even though their academic preparation would make them eligible for many other colleges and universities in other parts of the country.

IQ scores and other test scores vary considerably among Xavier students, but the average score of the school as a whole has fluctuated around the national norm—which is to say, higher than for Southerners of either race, higher than for black students nationally, and considerably higher than for black Southern children from the modest socioeconomic backgrounds of Xavier students. The mean IQ of the school as a whole ranged from 96 to 108 during the 1960s, and has been at or above 100 for each year surveyed during the 1970s.

In the earliest years of Xavier Prep, many of the students were from Creole backgrounds. But today the colors and conditions of the students represent a cross section of black America. Over the years about 40 to 50 percent of the students have come from low-income families, many entering with serious educational deficiencies, requiring remedial work. More than 60 percent of its students are eligible for the free lunch program. While Xavier is a private school, its tuition is only $35 a month. Our statistical tabulation of parental occupation shows that from one-half to four-fifths of the parents' occupations have been in the "unskilled or semiskilled" category, in the period from 1949 to 1972 for which we have data. Parents in professional or white-collar occupations put together added up to only 7 percent of the total during that same span. The principal, Sister Anne Louise Bechtold, recalls "one dentist" this year and "one lawyer last year" among the parents, but no engineers or college professors, and a small percentage of public school teachers— and otherwise parents of very modest socioeconomic backgrounds, with some of the mothers being domestics or store clerks and the fathers in similar occupations.

Unlike middle-class parents, the parents of Xavier students tend to be very cautious about their input into the school—even when invited and encouraged to participate. They seek discipline and an emphasis on basic education and seem particularly pleased when their children's teachers are nuns. The caution of the parents is also a factor in the narrow range of colleges which most Xavier graduates attend. Ivy League and other Northern colleges attempt to recruit Xavier graduates, but the parents are reluctant to have their daughters exposed to strange influences in faraway colleges. In some cases, the teachers or counselors fight a losing battle to get a promising student to accept an offer from a top-level college or university. This is not all the result of the limited cultural horizons of the parents. Economic pressures make it difficult for many of the parents to finance the travel involved, much less the living expenses, even if the student has a full scholarship.

Classes at Xavier Prep in the past tended to be large (35–40 students), but since boys were phased out in the mid-1960s, classes have been reduced to about 25 to 30 students. These students are "tracked" by academic ability. The less prepared students are given intensive and imaginative remedial work. Unlike St. Augustine, Xavier Prep has neither corporal punishment nor an emphasis on athletics. But the general atmosphere—described by one nun as "reserved but informal"—is very similar. Nuns and lay teachers are about equally represented on its faculty, and its principal is a nun. It is a quiet, low-key place where the changing of classes produces swarms of black teenagers in the halls, but little noise. The classes in session have students and teachers absorbed in mutual endeavor, but with a certain relaxed geniality. Discussions with Xavier teachers indicate that they put much thought and work, on their own time, into the preparation of their classes. Although subject to the guidance of superiors both inside and outside the school, the teachers seem to have more scope for personal initiative than do public school teachers. Among alumni of the school, their teachers' personal interest in them is a factor often cited as having given them the inspiration and self-confidence that came before the educational achievements themselves.

Brooklyn: P.S. 91

Perhaps the most remarkable of all the schools in this study is P.S. 91, an elementary school in a rundown neighborhood of Brooklyn. Here, where over half the students are eligible for the free lunch program and a significant proportion are on welfare, *every grade approximates or (usually) exceeds the national norms* in reading comprehension. A tour of the ancient school building is even more surprising than these statistics.

Here, in class after class, the students—overwhelmingly ghetto young-sters—work quietly, intently, and pleasantly under the direction of ob-viously intelligent and interested teachers and teacher aides who repre-sent a wide range of ages, races, and personal styles. The sheer silence of the school was eerie to one who had attended elementary school in central Harlem and had recently researched similar schools elsewhere.

In class after class, discussion periods brought lively exchanges between teachers and pupils—the children speaking in complete sen-tences, grammatically and directly to the point, and returning to the subject if the teacher's response was not clear or satisfactory to them. To see this happening with children identical in appearance and dress to those who are dull, withdrawn, or hostile in untold other ghetto schools can only be described as an emotional experience. After leaving one classroom where a lively discussion was still in progress, the principal said matter-of-factly: "That was our slow learners' class. They are doing all right, but I think there is need for improvement."

That was the remarkable attitude of a remarkable man. Martin Shor, the principal, is white and was principal of the school when the school was white. As the Crown Heights section of Brooklyn changed its racial composition and the socioeconomic level fell, the school population reflected these changes. Now there are only a few white or oriental children in P.S. 91. But unlike other schools whose academic standards have fallen along with the socioeconomic level of their neighborhoods, P.S. 91 has had a *rising* proportion of its students scoring above the national norms in reading. In 1971, just over 49 percent of its students exceeded the national norms, in 1972 it was 52 percent, in 1973 it was 54 percent, and in 1974 it was 57 percent. To put these numbers in perspec-tive, *none* of the 12 other schools in its district had even 40 percent of their students above the national norms, even though some of these other schools are in higher-socioeconomic-status neighborhoods. The highest percentage in the whole borough of Brooklyn—with more than 600 elementary schools—is 60 percent above the national norms.

The handicaps under which P.S. 91 operates include a very high turnover rate, characteristic of ghetto schools. There was a 34 percent turnover in just three months. This means that the school loses many of the good students it has prepared in the early grades and receives from other ghetto schools badly prepared youngsters whom it must re-educate in later grades. This is apparently a factor in the pattern of scores whereby the lower grades at P.S. 91 exceed the national norms by wider margins than the higher grades (see the table below). However, it should be noted that other black schools in other cities also tend to score relatively higher in their earlier grades—sometimes even exceeding the

READING SCORES, P.S. 91, BROOKLYN

Grade	National Norms	P.S. 91 Median
2	2.7	3.5
3	3.7	4.1
4	4.7	4.5
5	5.7	6.3
6	6.7	6.7

SOURCE: Compilation from District 17, Brooklyn.

national norms overall. How much of the later disastrous decline in scores in ghetto schools is the result of high turnover and how much is the result of the negative effects of the school itself, or the development of negative attitudes by the students toward the school (or life), is a subject which has scarcely been explored. Indeed, the phenomenon itself has hardly been recognized. It is well known that black children tend to fall progressively farther behind as they go through school systems, but just how well they do in the first or second grades—even in school systems with dreadful overall results, such as in Chicago or Philadelphia—is a largely unrecognized phenomenon.

Martin Shor puts heavy emphasis on teaching the P.S. 91 pupils to read well in the first grade. Indeed, half of the P.S. 91 children can read when they have finished kindergarten. While the school bears the imprint of his own special methods and approach, Shor argues that none of these methods would work unless the students first knew how to read. A disproportionate amount of the school's money and teaching talent goes into preparing the first graders to read, write, and express themselves orally.

The higher grades use a variety of self-teaching materials, including programmed books, teaching machines, and tape recorders. Many of these materials are *a year or more ahead* of the "age" or "grade" level of the students using them. Students are separated into small groups by ability within each class as well as between classes, and each group has its own assignment. "This may look like an 'open' classroom," Shor said. "But it's not. Every group is working on its own *assigned* task." When asked if this "tracking" system did not originally lead to certain racial imbalances in classes within the school, Shor pointed out that initially disadvantaged students advanced enough to produce more racial balance eventually.

"But if other schools followed your system," I asked, "wouldn't that mean that, in the interim, a multiracial school would have the appearance of internal segregation, which would lead to a lot of political flack?" "Then you just take the flack," he said. He had taken flack during the period of racial transition at P.S. 91, but the educational results silenced critics and gained parental support. How many other white principals in a ghetto neighborhood have that kind of courage is another question. A study of unusually successful ghetto schools by the Office of Educational Personnel Review in New York concluded that "the quality and attitude of the administrator seemed to be the only real difference" between these schools and less successful ones. A few hours with Martin Shor reinforce that conclusion. He is a quietly confident, forceful man, with an incisive mind, much experience and resourcefulness, and the implicit faith that the job *can* be done. His talk is free of the educational clichés and public relations smoothness normally associated with school administrators. He comes to the ghetto to do a job, does it well, and then goes home elsewhere—contrary to the emotional cries about the need for indigenous community leadership in the school.

P.S. 91 does not teach "black English" or black studies, though its many books and other materials do include a few items of special interest to black children. The school tries to *expand* the students' cultural horizons: Several hundred of these elementary school pupils study foreign languages. P.S. 91 students also read excerpts from translations of the classics of world literature, such as Cervantes or Aesop. They are constantly exposed to material that allows their minds to see beyond the drab school building, the decaying tenements, and the area that caused a friend to tell me, "You sure are brave to park a car in *that* neighborhood." The usual "middle-class" label used to dismiss black educational achievements is only a bad joke when applied to P.S. 91.

Washington, D.C.: Dunbar High School

The oldest and most illustrious of the black elite schools was Dunbar High School in Washington, D.C., during the period from 1870 to 1955. Over that 85-year span, most of its graduates went to college—rare for whites or blacks, then—and many went on to outstanding academic achievements and distinguished careers. Back at the turn of the century, Dunbar was sending students to Harvard, and in the period 1918-1923, Dunbar graduates earned fifteen degrees from Ivy League colleges, and ten degrees from Amherst, Williams, and Wesleyan. During World War II, Dunbar alumni in the Army included "nearly a score of Majors, nine Colonels and Lieutenant Colonels, and a Brigadier General"—a substantial percentage of all high-ranking black officers at that time.

Dunbar was the first black public high school in the United States.

Its unique position allowed it to select some of the best of the educated blacks in the country for its teachers and principals. Of its first nine principals, seven had degrees from either Harvard, Oberlin, Dartmouth, or Amherst. Of the remaining two, one was educated in Glasgow and London, and the other was a Phi Beta Kappa from Western Reserve. The principals included the first black woman in the United States to receive a college degree (from Oberlin, 1862) and the first black man to graduate from Harvard (in 1870). Clearly they were remarkable people even to attempt what they did, when they did.

So too was the man who spearheaded the drive that led to the founding of the school which ultimately became Dunbar High School (after several changes of name and location). William Syphax was a "free person of color," born in 1826 and active in civic affairs and civil rights issues, "fearing no man regardless of position or color." As a trustee of the Negro schools in Washington, Syphax preferred to hire black teachers, but only when their qualifications were equal to those of white teachers—for the trustees "deem it a violation of our official oath to employ inferior teachers when superior teachers can be had for the same money." He addressed demands not only to whites in power, but also to his own people, exhorting them to send their children to school with discipline, respect, and a willingness to work hard. These became hallmarks of Dunbar High School, as did the academic success that flowed from them. As early as 1899, Dunbar scored higher in city-wide tests than any of the white high schools in the District of Columbia. Down through the years its attendance records were generally better than those of the white high schools, and its rate of tardiness was lower. Dunbar meant business.

The teachers at Dunbar usually held degrees in liberal arts from top institutions, not education degrees from teachers colleges. The scarcity of alternative occupations for educated Negroes allowed Dunbar to pick the cream of the crop. As late as the 1920s, its staff included individuals with Ph.D.'s from leading universities, including the distinguished historian Carter G. Woodson. The teachers were as dedicated and demanding as they were qualified. Extracurricular tutoring, securing scholarships for graduating seniors, getting parents of promising students to keep them in school despite desperate family finances—all these were part of the voluntary workload of Dunbar teachers and principals. In a city that remained racially segregated into the 1950s, there were also constant efforts to bring cultural attractions to the school that were unavailable to black youngsters in theaters, concert halls, or other cultural and entertainment centers. While individual pride and racial awareness were part of the atmosphere at Dunbar High School, cultural expansion was the educational goal. Latin was taught throughout the period from 1870 to 1955, and in the early decades, Greek was taught as well. In the 1940s, Dunbar fought a losing battle with the superintendent of schools to have calculus added.

Throughout the 85-year period of its academic ascendancy, Dunbar never had adequate financial support. At its founding it was allowed to draw only on taxes collected in the black community. While this arrangement eventually gave way to drawing on the general taxes of the city, so too did the separate administration of Negro schools by black trustees give way to city-wide administration by an all-white board of education, which never provided equal support. Large classes were the norm from the 1870s, when there were more than 40 students per teacher, to the 1950s, when Dunbar's student/teacher ratio exceeded that of any white high school in Washington. The school was in operation more than 40 years before it had a lunchroom, which then was so small that many children had to eat lunch out on the street. Blackboards were "cracked with confusing lines resembling a map." It was 1950 before the school had a public address system.

The social origins of Dunbar students were diverse. For three decades, Dunbar was the only black high school in Washington, D.C., and for three more decades it was the only black academic high school in the city, so it drew on a broad cross section of students. As late as 1948, one-third of all black high school students in Washington were enrolled in Dunbar. Nevertheless, the "middle-class" label has been stuck on Dunbar, and no amount of facts dispels it. According to a *Washington Post* reporter, the one word "Dunbar" will divide any room of middle-aged black Washingtonians into "outraged warring factions." Some are fiercely loyal to Dunbar as a monumental educational achievement, while others see it as snobbish elitism for middle-class mulattoes who either excluded poor blacks from the school or ostracized them if they attended. A look through old yearbook photographs will disprove the myth of mulatto predominance, and our statistical tabulation of parental occupations from 1938 through 1955 shows 38 percent of known parental occupations to have been "unskilled and semiskilled" (including many maids), while "white-collar" and "professional" occupations together added up to only 17 percent.

Unquestionably, almost all middle-class Negroes in Washington sent their children to Dunbar during the period from 1870 to 1955, and for historical reasons, middle-class Negroes tended to be lighter in color—but that is very different from saying that most Dunbar students were either middle class or mulattoes. Former Dunbar principal Charles Lofton calls it all "an old wives' tale." "If we took only the children of doctors and lawyers," he asked, "how could we have had 1,400 black students at one time?" Yet the persistence and power of the myth suggests something of the depth of the hurt felt by those who either did not go to Dunbar because of fear of social rejection or did go and did not feel accepted. To this day, one Dunbar alumna has a policy at social gatherings in Washington of never mentioning where she went to high school.

Dunbar alumni claim that the school was at its academic peak in the 1920s or earlier—in particular that the "M Street School," which was the name prior to 1917, was superior to "Dunbar," which was the name attached to the building constructed that year. There is some inconclusive evidence—graduation years of distinguished alumni, numbers of graduates attending top colleges, etc.—supporting this view, but no standard tests were given in both eras that would permit a direct comparison. The earliest IQ records available are for 1938, so that our data cover only its supposedly declining years. Nonetheless, for this eighteen-year period, the average IQ in the school was below 100 for only one year (when it was 99) and was as high as 111 (in 1939).

There is general agreement that Dunbar declined precipitously and catastrophically after the school reorganization of 1955 made it a neighborhood school for the first time in its history. Its neighborhood was one of the worst in the city, and as its new students entered, advanced elective courses gave way to remedial math and English, and its quiet building now became the scene of "discipline problems." The past excellence of the school had caused many teachers to stay on past the retirement age, and now many of them began to retire at once. By the 1960s a newspaper story on the school was titled "Black Elite Institution Now Typical Slum Facility." It remains a typical slum school today—its past recalled only in the heat of a bitter controversy over the tearing down of the old building standing alongside a modern school bearing the same name. One of several city councilmen who favored demolition said that Dunbar "represents a symbol of elitism among blacks that should never appear again." But a Dunbar alumnus wondered if the real problem was that the new school fears the "silent competition" of the old building and the achievement it represents.

SOME CONCLUSIONS

Contrary to current fashions, it has not been necessary (or usual) to have a special method of teaching to "reach" black children in order to have high-quality education. Teaching methods used in the schools studied here have varied enormously from school to school, and even in particular schools the variation from teacher to teacher has been so great as to defy general characterization. Everything from religious principles to corporal punishment has been used to maintain order. The buildings have ranged from the most dilapidated wrecks to a sparkling plate-glass palace. The teachers and principals have been black and white, religious and secular, authoritarian and gentle, community leaders and visitors from another social world. Some have had a warm "human touch" and others would have failed Public Relations I. Their only common denominators have been dedication to education, commitment to the children, and faith in what it was possible to achieve. The institutional common denominators of these schools are a larger and more complex question.

In general, test scores have been significantly higher at these schools than at black schools in general and have been highest at the most elite and oldest—Dunbar High School in Washington, in its academic heyday. Yet all of the schools studied have included students well below national test score norms. In short, test scores are not "irrelevant" for black achievement, but neither are they the be-all and end-all. One of the tragedies in the wake of the Jensen controversy is that many schools and school systems avoid giving IQ tests for fear of political repercussions, when in fact much useful information can be obtained from this imperfect instrument, once its limitations are understood. Even where IQ tests are used, the results are often handled in a politicized way. For example, the Austin (Texas) public school system refused to release data on a school being considered for inclusion in this study because of "legal" reasons—but only after a lengthy cross-examination on my personal beliefs about various issues involved in the IQ controversy. Sometimes the data are suppressed for more directly institutional political reasons— as in the case of a large metropolitan black school on the West Coast whose outstanding performance is kept quiet for fear of citizen demands to know why other black schools in the same city cannot produce similar results.

Perhaps the most basic characteristic of all these schools could be called "law and order," if these had not become politically dirty words. Each of these schools currently maintaining high standards was a very quiet and orderly school, whether located in a middle-class suburb of Atlanta or in the heart of a deteriorating ghetto in Brooklyn. Schools formerly of high quality were repeatedly described by alumni, teachers, and others as places where "discipline problems" were virtually unheard of. "Respect" was the word most used by those interviewed to describe the attitudes of students and parents toward these schools. "The teacher was *always* right" was a phrase that was used again and again to describe the attitude of the black parents of a generation or more ago. Most Negro students of that era would not have dreamed of complaining to their parents after being punished by a teacher, for that would have been likely to bring on a second—and worse—punishment at home.

Even today, in those few instances where schools have the confidence of black parents, a wise student maintains a discreet silence at home about his difficulties with teachers, and hopes that the teachers do the same. The black culture is not a permissive culture. But in more and more cases, "student rights" activists among adults—particularly adults with an eye to political exposure—create a more contentious environment in which it is the teacher or the principal who maintains a discreet silence for fear of legal or physical retaliation. The sheer exhaustion of going through "due process" for every disruptive student who needs to be suspended is enough to discourage decisive action by many school officials.

The destruction of high-quality black schools has been associated with a breakdown in the basic framework of law and order. Nor did it require mass violence to destroy these or other black schools. Again and again, those interviewed who were working in the field of education pointed out that only a fraction—perhaps no more than one-tenth of the students—need to be hard-core troublemakers in order for good education to become impossible. Another way of looking at this is that only a small amount of initial selectivity (including student self-selection) or subsequent ability to suspend or expel is necessary to free a school of a major obstacle to education. At one time this small amount of selectivity was provided automatically for black (and other) high schools, because most uninterested students did not go on to high school. Those whose educational performances were substandard in the lower grades were left back often enough to reach the age to leave school before reaching high school. Moreover, that legal age was lower then; and, in addition, those utterly uninterested in school were unlikely to be zealously pursued by attendance officers in the era before the "dropout" problem became an emotionally important political issue.

Formal selectivity, in terms of entrace examination cutoff scores, was the exception rather than the rule for the schools studied here. Most of these were public schools serving all students in a given area; and for some period of their history, that area has included all black children in the city, in the cases of Dunbar, Douglass, and Booker T. Washington high schools. The private schools—St. Augustine, Xavier, and St. Paul—have entrance examinations, but these do not automatically admit or exclude, and the wide range of student test scores in these schools indicates that such scores are far from decisive in admissions. In short, no stringent "elitism" is necessary to achieve high-quality education. It is only necessary to select, or have students self-select, in such a way as to exclude the tiny fraction who are troublemakers.

At one time it was a relatively simple matter to suspend, expel, or transfer a disruptive student to some "special" class or "dumping ground" vocational school, allowing the rest of the educational system to proceed undisturbed. Now this has become more difficult with the growth of "student rights" and "parent power"—and, more generally, with an agonizing preoccupation with the question of what can be done for the disruptive student to "solve" his "problem." This mass projection of the academic paradigm of problem-solving to the whole society is part of the general spirit of the times, but it overlooks the vital question whether there is, in fact, a solution—whether we have it within our grasp today, and whether we shall allow the "problem" to take its fullest destructive toll before such indefinite time as we have it "solved." Recent campaigns to "get the drunk driver off the road" suggest that there are cases where the primary concern is to protect society, and where whatever remedies can be offered the individual are secondary. The enormous toll of a few destructive students on black education is one of the tragic untold stories of our time—perhaps because there is no political gain to be made by telling it, and much political capital to reap from championing "student rights."

While order and respect have been universal characteristics of the schools studied here, other ingredients have also been necessary to create academic excellence. Chief among these have been the character and ability of the principals. Some of these principals have been of heroic dimensions—fighters for civil rights at a time when that was a dangerous role—and others have been simply dedicated educators. The number of these principals who have trained at top colleges and universities in the country suggests that investments made in promising Negro youths more than half a century ago have paid off large and continuing dividends.

Ability-grouping has been a prominent feature of most of these schools during their periods of academic excellence—contrary to the "democratic" trends in contemporary education. For many reasons going back into history, there are very wide ranges of educational preparation and orientation among black children, and accommodating them all in one standard curriculum may often be impractical. Among Dunbar students in the period from 1938 to 1955, it was not uncommon to find individuals with IQs in the 80s and individuals with IQs in the 140s in the same grade, though not necessarily in the same classroom. In P.S. 91 today, the ability-grouping principle includes not only several different classes in the same grade but also several different ability groupings within each class—all told, perhaps two dozen ability levels in a single grade. This may not sound plausible as an educational policy, but it works—and it works in an unpromising social setting where many more popular ideas fail to show any results.

Perhaps the most disturbing aspect of contemporary education is the extent to which the very process of testing ideas and procedures by their actual *results* has been superseded by a process of testing them by their consonance with existing *preconceptions* about education and society. Father Grant, even after his remarkable successes as principal of St. Augustine, found no receptivity at the Ford Foundation either to his appeals for money for the school or to his ideas about education. He was out of step with the rhetoric of his time and did not use the "innovative" methods that were preconceived to be necessary or beneficial to black students. Xavier Prep, even after more than half a century of demonstrable results, is still looking for a modest sum of money to improve its library, but libraries are not "exciting" or "imaginative"—as "black English" or "black studies" are.

The social settings of the schools studied here are also significant. Every one of them was an urban school. This is remarkable because, during the academic heyday of most of these schools, most American Negroes lived in rural and small-town settings. This suggests that the rise of such prominent blacks as those who came from these schools— which is to say, most of the top black pioneers in the history of this country—seems a matter less of innate ability and more of special social settings in which individual ability could develop; and that the settings from which such black leadership arose were quite different from the social settings in which the mass of the black population lived. The second point needs emphasis only because of the recent mystique surrounding "grass-roots" origins and/or the faithful reflection of "grass-roots" attitudes by leaders. Much of this is nothing more than brazen presumption and reckless semantics: No one ever applies labels like "middle-class" to Angela Davis or LeRoi Jones (or others of their persuasion), though that is in fact their origin, while those with a more moderate philosophy are often condemned as "middle-class"—no matter how many polls show that their opinions are shared by the masses of blacks.

The particular cities in which the high-quality black schools arose were distinctive as centers of concentration for the "free persons of color" in the antebellum era. Except in the case of Dunbar High School in Washington, there was no unbroken historical line traceable back to the free Negroes of the early nineteenth century, but it seems more than coincidence that these schools took root in places where there had been schools for black children (usually private schools) for up to 100 years earlier. That is, an old black community with a demand for good education existed even before good schools became an institutional reality. It is not that the bulk of the Negroes in these cities necessarily wanted quality education, but that there was an important nucleus that understood what was needed, and that the others recognized and respected good education when it appeared.

Apparently the great bulk of black children who benefited from these schools were *not* descendants of "free persons of color" or of middle-class Negroes in general. But the knowledge, experience, and values of the more fortunate segment of the race became their heritage. While the black educated classes were not angels—they could be as snobbish and insufferable as any other privileged group—they were a vital source of knowledge, discipline, and competence. They opened a window on a wider world of human history and culture. They did not glorify provincialism or tribalism in the manner of some of today's black middle-class radicals who attempt to expiate their own past by being "blacker-than-thou." Those white officials who have successfully run high-quality black schools have, without exception, been men and women who were neither impressed nor intimidated by the militant vogues of the 1960s.

Whatever is the objective importance of social history in any final assessment of black education, that history must be dealt with—if only to counter the *fictitious* history that has become part of current stereotypes. Messianic movements of whatever place or time tend to denigrate the past as a means of making themselves unique and their vision glorious. Recent black messianic movements, and white messianic movements speaking in the name of blacks, have been no exception. The picture that emerges from these visions is of an inert, fearful, and unconcerned black leadership in the past—leaders only recently superseded by bold men of vision, like themselves. This is a libel on the men and women who faced up to far more serious dangers than our generation will ever confront, who took the children of slaves and made them educated men and women, and who put in the long hours of hard work required to turn a despised mass into a cohesive community. In many ways, those communities had far more cohesion, stability, mutual respect, and plain humanity than the ghettos of today.

NOTES

1. Thomas Sowell, "Black Excellence: The Case of Dunbar High School," *The Public Interest*, no. 35 (Spring 1974): 1–21.

2. Horace Mann Bond, "The Negro Scholar and Professional in America," *The American Negro Reference Book* (Englewood Cliffs, N.J.: Prentice-Hall, 1970), p. 562.

3. E. Franklin Frazier, *The Negro in the United States* (New York: Macmillan, 1971), p. 74.

4. Henry Reid Hunter, *The Development of the Public Secondary Schools of Atlanta, Georgia: 1845–1937* (Office of the School System Historian, Atlanta Public Schools, 1974), pp. 49–52.

5. "They Knew Charles L. Harper," *The Herald*, October 1955, p. 19.

6. Quoted in V. W. Hodges, "Georgians Join Atlantans in Tribute to Mr. Harper," *The Atlanta World*, June 14, 1950.

Assumptions
Versus History
in Ethnic Education

Even more important than the assumptions and beliefs that guide educational policy is the extent to which these assumptions and beliefs are tested against facts, rather than judged by their individual plausibility or by their consonance with some general vision of education or society. In the area of race and ethnicity, many key assumptions behind current policies remain untested against either current or historical facts.

Perhaps the best-publicized assumptions guiding judicial educational policy today are that segregated schools are inherently inferior (*Brown v. Board of Education*), and that the equalization of per-pupil expenditures is essential to an equalization of education (*Serrano v. Priest*). A more general assumption, encompassing these and other policies, is that the large disparities in school performances among racial or ethnic groups (1) are unusual and suspicious, and (2) reflect differences in the way those groups are treated by the schools and/or the society. These are not unreasonable assumptions, but reasonableness is no substitute for empirical verification, especially when so much is at stake. There is no *a priori* reason why statistics collected at a given institution must be solely the result of the policies of that institution, rather than the characteristics of the population in question.

Other common educational doctrines seldom seriously tested include the belief that school performance is greatly influenced by family

Reprinted from *Teachers College Record*, Fall 1981.

socioeconomic status, class size, teacher-student differences in ethnicity, and the cultural bias of tests. Statistical correlations are abundantly available in support of some of these doctrines, but the principle that "correlation is not causation" cannot be simply a pious disclaimer uttered in passing while proceeding *post haste* to equate the two in cognitive conclusion or policy application.

History is important because it allows a given principle to be tested under a far wider variety of conditions than are likely to be found contemporaneously. Despite the unplanned nature of historical "experiments," they can sometimes provide a richer set of data. At the very least, history provides an *additional* set of evidence.

SEGREGATION

There is no serious question that the segregated black schools long traditional in the South generally had educational results inferior to those in the white schools in the same communities. The Supreme Court in *Brown v. Board of Education* attributed causation, thereby making segregation the reason for educational and psychological problems in the black schools, and in turn this state-enforced educational inferiority constituted a denial of the "equal protection" required under the Fourteenth Amendment to the Constitution. But the mere contemporaneous existence of two striking social phenomena—rigid racial segregation and large differences in academic performance, in this case—does not automatically establish one as the cause of the other. At the very least, such a conclusion should await consideration of alternative hypotheses and the derivation of evidence that would distinguish one hypothesis from the other.

Among the best-known competing theories are that deficiencies in educational performance are the result of either (1) a unique black heredity or (2) a unique black environment or history. Tempting as it is to plunge into the Jensen controversy (as I have done elsewhere[1]), we must recognize how limited the significance of these hotly disputed theories is for the issue at hand. Before resorting to either hereditary or environmental theories which—even if true—would be applicable only to the special case of blacks, we must first determine whether the performance disparities between blacks and whites are themselves unique. In other words, we need to frame some general hypotheses, going beyond black-white differences, and at least see whether these larger patterns apply to racial as well as ethnic or other socioeconomic group differences. If such an attempt fails, there will then be time enough to formulate theories applying solely to blacks and whites. But we should not begin by presuming that such an attempt must fail, before even trying.

To present an alternative hypothesis: What would we expect to see if segregation were *not* a significant cause of educational differences? Unless we presume a genetic basis for unique black intellectual or educational results, we might expect to find at least three major phenomena:

1. Black intellectual or education performance would not be unique in level or pattern, but would be closely approximated by some other group(s).

2. Some groups who live in the same neighborhoods and attend the same schools together would be expected to exhibit intellectual or educational differences of a magnitude comparable to black-white differences in the segregated South.

3. Performance differences *within* the set of segregated black schools should be of a magnitude comparable to those *between* black and white schools in the segregated South.

A case could be made that the unique historical background of blacks might take the place of a unique genetic background in preventing these phenomena from emerging. However, if these phenomena do emerge, despite some unique features of black history, then the argument that segregation has had the devastating educational effect attributed to it is undermined all the more. That is, the uniqueness of racial segregation *plus* all the other unique features of black history—put together—would have been unable to present the emergence of a pattern found among other American ethnic groups not subject to these unique influences.

PERFORMANCE LEVELS

The habit of comparing black IQs, reading scores, or other indices of aptitude or performances with the "national average" glosses over the question of whether that "national average" is itself only an amalgam of results as disparate as the black-white differences under discussion. This is also true of comparisons of the economic or other indices for any given group with the so-called national average.

Despite a long and bitter controversy over how best to explain a supposedly unique black IQ level, neither the hereditary nor the environmental advocates have established that uniqueness in the first place. History presents an entirely different picture from that from which both sets of controversialists begin. There has been nothing unique about the black IQ level. The average IQ of blacks in the United States has been consistently around 85, compared with the national norm of 100. Group IQ averages at or below 85 have been common in history and currently. Back in the 1920s, for example, numerous studies showed similar IQ averages for such American ethnic groups as the Italians, Greeks, Poles, Hispanics, Slovaks, and Portuguese.[2] A more recent study shows Mexican Americans with lower average IQs than blacks in the 1940s, 1950s, and 1960s, and Puerto Ricans with lower average IQs than blacks in the 1970s.[3] Similar group averages have been found in white mountaineer communities in the United States and among culturally isolated people in the Hebrides Islands off Scotland and among children raised in canal boat communities in England.[4]

A similar picture emerges in comparisons of educational performances of black schools in Harlem in the 1940s and 1950s compared with (1) the city-wide average and (2) performances on the same tests given at the same time in the ethnic neighborhoods on New York's Lower East Side. Table 1 shows that schools in Harlem and on the Lower East Side were typically below the city-wide averages, but without any consistent or decisive advantage over each other in either verbal or mathematical areas.

Sometimes it is not the performance level but the performance pattern that is considered unique to blacks. The so-called Moynihan Report in the 1960s demonstrated that black female performance on tests and grades significantly exceeded black male performance, explaining this by a supposedly "matriarchial" black culture going back to slavery.[5] However, higher female performances have been common among low-IQ groups, now and in the past, in the United States and abroad.[6] Sex differences are especially pronounced among high-IQ members of low-IQ groups.[7] A plausible speculation is that this is an example of a more general phenomenon of greater female insulation from either the positive or the negative features of the environment.[8] But whatever the explanation, the pattern extends well beyond blacks. There was, for example, a time when Jews scored below the national average on mental tests,[9] and in that era Jewish girls scored higher than Jewish boys.[10] Today, Mexican American girls score higher than boys on IQ tests and are overrepresented among high-IQ Mexican American students.[11]

INTERGROUP DIFFERENCES
AMONG NONSEGREGATED ETHNICS

There are serious practical difficulties in testing the proposition that intergroup differences among nonsegregated ethnics would be compara-

Table 1:   NEW YORK CITY SCHOOLS

SCHOOL NEIGHBORHOOD	GRADE TESTED	GRADE EQUIVALENT SCORES			
		Paragraph Meaning	*Word Meaning*	*Arithmetic Reasoning*	*Arithmetic Computation*
APRIL 1941					
Harlem					
P.S. 5	6B	4.8	5.3		
P.S. 90	6B	6.0	5.9		
P.S.136	6B	4.5	4.7		
Lower East Side					
P.S. 23	6B	5.4	5.4		
P.S. 130	6B	5.7	5.4		
DECEMBER 1941					
Harlem					
P.S. 5	6B	5.2	5.2		
P.S. 90	6B	5.8	5.6		
P.S. 136	6B	5.4			
P.S. 194	6B	5.6			
Lower East Side					
P.S. 23	6B	5.1	4.5		
P.S. 130	6B	5.1	4.7		
City-wide Average	6B	6.8	6.5		
MAY 1947					
Harlem					
P.S. 5	3	3.5	3.5	3.9	3.9
P.S. 90	3	2.9	2.9	2.9	3.5
P.S.194	3	2.8	2.6	2.7	3.0
Lower East Side					
P.S. 23	3	3.1	3.2	3.3	3.6
P.S. 130	3	2.9	2.8	3.1	3.5
City-wide Average	3	3.5	3.5	3.5	3.7
FEBRUARY 1951					
Harlem					
P.S. 139	8	6.6	7.2		
P.S. 136	8	7.2	7.3		
Lower East Side					
P.S. 65	8	7.2	7.4		
City-wide Average	8	8.1	8.0		

SOURCE: New York City Board of Education.

ble to black-white differences, in the absence of the segregation effect postulated in *Brown v. Board of Education*. Interethnic comparisons of educational performance among European-origin groups have become rare since the 1920s, though there was a substantial literature before then, during the immigration controversy preceding the restrictive laws that went into force in 1924. These early studies did, however, show IQ differences, for example, as great as (or greater than) those between blacks and whites. While Polish and Italian youngsters, for example, scored in the low to middle 80s in IQ, scores at or above 100 were common among youngsters who were German or Irish or from a number of other groups that had immigrated far enough in the past to be assimilated to American norms in general.[12] Diane Ravitch's history of the New York City school system showed German and Jewish schoolchildren in the early twentieth century completing high school at a rate more than one hundred times greater than that of Irish or Italian schoolchildren.[13]

A recent study by the present writer has attempted to trace the IQ records of a number of ethnic groups from that early period to the present. The research has involved the collection of more than 70,000 IQ records for students attending 58 schools in communities across the country. The general results of that survey have already been published,[14] but what is relevant here is the performance of different groups in the *same schools* at the same time.

The two European immigrant groups with the most pronounced cultural differences in their approach to education were the Jews and the Italians. The centuries-old tradition of reverence for learning in the Jewish culture is well known. Among the people of southern Italy—from whom most Italian Americans are descended—an opposite tradition of hostility to formal schooling existed. For example, the introduction of compulsory school attendance laws in Italy in 1877 provoked riots in southern Italy, in the course of which some schoolhouses were burned to the ground.[15] Much of the literature on the Italian immigrants to the United States mentions various indicators of their low esteem for formal schooling.[16] Moreover, the peak of the Italian and the Jewish immigrations coincided in time (late nineteenth and early twentieth centuries), so that they would have been present in the immigrant ghettos at the same time and their assimilation processes would not have been out of phase, as would those of the Jews and the Irish, for example.

The Italians and the Jews would then clearly be among the candidates for testing whether nonsegregated ethnics have had as substantial differences in their performances in the same school as segregated races have had in different schools. Another pair who would have been in the same schools at the same time and at a similar phase of their assimilation would be the Japanese Americans and the Mexican Americans in the West. They also have many cultural contrasts, well documented in the literature. For example, over half of all Mexican American women get married in their teens, while only 10 percent of Japanese American women get married that young.[17] The implications of this for higher education and subsequent careers is obviously important. Here we are concerned about the differences in cultural values implied.

The nationwide sample of 58 schools was searched to find schools in which students from either of these pairs (Italian-Jewish or Japanese-Mexican) were present, with at least ten students per year from each group for at least five years. Only two sets of data in the nationwide sample proved to meet these specifications—one for each ethnic pair. One was a school (coded 0918) in a northeastern metropolis with a population of more than one million. An unexpected bonus was that the same school also turned out to contain a significant Puerto Rican population during the same years as the Italian and Jewish populations, and their data are included in Table 2 to extend the intergroup comparisons. The other data (coded 0610) are for a unified school district in a western community with fewer than 20,000 inhabitants. The data for the nationwide survey were collected under a pledge of confidentiality, so no institutional identification is possible.

How do these data bear on our hypothesis concerning the effect of segregation on education? Table 2 shows substantial and persistent IQ differences between nonsegregated ethnic groups—differences comparable in magnitude to national black-white differences. As already noted, the national black-white IQ difference is 15 points. In the segregated southern schools, black-white IQ differences have been slightly greater—almost 20 points.[18] Over a period of more than twenty years, Jewish youngsters averaged 13 points higher IQs than Italian youngsters attending the same school. Indeed, the highest Italian IQ average for any of these years is lower than the lowest Jewish IQ average for any of these years. Puerto Rican IQs averaged 26 points lower than the Jewish IQ. In short, the Jewish-Italian IQ difference was almost the same as the national black-white IQ differences, and the Jewish–Puerto Rican IQ difference was even greater than black-white IQ difference in segregated Southern schools. These huge disparities existed among children living in the same neighborhoods and sitting side-by-side in the same classrooms.

The data coded 0610 show a similar pattern of difference between Japanese Americans and Mexican Americans (see Table 3).

Although these were school district data rather than individual

Table 2: SCHOOL CODE 0918

Year	Jews		Italians		Puerto Ricans	
	Mean IQ	Sample Size	Mean IQ	Sample Size	Mean IQ	Sample Size
1931	–	–	90	32	–	–
1932	100	49	90	113	–	–
1933	108	58	90	125	84	11
1934	103	100	91	222	87	12
1935	102	179	92	364	–	–
1936	102	149	91	267	–	–
1937	108	114	89	228	–	–
1938	108	118	92	290	–	–
1939	107	105	91	327	80	24
1940	111	103	94	239	87	12
1941	111	85	97	224	90	10
1942	106	71	93	160	95	11
1943	106	110	94	324	88	20
1944	108	66	92	188	90	19
1945	108	74	94	178	89	10
1946	101	63	92	199	78	12
1947	106	67	92	149	79	24
1948	104	51	89	142	74	38
1949	102	50	94	122	78	42
1950	102	37	92	152	79	55
1951	102	22	88	92	77	49
1952	102	50	89	109	77	81
1953	103	41	89	131	78	98
1954	–	–	87	21	74	20
1955	–	–	84	22	72	42
1956	–	–	–	–	71	11
Totals*	105	1,790	92	4,434	79	637

*Individual year data shown may not add up to the total, which includes data for years during which sample was too small (less than 10) to be shown separately.

Source: Ethnic Minorities Research Project, The Urban Institute. Raw data and explanation of research methods available from National Technical Information Service, U.S. Department of Commerce, Springfield, Va. 22161 (Accession number PB 265 8.13).

school data, children of Japanese and Mexican ancestry were not separated from each other in different schools, either *de jure* or *de facto*. These data include parental occupation, which was unavailable in school 0918, and these occupations indicate that the large IQ differences between Japanese and Mexican children were not due to "middle class"

Table 3:   SCHOOL CODE 0610

	JAPANESE			MEXICANS		
YEAR	Mean IQ	Sample Size	Low-skill Parents (%)	Mean IQ	Sample Size	Low-skill Parents (%)
1944	–	–	–	86	51	86
1945	–	–	–	80	39	82
1946	106	14	79	82	92	88
1947	–	–	–	81	68	81
1948	–	–	–	84	212	84
1949	–	–	–	83	71	80
1950	–	–	–	83	127	80
1951	–	–	–	87	107	79
1952	–	–	–	79	110	83
1953	106	14	72	82	227	70
1954	100	26	85	84	173	80
1955	99	16	88	75	103	61
1956	100	17	89	81	204	69
1957	109	12	92	79	199	65
1958	–	–	–	81	166	65
1959	–	–	–	79	324	56
1960	–	–	–	73	278	42
1961	–	–	–	79	277	57
1962	–	–	–	77	270	66
1963	–	–	–	79	306	63
1964	–	–	–	83	351	72
1965	–	–	–	83	371	64
1966	–	–	–	79	147	74
1967	–	–	–	74	117	54
1968	–	–	–	78	149	58
1969	–	–	–	76	122	52
1970	–	–	–	80	82	44
1971	–	–	–	77	37	49
Totals*	100	172	77%	80	4,852	66%

*Individual year data shown may not add up to the total, which includes data for years during which sample was too small (less than 10) to be shown separately.

SOURCE: Ethnic Minorities Research Project, The Urban Institute. Raw data and explanation of research methods available from National Technical Information Service, U.S. Department of Commerce, Springfield, Va. 22161 (Accession Number PB265 8.13).

occupations or incomes of the Japanese parents during the 1950s, when data were available for both groups. The parents of the high-IQ Japanese Americans were generally "unskilled and semiskilled" workers to an even greater extent than the parents of low-IQ Mexican American young-

sters. Only 2 percent of the parents of either group of children in this
school were white-collar workers, and another 2 percent had skilled or
supervisory occupations. Nevertheless, the average IQ differences between these Japanese American and Mexican American schoolchildren
ranged from 16 to 30 points for the six years for which data are available
for both—averaging 20 points difference for the whole period. Again, this
is larger than national black-white IQ differences, and about the same as
the IQ difference between Southern blacks and whites in racially segregated schools.

INTERGROUP DIFFERENCES
AMONG SEGREGATED BLACKS

If racial segregation is not the crucial determinant of disparate educational performances that it has been assumed to be, we should expect to
find performance disparities among all-black schools comparable in
magnitude to black-white disparities. The same survey of 58 schools
shows the two highest IQ and two lowest IQ all-black schools to differ by
more than 20 points—that is, by more than the IQ differences found in
racially segregated schools in the South. Nor are the two high-IQ black
schools unique. Similar IQ levels have been found in other all-black
schools surveyed elsewhere.[19] The low-IQ schools are likewise not
unique. Just among the all-black schools in this study, there were five
more with IQs at least 20 points below the IQ level of school 0508/0598
(see Table 4).[20]

The school coded 0508/0598 is a public high school in a northeastern city of between half a million and one million population.
(Because it was handpicked for special study, its data are not included in
the published national data for blacks in the IQ study already mentioned.) The school coded 3169 is a private elementary school in the
South, in a city of between 100,000 and 500,000 population. The schools
coded 2756 and 2757 are both public schools in the same southern town
of less than 20,000 population. These various schools are not alleged to
be comparable in any way other than being all-black schools. No doubt
there are many reasons for their large IQ differences. Segregation is not
among them.

SEGREGATED NONBLACK ETHNIC GROUPS

Blacks have not been the only group segregated even *de jure*, much
less *de facto*. Other groups have attended schools whose student bodies

Table 4: ALL-BLACK SCHOOLS

Year	Mean IQ	Sample Size
SCHOOL CODE 0508/0598**		
1938	105	365
1939	111	373
1940	108	361
1941	109	365
1942	105	289
1943	101	370
1944	106	388
1945	99	371
1946	102	425
1947	103	461
1948	105	240
1949	106	238
1950	111	306
1951	103	405
1952	102	426
1953	101	460
1954	102	477
1955	100	402
Totals*	104	6,701

Year	Mean IQ	Sample Size
SCHOOL CODE 3169		
1960	99	92
1961	100	158
1962	102	44
1963	101	60
1964	99	61
1965	100	74
1966	100	48
1967	106	111
1968	95	16
1969	–	–
1970	105	41
1971	–	–
1972	107	61
Totals*	102	789

Year	Mean IQ	Sample Size
SCHOOL CODE 2756		
1967	73	20
1968	70	46
1969	90	201
1970	70	78
1971	71	171
Totals*	78	526

Year	Mean IQ	Sample Size
SCHOOL CODE 2757		
1966	86	23
1967	68	49
1968	77	46
1969	86	56
1970	74	55
1971	78	101
Totals*	77	331

*Individual year data shown may not add up to the total, which includes data for years during which sample was too small (less than 10) to be shown separately.

**The graduates and dropouts from this school were coded separately. The data shown are for the whole student body.

SOURCE: Ethnic Minorities Research Project, The Urban Institute. Raw data and explanation of research methods are available from National Technical Information Service, U.S. Department of Commerce, Springfield, Va. 22161 (Accession Number PB265 8.13).

have consisted exclusively, or almost exclusively, of members of their own ethnic group. In our nationwide IQ sample, there were two school codes that were more than 95 percent Chinese, one that was 95 percent Puerto Rican, one that was 100 percent American Indian, and one that was more than 99 percent Mexican American. Did these segregated schoolchildren of various ethnicities have test performances inferior to their respective compatriots in nonsegregated schools? Let us consider these groups one by one.

Chinese

The above-average IQ of the more than 1,500 segregated Chinese schoolchildren in our sample (Table 5) is in complete contradiction to the *Brown v. Board of Education* doctrine that separate schools are inherently inferior. The IQs of the segregated Chinese are certainly no lower than the IQs of Chinese Americans in general nor Americans in general.

The segregated Chinese children in our sample come from four schools in the same city (population between half a million and one million) in the West—three public elementary schools coded together as 0115 and one private school coded 0106 (see Table 5). Like most other private schools in our sample, it is *not* located in an affluent area. Such schools, in this study at least, are much more likely to be Catholic parochial schools than the academically selective and socially exclusive schools conjured up as the image of "private" schools. The median family income of the census tract in which school 0106 was located was about half the national average in the 1950 census, and just under a third of the national average in the 1960 and 1970 censuses. Such income disparities have been common in Chinatown neighborhoods, even after the Chinese rose above the national average in income, for the more affluent Chinese tend to live away from Chinatowns.

Puerto Ricans

Our Puerto Rican school sample was only one school (0921) and for only one year (1952). The mean IQ there was 81—compared with 79 for Puerto Ricans nationally in the same sample for the decade of the 1950s.[21] Although the IQs here are below the national average, the all–Puerto Rican school did *not* have results inferior to those of Puerto Ricans scattered through other schools, which is the point at issue. As might be expected, this all–Puerto Rican public school was in a low-income urban neighborhood. The median family income in its census

Table 5: CHINESE AMERICAN IQs

	CHINESE SCHOOLS				
	CODE 0106			CODE 0115	
Year	Mean IQ	Sample Size		Mean IQ	Sample Size
1949	100	172		–	–
1950	108	22		–	–
1951	101	45		99	85
1952	–	–		–	–
1953	96	11		102	92
1954	109	83		–	–
1955	–	–		–	–
1956	–	–		–	–
1957	107	73		–	–
1958	–	–		104	136
1959	–	–		–	–
1960	109	66		–	–
1961	–	–		–	–
1962	109	160		–	–
1963	103	80		–	–
1964	110	24		–	–
1965	–	–		–	–
1966	109	157		–	–
1967	103	60		–	–
1968	–	–		–	–
1969	108	124		–	–
1970	114	34		–	–
1971	107	47		–	–
Totals*	106	1,198		102	313

CHINESE AMERICANS NATIONALLY

Decades	Median IQ	Sample Size
1930s	103	107
1940s	101	277
1950s	102	1,016
1960s	107	765
1970s	108	105
Totals	103	2,580

*Individual year data shown may not add up to the total, which includes data for years during which sample was too small (less than 10) to be shown separately.

SOURCE: Ethnic Minorities Research Project, The Urban Institute. Raw data and explanation of research methods are available from National Technical Information Service. U.S. Department of Commerce, Springfield, Va. 22161 (Accession Number PB265 8.13).

Table 6:   AMERICAN INDIAN IQs

AMERICAN INDIAN SCHOOL (CODE 1016)		
Year	Mean IQ	Sample Size
1956	111	10
1957	—	—
1958	—	—
1959	—	—
1960	115	41
1961	—	—
1962	101	46
1963	104	37
1964	104	13
1965	110	15
1966	109	20
1967	107	22
1968	113	21
1969	—	—
1970	107	18
Totals*	107	244

*Individual year data shown may not add up to the total, which includes data for years during which sample was too small (less than 10) to be shown separately.

SOURCE: Ethnic Minorities Research Project, The Urban Institute. Raw data and explanation of research methods are available from National Technical Information Service, U.S. Department of Commerce, Springfield, Va. 22161 (Accession Number PB265 8.13).

tract in 1950 was just under half the national average. The city was in the Northeast, and had a population of more than one million.

American Indians

Our American Indian sample was also for only one school (and only one tribe), but included data for a number of years (see Table 6).

For this tribe of Indians, at least, an all-Indian school did not mean an inferior performance. Their IQs were consistently just above the national norms. They were also just above the national IQ level found among American Indians in this survey (106)—not significantly above, but not below, which is what is relevant to the *Brown v. Board of Education* doctrine. School 1016 was a public school located in the Northeast in a community of fewer than 20,000 inhabitants. No income data were available, and 90 percent of the parents' occupations were unknown. This one school provided 86 percent of all the American Indian IQs found in our nationwide survey, so a comparison among Indians would mean somewhat less than otherwise, and no conclusions about the national IQ level of Indians in general are drawn from them here, nor were any of these data presented in the published IQ study referred to,[22] because of the narrowness of the sample. But for our more limited purpose here, this sample is one more piece of evidence at odds with the doctrine that separate is inferior.

Mexican Americans

With Mexican Americans as well, the evidence goes directly counter to the doctrine that segregation reduces the group's performance. The Mexican American mean IQ of 90 in school 3167 is below the national average, but *above* the average of Mexican Americans nationally in the same study (see Table 7).

No income data are available for school 3167, a public school in the West, in a community of between 20,000 and 50,000 inhabitants. Parental occupations were slightly higher than for Mexican Americans nationally. While only 2 percent of the parents were professionals and 4 percent small businessmen, about a quarter were skilled or supervisory workers. However, the mean IQ of the children whose parents fell into the "small business" or the "skilled or supervisory" category was the same as the school average, and the children of the "unskilled and semiskilled" were only one point below. The children whose parents were professionals had mean IQs of 102, but because they were only 2 percent of the study body, this could hardly explain the school's IQ level. For this 99-percent Mexican school at least, economic status seems to have had as little overall effect as segregation.

SOCIOECONOMIC VARIABLES

We are well familiar with the fact that the social class and economic position of the parents affects the school performance of the child, and that the quantity and quality of schooling affects the eventual socioeconomic position of the child. Perhaps we are *too* well acquainted with these relationships, and therefore too inclined to be deterministic in our thinking about education.

Table 7: MEXICAN AMERICAN IQs

SCHOOL CODE 3167		
Year	Mean IQ	Sample Size
1945	92	13
1946	–	–
1947	–	–
1948	93	11
1949	83	12
1950	–	–
1951	89	41
1952	–	–
1953	88	14
1954	80	135
1955	80	87
1956	81	55
1957	90	18
1958	94	99
1959	93	201
1960	96	51
1961	96	69
1962	94	77
1963	96	85
Totals	90	991

MEXICAN AMERICANS NATIONALLY		
Decades	Median IQ	Sample Size
1940s	83	724
1950s	83	2,666
1960s	82	2,916
1970s	87	193
Totals	83	6,523

*Individual year data shown may not add up to the total, which includes data for years during which sample was too small (less than 10) to be shown separately.

SOURCE: Ethnic Minorities Research Project, The Urban Institute. Raw data and explanation of research methods are available from National Technical Information Service, U.S. Department of Commerce, Springfield, Va. 22161 (Accession Number PB265 8.13).

School Performance

One of the problems in trying to disentangle the effects of family background on school performance is that so many of the relevant variables vary together. High-income parents tend to live in high-income neighborhoods, with higher-quality schools, and have homes where books, magazines, conversation, and child-rearing patterns all enhance the development of the child's intellectual potential. Sorting out which of these factors is most responsible is like trying to unscramble an egg.

A more manageable analysis may be possible when dealing with historical data. At particular times in history, there have been groups with the values and aspirations that go with good educational performance, but that had not yet acquired the parental education, incomes, or occupations considered "middle class." Have their children's school performances matched their parents' socioeconomic realities or their parents' aspirations and pressures?

Two of the classic cases of groups whose history in America began in poverty and ended in affluence are the Jews on the East Coast and the Japanese on the West Coast.[23] We have already seen, from the record of Japanese American children in one school district (0610), that parental occupations overwhelmingly in the unskilled and semiskilled category did not prevent their offspring from meeting or exceeding national test norms. For our nationwide sample as well (see Appendix), Japanese American youngsters whose parents' occupations were low skilled still had IQs of 102 for the one decade (1950–1959) for which we have a national sample size of 50 or more. The national sample of Jewish schoolchildren likewise shows that those whose parents were unskilled and semiskilled had mean IQs of 104 through 106 for the three decades for which sufficient data are available.

While our historical data (see Appendix) for ten ethnic groups generally shows a higher IQ for the children of professionals than for the children of low-skilled workers, it is difficult to explain the substantial intergroup differences by parental occupations. For example, the children of Irish, German, or Chinese low-skilled workers scored consistently higher than the children of Mexican white-collar workers, small businessmen, or skilled and supervisory personnel. This is not to say that parental background meant nothing and the school everything. Clearly the school is not everything, for we have already seen (Tables 2 and 3) different ethnic groups with very different test performances in the same schools. The point here is simply that the kinds of parental backgrounds we traditionally measure—occupations or income—seem to explain little. No doubt the values and attitudes of the parents meant

Table 8:   DISTRICT 17 (BROOKLYN) ELEMENTARY SCHOOLS

School	Percent At or Above Reading Norm, 1974
91	56.5%
161	39.2
181	38.8
167	37.5
249	37.2
241	34.9
289	32.1
92	31.6
221	31.3
189	28.3
316	22.1
138	22.0
191	20.2

SOURCE: New York City Board of Education

much. That, however, does not mean that good schooling requires parental "participation" in school decisions. Neither the immigrant Jewish parents nor the immigrant Japanese parents participated in school decisions—except to back up whatever the teacher said.[24] The same was true of the role of the parents in high-quality black schools.[25]

What of the effectiveness of schools? Do they make little difference, as many studies suggest? Before determining the potential effectiveness of school differences, we must first have some idea of how different the schools are in the first place. For example, if most ghetto public schools differ little among themselves in the first place, we should expect little difference in their pupils' performances—but this in no way indicates that it is futile to expect them to make a real difference, *if they were to be themselves very different from what they are*, or even to vary more than they do. A growing literature has shown numerous ghetto schools with good-to-high academic performance,[26] often among children either wholly unselected or differing in no demonstrable socioeconomic way from other ghetto children. The example I studied was P.S. 91 in Brooklyn, where over half the children were eligible for the free lunch program and where many came from families on welfare. Yet whole grades were reading above the national norms, and the school's performance was far above the performances of the other schools in the same school district (see Table 8).

Parental occupational data from a number of high-performance black schools (see Table 9) reinforce the point that socioeconomic background is no more of an insurmountable handicap to good school performance among blacks than among other groups. These are children whose parents' occupations fall in the "unskilled and semiskilled" category. The children's IQs around the national norm are all the more significant because three of the schools are in the South as commonly understood, and all four are in the South as defined by the census.

As already noted, the average IQ of Southern blacks has usually been around 80. These four schools could all be considered "selective," in that the individual student had to choose to attend them, unlike P.S. 91, which is a neighborhood school to which students were automatically assigned. However, they are by no means selective in the sense in which Andover or Exeter is selective. None had cut-off scores that students had to meet to gain admission, all admitted substantial numbers of students with IQs in the 80s or below, and one (0508/0598) enrolled at least one-third of all the black students in its city during most of the period covered by our data.

"Selective," like "private," is a label that must be used cautiously. Parental occupational data for P.S. 91—a nonselective school—would have been more appropriate, but were unavailable. However, by all available indicators of socioeconomic status, those occupations are very unlikely to be higher than those for the schools shown in Table 9.

The point here is not to claim that schools can achieve success in spite of parents, or even to apportion the blame for low-performance ghetto schools between the parents and the schools. There is plenty of blame to go around. Instead, the point is to determine which of the many factors that differ among groups make no major demonstrable difference in results so that we can concentrate attention on those that do. Clearly schools cannot do it alone, as shown by the historical examples of groups with vast performance difference in the same schools. But clearly, too, poverty and low parental status are not fatal either.

Nothing is easier than to put together a list of desired things and call them the "prerequisites" for quality education, and to blame the absence of these things for all present shortcomings. But, historically, many of these prerequisites have been missing in high-performance schools as well as low-performance schools. Adequate physical plant, small class size, parental participation in the school, teacher "role models" of the student's own ethnic background, bilingual education—these are among the many prerequisites almost universally *lacking* in the schools from which the children of Jewish or Japanese immigrants emerged and in the high-quality black schools I have studied.

My study of high-performance black schools repeatedly took me

Table 9: IQs OF BLACK CHILDREN WITH LOW-SKILL PARENTS
AND HIGH-QUALITY SCHOOLS

Year	IQ	Year	IQ
SCHOOL 0508/0598		SCHOOL 3169	
1938	104	1960	101
1939	111	1961	96
1940	108	1962	99
1941	109	1963	100
1942	106	1964	100
1943	100	1965	103
1944	105	1966	—
1945	97	1967	106
1946	101		
1947	104	Year	IQ
1948	105		
1949	104	XAVIER PREP.*	
1950	113	1946	105
1951	102	1947	93
1952	102	1948	97
1953	98	1949	98
1954	102	1950	100
1955	98	1951	96
		1952	100
Year	IQ	1953	93
		1954	96
ST. AUGUSTINE*		1955	95
1954	91	1956	94
1955	90	1957	95
1956	94	1958	98
1957	87	1959	96
1958	—	1960	97
1959	89	1961	101
1960	93	1962	102
1961	96	1963	100
1962	97	1964	103
1963	98	1965	103
1964	103	1966	107
1965	103	1967	99
1966	101	1968	100
1967	102	1969	—
1968	103	1970	103
1969	102	1971	100
1970	97	1972	101
1971	102	1973	94
1972	101		

*See Thomas Sowell, "Patterns of Black Excellence," The Public Interest, Spring 1976.
SOURCE: Surveys for The Public Interest and Ethnic Minorities Research Project, The Urban Institute.

into ancient school buildings—including P.S. 91 in Brooklyn, where there were still gas jets in the halls, from the era before there was electric lighting. Others have found good academic performances in "storefront" ghetto schools. At least one of the schools in my study had lacked central heating for most of its history and relied on potbellied stoves in each classroom. This was neither desirable nor morally right. But it did not prevent good education from taking place.

Historically, the most outstanding of all black schools—whether measured by IQ or by the later achievements of its alumni—was Dunbar High School in Washington, D.C., during the period from 1870 to 1955. In the nineteenth century, the average class size at Dunbar was over 40, and it continued to have the largest class size of any high school in Washington on into the twentieth century. In New York at the turn of the century, it was not unusual for Jewish schoolchildren to be in classes of 60 or more pupils. [27] And there were no teacher's aides.

Teacher role models of the student's own ethnic background have been equally rare in history. When the Irish Catholic immigrant children went to public school in the middle of the nineteenth century, they were likely to be taught by Protestant Anglo-Saxon teachers. By the time the Jewish immigrant children were flooding into the public schools of New York at the turn of the century, they were far more likely to be taught by Irish Catholic teachers than by Jewish teachers. By the time I went to school in Harlem in the early 1940s, Jewish teachers outnumbered black teachers many times over. Similar patterns of group succession existed in labor unions and other organizations. All that is different about today is our naive insistence that all statistical disparities are unusual and/or evidence of sinister designs.

Among the high-performance black schools in my study for *The Public Interest*, some had all-black teaching staffs, some all-white, some predominantly clerical, some exclusively laymen. Some of the principals were warm and friendly, others tough and blunt. The notion that there is one formula that can be applied simply does not fit the facts, either as regards schools or homes. Much has been made of the home well-stocked with books and magazines and enriched with a continuous stream of conversation between parents and children. This model fits the history of Jewish immigrants on the East Coast, but not the history of Japanese immigrants on the West Coast. Books were rare in their homes, and conversation between the generations infrequent and usually unilateral. [28] But the Japanese children were the delight of their teachers, [29] even in an era of anti-Japanese sentiment in the society at large, and their educational performances demonstrated the payoff to diligent application, even in the absence of other "prerequisites" of good education.

Among the many fashionable "prerequisites" for good minority education (or excuses for its absence) is bilingual schooling. As in so many other areas of social policy discussion, this expression defines a process not by its own characteristics, but by its hopes. Described as a process, so-called bilingual education in practice means that a certain portion of the school work (sometimes a majority or virtually all) is taught in the student's native language, rather than in English. Whether or not that leads to bilingual students is a question, not a foregone conclusion. History does show that preceding generations of students—from the Jews and Italians on the East Coast to the Chinese and Japanese on the West Coast—became bilingual through opposite policies: teaching exclusively in English in school and speaking their respective native tongues at home.

The argument here is not over whether decent buildings, smaller class sizes, and so forth are desirable but over whether they are prerequisites—or (more to the point) whether their absence provides blanket excuses for educational failure.

UPWARD MOBILITY

The effect of the school on socioeconomic mobility has become as deeply embedded in folklore as the effect of socioeconomic variables on the schools. The strength of this belief is demonstrated, not by the evidence marshaled to support it, but by the lack of any felt necessity to produce evidence. Most prosperous groups are of course well-educated—and usually well-housed, well-clothed, and well-entertained. Yet no one regards that as proof that housing, clothing, or entertainment produces economic advancement. History again permits us to see various ethnic groups *before* they became prosperous, to find out which came first, the chicken or the egg.

It is by now a familiar story how the immigrant Jews brought to New York a long tradition of reverence for learning, how they crowded into the public libraries, the lecture halls, and the free colleges and universities of the city.[30] What is not so familiar is that the occupations through which they rose out of poverty were *not* primarily occupations requiring or utilizing formal schooling. In 1880 and in 1905, over half the Russian Jews in New York worked in manual occupations—and that is not counting the large number who were pushcart peddlers, who were officially classified as "white-collar" workers. Only 2 percent of the Russian Jews in 1880 were clerks or semiprofessionals[31]—the kinds of occupations normally thought of as "white collar." After a quarter of a century of upward mobility, there was a *smaller* proportion of Russian Jews in lower white-collar jobs, because pushcart peddling had declined.[32] But although Jewish upward mobility was well under way by the early twentieth century, Jewish children at the turn of the century seldom went far in school, because they were working—at home or outside. In 1908, 38 percent of all clothing workers in New York City were teenage Jews.[33] Even among Jewish children under ten years of age, between 7 and 10 percent were out of school and working at home[34]—in the "sweatshops."

The upward mobility of Jews in the last two decades of the nineteenth century could hardly have been due to education, and certainly not to higher education. No Jewish youngster graduated from a New York City public high school in the nineteenth century, for the first graduating class for any New York City public high school was the class of 1902.[35] A 1951 survey of City College students (mostly Jewish) showed that only 17 percent of their fathers born before 1911 had completed the eighth grade.[36] The massive Eastern European influx into City College and Hunter College occurred later, in the 1920s and 1930s.[37] By then their parents could afford to support them through high school.

The experience of the Japanese immigrants on the West Coast demonstrates even more dramatically that upward mobility occurred first, and the sending of the next generation to college was the consequence— not the cause—of that socioeconomic rise. As late as 1940, a majority of Japanese American males were in farming—and they produced about a third of all the commercial truck crops grown in California.[38] They were also successful as small businessmen. As early as 1919, Japanese Americans owned almost half the hotels and one-fourth of the grocery stores in Seattle.[39] First-generation Japanese also owned hundreds of produce markets in Los Angeles,[40] and more than a thousand were contract gardeners in southern California.[41] None of this required education, and most of the first-generation Japanese immigrants spoke little English.[42] Education was one of the things the next generation acquired with its affluence—not the cause of it.

SUMMARY

The dire state of American public education has been well documented, as is the fact that it has generally been getting worse, rather than better, over the past decade or more. As public trust—and public money—threaten to ebb away, many panicky "explanations" of failure or "prerequisites" for success have emerged. The quarter-of-a-century-old crusade for racial integration overlaps and complicates the educational picture and generates its own explanations and "prerequisites."

What is "the" answer? It is not clear that there is any single answer. The constant grasping for one answer or some magic formula or "innovation" may itself be part of the problem. What should be clear, however, is that self-serving mythology is not the answer. We are never going to solve the problem unless we can first face the problem as it is—not with a long list of excuses, pious hopes, or open-ended demands for "more."

More generally and more fundamentally, how have we all managed for decades to repeat dogmas and mount crusades without first testing our facts? Much of the discussion of the educational effects of segregation, or of socioeconomic status, has proceeded as if these were irrefutable facts rather than fashionable assumptions and moralistic pronouncements. They were never facts but only what the great sociologist Robert Merton has called "pseudofacts." The problem with pseudofacts, as Merton warns, is that they "have a way of inducing pseudoproblems which cannot be solved because matters are not as they purport to be."[43] The problems of education, and particularly of minority education, are all too real. But what we are trying to solve are the pseudoproblems— how to extract more government money for more projects, studies, and "innovative" gimmicks. The taxpayers' revolt, symbolized by spending limitations initiatives (beginning with California's celebrated Proposition 13) and by the defeat of school bond issues that used to pass routinely, suggests that the pseudoproblem may not be solved for many years, if at all. The real problem—teaching youngsters to read and think—has already been solved by many institutions in both rich and poor neighborhoods, by people with varying ethnicities, personalities, and approaches. The real problem can be solved, but it must first be addressed.

APPENDIX

A strong word of caution is necessary before presenting the nationwide IQ data that follow. Unlike the coded school data tabulated from the same study, the data in the following tables do not represent ethnic performance differences in the same schools on the same tests, or even in the same neighborhoods or geographic regions of the country. Intergroup comparisons from the national tables are therefore very hazardous, for many relevant variables—socioeconomic status, test type, geographic mix—are *not* held constant from one group to another though they could be if someone wished to retabulate the data from the computer tape. However, the tables may be useful in a variety of other ways, including showing patterns of internal IQ differences (by parental occupation) for a given group, and following the changes that have occurred in that group's scores over time. Other uses and more detailed breakdowns of these data (by sex, test types, etc.) may be found in Thomas Sowell, "Race and I.Q. Reconsidered," in Thomas Sowell, ed., *Essays and Data on American Ethnic Groups* (Washington, D.C.: The Urban Institute, 1978), pp. 203-38; and Leon J. Kamin, "Sibling IQ Correlations Among Ethnic Groups," in ibid., pp. 239-49. The raw data itself, including information not included in any of the published studies (foreign-born parents, for example) and a more detailed description of the data categories and collection methods are all available from National Technical Information Service, U.S. Department of Commerce, Springfield, VA 22161 (Accession Number PB265 8.13).

In the tables that follow the Notes, a dash is entered in any cell for which the national IQ sample for the whole group is less than 50, or in which the sample is less than 10 for any given parental occupation. An asterisk indicates that while the sample in the occupational cell was 10 or more, this was less than one-half of 1 percent of the parental occupations for that decade.

NOTES

1. Thomas Sowell, "Race and I.Q. Reconsidered," in Thomas Sowell, ed., *Essays and Data on American Ethnic Groups* (Washington, D.C.: The Urban Institute, 1978), pp. 203-38.
2. See studies cited in ibid., pp. 207-8.
3. Ibid., pp. 214, 217.
4. Ibid., pp. 210-11.
5. U.S. Department of Labor, *The Negro Family: The Case for National Action* (Washington, D.C.: U.S. Government Printing Office, March 1965).
6. Sowell, "Race and I.Q. Reconsidered," pp. 219-24.
7. Ibid., pp. 222, 223, 224.
8. Ibid., pp. 219-20.
9. Ibid., pp. 207-8.
10. Ibid., p. 222.
11. Ibid., p. 223.
12. Ibid., p. 210.
13. Diane Ravitch, *The Great School Wars* (New York: Basic Books, 1974), p. 178.

14. Sowell, "Race and I.Q. Reconsidered," pp. 203–38.

15. Richard Gambino, *Blood of My Blood* (Garden City, N.Y.: Anchor Books, 1974), p. 249.

16. Ibid., pp. 246–57; Herbert J. Gans, *The Urban Villagers* (New York: Free Press, 1962), pp. 130–31; and Sr. Mary Fabian Matthew, C.S., "The Role of the Public Schools in the Assimilation of the Italian Immigrant Child in New York City, 1900–1914," in S. M. Tomasi and M. H. Engels, eds., *The Italian Experience in the United States* (New York: Center for Migration Studies, 1970), pp. 139–40.

17. Peter Uhlenberg, "Demographic Correlates of Group Achievement: Contrasting Patterns of Mexican-Americans and Japanese-Americans," in Robert K. Yin, ed., *Race, Color, or National Origin* (Itasca, Ill.: F. E. Peacock, 1973), p. 91.

18. Audrey M. Shuey, *The Testing of Negro Intelligence*, 2nd ed. (New York: Social Science Press, 1966), p. 500.

19. Thomas Sowell, "Patterns of Black Excellence," *The Public Interest*, Spring 1976, pp. 26–58.

20. Their schools codes are 1734, 1839, 2968, 3062, 3063, and 3064. The last-named had an average IQ of 77, but its table was not printed here because it did not meet the criterion used in the other tables—at least five years with ten or more student IQs recorded.

21. Sowell, "Race and I.Q. Reconsidered," p. 214.

22. Ibid., pp. 203–38.

23. See, for example, Harry H. L. Kitano, *Japanese Americans* (Englewood Cliffs, N.J.: Prentice-Hall, 1969); and Irving Howe, *World of Our Fathers* (New York: Harcourt Brace Jovanovich, 1976).

24. Kitano, *Japanese Americans*, pp. 23, 76n; and Howe, *World of Our Fathers*, p. 273.

25. Sowell, "Patterns of Black Excellence," pp. 54–55.

26. Ibid. See also Derrick A. Bell, Book Review, *Harvard Law Review* 92 (1979): 1841n.

27. Ravitch, *The Great School Wars*, p. 678.

28. Kitano, *Japanese Americans*, pp. 23–24, 72–73.

29. Ibid., pp. 23, 72–73.

30. Howe, *World of Our Fathers*, chap. 7.

31. Thomas Kessner, *The Golden Door* (New York: Oxford University Press, 1977), p. 61.

32. Ibid., pp. 60, 64.

33. Selma C. Berrol, "Education and Economic Mobility: The Jewish Experience in New York City, 1880–1920," *American Jewish Historical Quarterly*, March 1976, p. 262.

34. Ibid.

35. Ibid., p. 261.

36. Ibid.

37. Ibid., p. 262.

38. Robert Higgs, "Landless by Law: Japanese Immigrants in California Agriculture to 1941," *Journal of Economic History*, March 1978, p. 207.

39. Ivan H. Light, *Ethnic Enterprise in America* (Berkeley: University of California Press, 1972), p. 10.

40. Ibid., p. 17.

41. Kitano, *Japanese Americans*, p. 22.

42. William Peterson, *Japanese Americans* (New York: Random House, 1971), p. 183.

43. Quoted in Herbert Gutman, *The Black Family in Slavery and Freedom* (New York: Vintage Books, 1977), p. 463.

Table 10: BLACK AMERICANS

Decades	Mean IQ	Unskilled and Semi-skilled		White Collar		Skilled and Supervisory		Small Business		Professional		Executives		Unknown	
		IQ	%	IQ	%	IQ	%	IQ	%	IQ	%	IQ	%	IQ	%
1920s	–	–	–	–	–	–	–	–	–	–	–	–	–	–	–
1930s	91	89	56	–	–	–	–	–	–	–	–	–	–	92	34
1940s	92	91	60	101	2	94	2	–	–	–	–	–	–	94	35
1950s	92	91	59	97	2	91	1	103	*	112	*	–	–	92	37
1960s	88	85	66	102	7	94	4	99	1	106	1	–	–	88	21
1970s	82	79	35	103	2	95	1	–	–	111	*	–	–	82	61

*Less than half of one percent.

(A large shift in the geographic mix of the data sources is partly responsible for the appearance of a decline in black IQ in this table. See Thomas Sowell, "Race and IQ Reconsidered," *Essays and Data on American Ethnic Groups* [Washington, D.C.: The Urban Institute, 1978], p. 217.)

Table 11: CHINESE AMERICANS

		PARENTAL OCCUPATION														
DECADES	MEAN IQ	UNSKILLED AND SEMI-SKILLED		WHITE COLLAR		SKILLED AND SUPERVISORY		SMALL BUSINESS		PROFESSIONAL		EXECUTIVES		UNKNOWN	
		IQ	%	IQ	%	IQ	%	IQ	%	IQ	%	IQ	%	IQ	%
1920s	–	–	–	–	–	–	–	–	–	–	–	–	–	–	–
1930s	103	–	–	–	–	–	–	–	–	–	–	–	–	103	97
1940s	98	98	15	103	7	–	–	–	–	–	–	–	–	97	77
1950s	102	104	11	110	7	–	–	–	–	114	2	–	–	101	80
1960s	107	105	40	110	23	–	–	–	–	120	4	–	–	105	33
1970s	108	106	48	111	20	–	–	–	–	–	–	–	–	108	24

Table 12: GERMAN AMERICANS

| | | Parental Occupation | | | | | | | | | | | | | |
| | Mean | Unskilled and Semi-skilled | | White Collar | | Skilled and Supervisory | | Small Business | | Professional | | Executives | | Unknown | |
Decades	IQ	IQ	%	IQ	%	IQ	%	IQ	%	IQ	%	IQ	%	IQ	%
1920s	101	100	60	98	10	97	6	—	—	—	—	—	—	104	24
1930s	101	101	56	102	8	103	5	106	1	110	1	—	—	101	29
1940s	103	100	45	103	9	104	6	108	1	105	1	—	—	105	37
1950s	102	102	51	103	9	104	6	107	1	111	1	—	—	102	32
1960s	106	104	32	105	10	111	6	—	—	117	3	—	—	106	49
1970s	105	106	40	98	9	101	13	—	—	—	—	—	—	105	31

Table 13:   IRISH AMERICANS

DECADES	MEAN IQ	PARENTAL OCCUPATION													
		UNSKILLED AND SEMI-SKILLED		WHITE COLLAR		SKILLED AND SUPERVISORY		SMALL BUSINESS		PROFESSIONAL		EXECUTIVES		UNKNOWN	
		IQ	%	IQ	%	IQ	%	IQ	%	IQ	%	IQ	%	IQ	%
1920s	102	105	61	–	–	–	–	–	–	–	–	–	–	99	24
1930s	102	102	55	104	4	103	2	–	–	102	2	–	–	103	37
1940s	104	104	52	104	5	103	3	–	–	109	2	–	–	104	38
1950s	105	104	45	108	8	106	7	106	1	109	2	–	–	104	37
1960s	107	106	36	110	11	108	12	113	2	113	2	–	–	105	37
1970s	105	100	33	107	21	103	14	–	–	–	–	–	–	109	25

Table 14: ITALIAN AMERICANS

| | | PARENTAL OCCUPATION | | | | | | | | | | | | | | |
| | Mean | Unskilled and Semi-skilled | | White Collar | | Skilled and Supervisory | | Small Business | | Professional | | Executives | | Unknown | |
Decades	IQ	IQ	%	IQ	%	IQ	%	IQ	%	IQ	%	IQ	%	IQ	%
1920s	92	91	62	—	—	98	16	—	—	—	—	—	—	93	16
1930s	93	94	21	97	1	95	5	93	2	—	—	—	—	92	72
1940s	95	97	26	102	2	96	4	101	1	104	*	—	—	95	66
1950s	99	99	37	102	6	102	11	103	3	112	1	—	—	97	43
1960s	103	101	41	107	8	104	15	107	4	109	2	—	—	104	31
1970s	100	99	52	95	8	102	9	—	—	—	—	—	—	102	28

*Less than half of one percent.

Table 15: JAPANESE AMERICANS

| DECADES | MEAN IQ | PARENTAL OCCUPATION | | | | | | | | | | | | |
| | | UNSKILLED AND SEMI-SKILLED | | WHITE COLLAR | | SKILLED AND SUPERVISORY | | SMALL BUSINESS | | PROFESSIONAL | | EXECUTIVES | | UNKNOWN | |
		IQ	%	IQ	%	IQ	%	IQ	%	IQ	%	IQ	%	IQ	%
1920s	—	—	—	—	—	—	—	—	—	—	—	—	—	—	—
1930s	—	—	—	—	—	—	—	—	—	—	—	—	—	—	—
1940s	—	—	—	—	—	—	—	—	—	—	—	—	—	—	—
1950s	101	102	83	—	—	—	—	—	—	—	—	—	—	92	9
1960s	—	—	—	—	—	—	—	—	—	—	—	—	—	—	—
1970s	—	—	—	—	—	—	—	—	—	—	—	—	—	—	—

Table 16: JEWISH AMERICANS

| Decades | Mean IQ | Parental Occupation | | | | | | | | | | | | |
| | | Unskilled and Semi-skilled | | White Collar | | Skilled and Supervisory | | Small Business | | Professional | | Executives | | Unknown | |
		IQ	%	IQ	%	IQ	%	IQ	%	IQ	%	IQ	%	IQ	%
1920s	112	104	15	110	21	111	11	114	14	–	–	–	–	115	39
1930s	104	106	5	108	6	108	8	112	3	109	1	–	–	103	76
1940s	104	105	5	107	6	109	7	107	2	–	–	–	–	103	79
1950s	102	–	–	–	–	–	–	–	–	–	–	–	–	102	98
1960s	–	–	–	–	–	–	–	–	–	–	–	–	–	–	–
1970s	–	–	–	–	–	–	–	–	–	–	–	–	–	–	–

(The apparent decline in Jewish IQs from the 1920s to the 1930s reflects in part a sharply changing geographic mix—from almost entirely midwestern data in the 1920s to a majority of northeastern data for later decades.)

Table 17: MEXICAN AMERICANS

Decades	Mean IQ	Parental Occupation												
		Unskilled And Semi-skilled		White Collar		Skilled And Supervisory		Small Business		Professional		Executives		Unknown	
		IQ	%	IQ	%	IQ	%	IQ	%	IQ	%	IQ	%	IQ	%
1920s	—	—	—	—	—	—	—	—	—	—	—	—	—	—	—
1930s	—	—	—	—	—	—	—	—	—	—	—	—	—	—	—
1940s	83	82	78	—	—	92	5	80	2	—	—	—	—	84	14
1950s	83	84	60	92	2	88	8	84	1	103	1	—	—	79	28
1960s	82	83	57	97	5	97	3	—	—	—	—	—	—	77	34
1970s	87	90	53	114	5	—	—	—	—	—	—	—	—	80	40

Table 18: POLISH AMERICANS

Decades	Mean IQ	Unskilled and Semiskilled		White Collar		Skilled and Supervisory		Small Business		Professional		Executives		Unknown	
		IQ	%	IQ	%	IQ	%	IQ	%	IQ	%	IQ	%	IQ	%
1920s	91	91	76	–	–	93	9	99	2	–	–	–	–	93	12
1930s	95	95	74	101	1	98	6	100	1	100	*	–	–	94	18
1940s	99	98	72	105	1	101	3	100	1	–	–	–	–	101	23
1950s	104	104	50	108	6	104	4	107	1	–	–	–	–	103	39
1960s	107	106	19	110	4	108	1	–	–	–	–	–	–	107	76
1970s	109	106	16	–	–	104	5	–	–	–	–	–	–	109	76

*Less than half of one percent.

Table 19: PUERTO RICANS

| | | PARENTAL OCCUPATION | | | | | | | | | | | | | |
| DECADES | MEAN IQ | UNSKILLED AND SEMI-SKILLED | | WHITE COLLAR | | SKILLED AND SUPERVISORY | | SMALL BUSINESS | | PROFESSIONAL | | EXECUTIVES | | UNKNOWN | |
		IQ	%	IQ	%	IQ	%	IQ	%	IQ	%	IQ	%	IQ	%
1920s	–	–	–	–	–	–	–	–	–	–	–	–	–	–	–
1930s	85	–	–	–	–	–	–	–	–	–	–	–	–	85	100
1940s	82	–	–	–	–	–	–	–	–	–	–	–	–	82	99
1950s	79	91	4	–	–	–	–	–	–	–	–	–	–	78	95
1960s	84	87	35	–	–	96	4	–	–	–	–	–	–	81	59
1970s	80	85	19	–	–	97	2	–	–	–	–	–	–	79	79

Affirmative Action in Faculty Hiring

There is little real question that if one goes back a number of years one finds a pervasive pattern of discrimination against minorities in academic employment. This applies not only to blacks and other minorities regarded as "disadvantaged," but also to Jews, who were effectively excluded from many leading university faculties before World War II.[1] The situation of women is somewhat more complicated and so will be deferred for the moment. However, the question that is relevant to affirmative action programs for both minorities and women is: What was the situation at the onset of such programs, and how has the situation changed since?

While colleges and universities were subject to the general provisions of the Civil Rights Act of 1964 and to subsequent executive orders authorizing cancellation of federal contracts for noncompliance,[2] the numerical proportions approach dates from the Labor Department's 1968 regulations as applied to academic institutions by the Department of Health, Education, and Welfare (HEW).[3] More detailed requirements—including the requirement of a written affirmative action program by each institution—were added in Revised Order No. 4 of 1971,[4] which contains the crucial requirement that to be "acceptable" an institution's "affirmative action program must include an analysis of areas

Reprinted from *Affirmative Action Reconsidered* (Washington, D.C.: American Enterprise Institute, 1975).

within which the contractor is deficient in the utilization of minority groups and women" and must establish "goals and timetables" for increasing such "utilization" so as to remedy these "deficiencies."[5]

BEFORE AFFIRMATIVE ACTION

For purposes of establishing a chronology, 1971 may be taken as the beginning of the application of numerical goals and timetables to the academic world. The question thus becomes: What were the conditions in academic employment, pay, and promotions as of that date? For minorities in general, and blacks in particular as the largest minority, virtually nothing was known about academic employment conditions at that point. Assumptions and impressions abounded, but the first national statistical study of the salaries of black academics is that published in 1974 by Professor Kent G. Mommsen of the University of Utah.[6] In short, affirmative action programs had been going full blast for years before anyone knew the dimensions of the problem to be solved. Professor Mommsen's data for the academic year 1969-70 show a grand total of $62 per year salary difference between black Ph.D.'s and white Ph.D.'s.[7] An earlier study by Professor David Rafky found that only 8 percent of black academics in white institutions regarded themselves as having personally experienced discrimination in their careers.[8]

These data may seem to be sharply at variance with data showing numerical "underutilization" of minorities in the white academic world, and it is these latter data which HEW and other supporters of affirmative action rely upon. There are some rather simple and straightforward reasons why the percentage of blacks (or minorities in general) in the academic world (or at white institutions) is smaller than their percentage in the general population:

1. Only a very small proportion of blacks meet the standard requirements of a Ph.D. for an academic career. Less than 1 percent of the doctorates earned in the United States are received by blacks and, despite many special minority programs and much publicity, less than 2 percent of graduate students are black.[9] Various surveys and estimates show less than 4,000 black Ph.D.'s in the United States.[10] This is less than two black Ph.D.'s for every American college or university—regardless of what goals and timetables may be set.

2. Most black academics teach at black colleges and black universities,[11] and so do not show up in the predominantly white insti-

tutions where affirmative action data are collected. Nor are these black academics eager to leave and join white faculties elsewhere: the average salary increase required to induce black academics to move was over $6,000 a year in 1970.[12] The crucial element of individual choice is left out of the affirmative action syllogism that goes from numerical "underrepresentation" to "exclusion." One study (by strong supporters of affirmative action) showed that some black academics refuse even to go for an interview at institutions that do not have a black community nearby.[13]

3. The career characteristics of most black academics do not match the career characteristics of white (or black) faculty at the leading research universities that are the focus of affirmative action pressures. This is particularly true of the two key requirements at research universities—the Ph.D. and research publications. A survey of the faculty at black private colleges and universities found that only 25 percent had a doctorate and only 4 percent had ever published in a scholarly journal.[14] None of this is surprising, given the history of blacks in the United States. Nor should it be surprising that academics with those characteristics prefer to remain at teaching institutions, rather than move to research universities.

None of this disproves the existence of discrimination in the academic world. It merely indicates that numerical underrepresentation is not automatically equivalent to discrimination. More fundamentally, it makes discrimination an empirical question—not something to be established intellectually by sheer force of preconception or to be established administratively by simply putting a never-ending burden of proof (or disproof) on institutions. For both minorities and women, a distinction must be made between saying that there is discrimination in general and establishing the particular *locus* of that discrimination. Even the most casual acquaintance with American history is sufficient to establish the existence of discrimination against blacks. The question is whether the statistical end results so emphasized by HEW are caused by the institutions at which the statistics were gathered.

The extent to which the patterns of minorities can be generalized to women is also ultimately an empirical question. In some specific and important respects, academic women are quite different from minority academics:

1. Women have not risen to their present proportions among college and university faculty from lower proportions in earlier eras, despite a tendency towards such fictitious parallelism in the liter-

ature.[15] Women constituted more than 30 percent of all faculty members in 1930, and the proportion declined over the next thirty years to about 20 percent in 1960. Women reached a peak of nearly 40 percent of all academic personnel (faculty and administrators) in 1879, with fluctuations, generally downward, since then.[16] Similar declines have occurred in the representation of women in other high-level professions over a similar span, both in the United States and in Europe.[17] It is not merely that much of the assumed history of women is false but, more important, that the reasons for current female disadvantages in employment, pay, and promotion are misunderstood as a result. The declining proportions of female academics occurred over a period of rising rates of marriage among academic women,[18] and a period of rising birthrates among white women in general.[19] In short, there is at least *prima facie* evidence that domestic responsibilities have had a major impact on the academic careers of women over time—which raises the question whether domestic responsibilities should not be investigated further as a factor in current female career differences from males, rather than going directly from numerical "underrepresentation" to "exclusion" and "discrimination."

2. Women have administered and staffed academically top-rated colleges for more than a century,[20] in contrast to the black colleges which have never had top-rated students or faculty.[21] Although women's colleges such as Bryn Mawr, Smith, and Vassar have been teaching institutions rather than research universities, their students have been quite similar academically to those in the research universities and their faculty typically has had training similar to that of the faculties of research institutions. In fact, in some instances, these women's colleges have been part of research universities (Radcliffe, Barnard, Pembroke, etc.). In short, academic women have had both higher academic standing than minorities and readier access to faculty positions at research universities. Information barriers in particular have been far less important in the case of women than in the minority case, and word-of-mouth methods of communication among prestige institutions have included women for a longer time.

The point here is not to minimize women's problems but to point out that they are in some ways distinct from the problems of minorities. In other ways, of course, they are similar. For example, women academics also do not publish as much as academics in general,[22] and women academics do not have a Ph.D. as often as other academics.[23] In the crucial area of salary, not only do women academics average less than men,[24] but also female Ph.D.'s average significantly less than male Ph.D.'s.[25] In short, women in academia face a different, though overlapping, set of problems from those faced by minorities in academia.

In addition to questions about the HEW "solution" for minorities, there may be additional questions about the simple extension of the minority solution to women by Executive Order No. 11375.

It must be emphasized that all the statistics cited thus far are for the academic world *prior* to affirmative action. They are intended to give a picture of the dimensions and nature of the problem that existed so as to provide a basis for judging the necessity of what was done under affirmative action programs. Now the results of those programs can also be considered.

AFTER AFFIRMATIVE ACTION

The academic employment situation has been described in terms of rough global comparisons—black-white or male-female. Finer breakdowns are necessary in order for us to determine the effects of many variables which differ between the groups whose economic conditions are being compared. Some of these intergroup differences have already been mentioned—educational differences and differences in publications, for example—but there are others as well.

If discrimination is to mean unequal treatment of equal individuals, then comparisons must be made between individuals who are in fact similar with respect to the variables which generally determine employment, pay, and promotion. Only insofar as we succeed in specifying all these variables can we confidently refer to the remaining economic differences as "discrimination." One of the perverse aspects of this residual method of measuring discrimination is that the more determining variables that are overlooked or ignored, the more discrimination there seems to be. Since no study can specify all relevant variables, the residual pay differences between minority and female academics, on the one hand, and white males, on the other, must be understood as the upper limit of an estimate of discriminatory differences.

For both sets of comparisons, the data sources are the American Council on Education (ACE) and the National Academy of Sciences (NAS). The ACE data are based on a sample of 60,018 academicians surveyed in 1969 and a sample of 50,034 academicians surveyed in 1972. The NAS data are from (1) a National Science Foundation survey conducted in 1973, based on a stratified sample of 59,086 doctorates in the social and natural sciences and engineering[26] and (2) a longitudinal compilation by NAS of biennial surveys of the same target population by the National Science Foundation during 1960–1970.

Minorities

Existing studies of black faculty members show many ways in which their job-related characteristics differ from those of faculty members in general. All these differences tend to have a negative impact on employment, pay, and promotion for academics in general:

1. A smaller proportion of black faculty than of white faculty holds a doctoral degree.[27]

2. The distribution of black doctoral fields of specialization is biased towards the lower-paying fields—particularly education (roughly one-third of all black doctorates) and the social sciences (one-fourth)—with very few (about 10 percent) of the doctorates in the natural sciences.[28]

3. The bulk of black faculty is located in the South[29]—a lower-paying region for academics in general,[30] as well as for others.

4. Blacks complete their Ph.D.'s at a later age than whites[31]—a reflection of both financial and educational disadvantages—and academics in general who complete their Ph.D.'s at a later age tend to be less "productive" in research publications.

5. Black academics, both at black colleges and at white institutions, publish much less than white academics.[32] Among the factors associated with this are much higher teaching loads and late completion of the Ph.D.

6. Black academics are less mobile than white academics—and less mobile academics tend to earn lower salaries. Forty percent of the black professors in the Mommsen study had not moved at all, despite an average of three or four job offers per year,[33] and the median pay increase which they considered necessary to make them move was a $6,134 per year raise.[34] By contrast, among faculty in general, "the academic career is marked by high mobility,"[35] and "professors expect to switch schools several times, at least, during their careers."[36]

7. Women constitute a higher proportion (20 percent) of black doctorates than of doctorates in general (13 percent)[37]—and women earn less than men among both blacks and whites.

With all these downward biases, it is worth noting once again that the academic salaries of white doctorates averaged only $62 per year more than those of black doctorates in 1970. On a field-by-field basis, black doctorates were generally earning more than white doctorates in the same area of specialization and receiving more job offers per year[38]— all this before the affirmative action program under Revised Order No. 4 in 1971. In other words, the effect of the straightforward antidiscrimination laws of the 1960s and of the general drive toward racial integration had created a premium for qualified black academics, even before HEW's goals and timetables.

The data from the American Council on Education permit a standardization for degree level, degree quality, field of specialization, and number of articles published, so that the salaries of blacks, whites, and Orientals who are comparable in these respects may be compared. Table 1 omits field of specialization to give a general view of race and salary in the academic world as a whole. Degree rankings in the table are based on surveys conducted by the ACE to determine the relative rankings of Ph.D.-granting departments in 29 disciplines, as ranked by members of those respective disciplines. (I have collapsed the two departmental rankings, "distinguished" and "strong," into one category in order to maintain a large sample size.) Articles published were selected as a proxy for publication in general, avoiding the problem of trying to convert books, monographs, conference papers, and articles into some equivalent.

My results for 1973 (Table 1) are generally not very different from those of Professor Mommsen for 1970: white faculty earned slightly more than black faculty in general ($16,677 versus $16,037). But when degree level and degree quality are held constant, blacks earned more than whites with doctorates of whatever ranking, while whites had an edge of less than $100 per year among academics without a doctorate. The overall salary advantage of whites over blacks—$640 per year—is a result of a different distribution of the races among degree levels and degree qualities, as well as a different distribution among publication categories. For example, 11 percent of the white faculty members in the ACE samples had Ph.D.'s from departments ranked either "distinguished" or "strong" by their respective professions, while only 4 percent of the black faculty came from such departments. Only 18 percent of the black academics in this sample had a doctorate at all, compared to 38 percent of the white academics. Thirty-one percent of the white faculty had published five or more articles, while only 12 percent of the black faculty had done so. Blacks who had published at all had higher salaries than whites with the same number of publications.

Orientals present a somewhat different picture. Only those Orien-

Table 1: MEAN ANNUAL SALARIES OF FULL-TIME FACULTY, 1972–73

| | TOTAL | | DEGREE QUALITY | | | | | | | |
| | | | "DISTINGUISHED" AND "STRONG" PH.D.'s | | LOWER-RANKED PH.D.'s | | UNRANKED DOCTORATES | | LESS THAN PH.D. | |
RACE AND ARTICLES PUBLISHED	Salary	Population size	Salary	Population size	Salary	Population size	Salary	Population size	Salary	Population size
WHITES	$16,677	359,828	$17,991	39,603	$17,414	51,490	$18,179	44,224	$15,981	224,510
5 or more	19,969	111,160	20,073	22,741	19,334	28,014	20,008	24,886	20,376	35,519
1–4 articles	15,702	101,132	15,486	11,700	15,252	15,820	16,153	12,457	15,767	61,156
No articles	14,780	142,869	14,013	4,653	14,507	6,948	14,977	6,348	14,814	124,920
No response	17,488	4,667	18,918	509	18,323	709	18,285	534	16,889	2,915
BLACKS	16,037	9,273	20,399	352	19,014	550	20,499	730	15,195	7,640
5 or more	22,583	1,115	21,211	181	21,877	293	28,783	249	19,797	391
1–4 articles	16,430	2,348	19,124	100	16,139	158	17,165	279	16,194	1,812
No articles	14,586	5,559	16,557	54	15,188	93	13,853	173	14,580	5,240
No response	15,403	251	31,000	18	14,000	6	20,896	29	13,244	197
ORIENTALS	15,419	4,678	18,235	740	17,035	1,248	16,724	785	12,727	1,905
5 or more	17,190	2,029	17,485	467	18,158	740	18,035	503	13,182	319
1–4 articles	15,082	948	21,084	220	14,869	224	14,539	155	11,674	348
No articles	13,200	1,651	13,091	46	15,813	276	13,899	120	12,538	1,209
No response	23,176	50	13,000	7	15,909	7	19,131	7	28,679	28

SOURCE: American Council on Education.

tals with "distinguished" and "strong" Ph.D.'s received slightly higher salaries than their white counterparts ($18,235 versus $17,991), and even this difference was not uniform across publications categories. Among the lower-ranked doctorates, both whites and blacks earned more than Orientals, and among those with less than a doctorate, considerably more. The overall salary average of Orientals was slightly below that of blacks, though Orientals were far more concentrated in the higher degree levels and higher degree qualities. Less than half of the Oriental faculty members lacked the Ph.D., and more than 40 percent of all Oriental faculty had published five or more articles. In short, just as group differentials do not imply discrimination, so an absence of such differentials does not imply an absence of discrimination. Orientals receive less than either blacks or whites with the same qualifications, and only the fact that the Orientals have generally better qualifications than either of the other two groups conceals this.

When field-by-field comparisons are made, very similar patterns emerge. In the social sciences, blacks have higher salaries than whites or Orientals, and especially so among holders of Ph.D.'s from "distinguished" and "strong" departments (Table 2). In the natural sciences (Table 3) and the humanities (Table 4), whites lead, with blacks second in the humanities and Orientals second in the natural sciences. A comparison of overall sample size from one table to another reveals very different distributions of these racial groups among academic fields: 37 percent of all black faculty members were in the social sciences, 23 percent were in the humanities, and only 16 percent were in the natural sciences. By contrast, 44 percent of the Orientals were in the natural sciences, 28 percent in the social sciences, and only 16 percent in the humanities. Whites were distributed more or less midway between blacks and Orientals: 30 percent in the social sciences, 24 percent in the humanities, and 25 percent in the natural sciences. Again, the net effect of these distributions is to exaggerate the overall salary differences between blacks and whites and to understate salary differences between Orientals and whites.

The National Academy of Sciences data confirm some of these patterns and reveal some new ones. NAS data for full-time doctoral scientists and engineers (academic and nonacademic) show blacks earning slightly more than whites, with Orientals last—and a spread of only $1,500 per year over all three groups (Table 5).

Publications data are not available for this survey, but age was tabulated as a proxy for experience. Degree quality was again available, and again Orientals with given credentials quality had lower salaries than either blacks or whites in the same categories. In all three groups, salary

Table 2: MEAN ANNUAL SALARIES OF FULL-TIME FACULTY IN THE SOCIAL SCIENCES, 1972–73

	DEGREE QUALITY									
	TOTAL		"DISTINGUISHED" AND "STRONG" PH.D.'S		LOWER-RANKED PH.D.'S		UNRANKED DOCTORATES		LESS THAN PH.D.	
RACE AND ARTICLES PUBLISHED	Salary	Population size	Salary	Population size	Salary	Population size	Salary	Population size	Salary	Population size
WHITES	$16,872	108,733	$18,369	17,307	$17,192	16,680	$18,132	10,417	$16,182	64,329
5 or more	19,924	30,623	20,753	9,563	19,161	7,939	20,105	4,295	19,623	8,827
1–4 articles	16,117	34,213	15,618	5,339	15,620	5,930	17,508	3,362	16,165	19,582
No articles	15,263	42,216	14,413	2,141	14,618	2,579	15,770	2,626	15,325	34,870
No response	17,040	1,681	19,728	264	18,583	232	16,832	135	16,050	1,050
BLACKS	17,527	3,373	20,451	186	20,344	222	20,487	326	16,718	2,639
5 or more	24,088	381	21,370	109	22,676	128	31,434	97	19,240	48
1–4 articles	15,162	977	19,688	66	17,919	54	18,176	103	14,154	754
No articles	17,793	1,914	15,813	11	16,232	40	13,324	121	18,152	1,742
No response	10,540	100	—	—	—	—	30,000	5	9,509	95
ORIENTALS	15,089	1,313	18,844	203	16,449	324	13,338	70	13,581	717
5 or more	15,653	350	18,204	101	18,700	95	16,216	7	11,931	148
1–4 articles	17,042	253	22,897	69	14,836	96	12,445	22	15,649	67
No articles	14,115	710	12,317	33	16,004	134	13,351	41	13,793	502
No response	—	—	—	—	—	—	—	—	—	—

SOURCE: American Council on Education.

Table 3: MEAN ANNUAL SALARIES OF FULL-TIME FACULTY IN THE NATURAL SCIENCES, 1972–73

RACE AND ARTICLES PUBLISHED	TOTAL		"DISTINGUISHED" AND "STRONG" PH.D.'S		LOWER-RANKED PH.D.'S		UNRANKED DOCTORATES		LESS THAN PH.D.	
	Salary	Population size	Salary	Population size	Salary	Population size	Salary	Population size	Salary	Population size
WHITES	$17,225	91,411	$18,377	12,457	$18,130	25,282	$18,361	12,575	$15,972	41,098
5 or more	19,469	43,243	19,535	8,946	19,527	16,746	19,339	9,228	19,426	8,324
1–4 articles	15,735	22,667	15,442	2,863	15,259	6,446	15,342	2,739	16,203	10,619
No articles	14,618	24,571	14,268	487	15,206	1,774	16,030	427	14,551	21,882
No response	18,090	929	18,646	160	19,069	316	19,651	181	15,589	272
BLACKS	15,176	1,474	20,436	78	17,950	243	18,383	167	13,535	986
5 or more	20,640	366	20,837	51	20,445	136	24,069	57	19,180	122
1–4 articles	14,562	410	18,023	16	14,560	76	16,444	70	13,817	248
No articles	12,051	639	22,000	11	15,672	25	13,779	41	11,572	562
No response	19,365	60	—	—	14,000	6	—	—	20,000	53
ORIENTALS	16,797	2,035	18,145	490	17,709	754	17,132	441	12,520	349
5 or more	17,852	1,320	17,276	342	18,301	588	18,135	319	15,646	71
1–4 articles	16,417	415	20,672	137	15,793	101	14,568	84	12,498	93
No articles	12,466	281	15,000	4	15,344	61	13,311	31	11,333	186
No response	15,902	19	13,000	7	15,000	4	19,131	7	—	—

SOURCE: American Council on Education.

Table 4: MEAN ANNUAL SALARIES OF FULL-TIME FACULTY IN THE HUMANITIES, 1972–73

| | DEGREE QUALITY | | | | | | | | | |
| RACE AND ARTICLES PUBLISHED | TOTAL | | "DISTINGUISHED" AND "STRONG" PH.D.'s | | LOWER-RANKED PH.D.'s | | UNRANKED DOCTORATES | | LESS THAN PH.D. | |
	Salary	Population size	Salary	Population size	Salary	Population size	Salary	Population size	Salary	Population size
WHITES	$15,572	85,904	$16,832	9,765	$15,659	9,084	$15,925	8,810	$15,293	58,245
5 or more	18,425	17,001	19,707	4,165	18,399	2,954	18,414	3,681	17,584	6,202
1–4 articles	15,419	23,923	15,315	3,490	14,573	3,381	14,776	3,048	15,789	14,004
No articles	14,497	43,751	13,530	2,025	13,920	2,594	13,059	1,943	14,667	37,149
No response	17,313	1,228	16,911	85	16,227	154	16,173	99	17,666	890
BLACKS	15,034	2,177	20,259	89	16,743	74	17,650	99	14,590	1,915
5 or more	16,221	135	22,296	21	21,513	19	21,507	15	12,658	80
1–4 articles	21,354	604	18,000	18	16,972	28	16,172	61	22,348	498
No articles	11,869	1,347	14,955	32	13,201	27	—	—	11,764	1,288
No response	18,175	91	31,000	18	—	—	19,000	24	13,161	49
ORIENTALS	13,005	757	16,561	47	14,860	146	16,003	90	11,509	473
5 or more	14,629	199	17,443	24	14,922	33	17,544	63	11,294	79
1–4 articles	10,317	239	16,110	14	11,557	27	11,738	15	9,579	183
No articles	13,000	306	15,000	9	15,487	82	13,000	12	11,753	203
No response	39,032	12	—	—	17,000	3	—	—	47,393	9

SOURCE: American Council on Education.

Table 5:　MEDIAN ANNUAL SALARIES OF FULL-TIME SCIENTISTS AND
ENGINEERS BY RACIAL GROUP AND DEGREE QUALITY, 1973

RACE AND AGE GROUP	TOTAL		"DISTINGUISHED" AND "STRONG" PH.D.'s		OTHER	
	Salary	Sample size	Salary	Sample size	Salary	Sample size
WHITES	$20,988	28,048	$22,146	8,589	$20,275	19,459
Under 35 years	17,228	6,615	17,879	1,827	16,933	4,788
35–49	21,757	14,024	22,480	4,167	21,342	9,857
50+	25,357	7,409	26,333	2,595	24,704	4,814
BLACKS	21,445	261	23,268	54	20,597	207
Under 35 years	18,660	44	20,476	4	18,396	40
35–49	21,256	149	22,998	26	20,668	123
50+	23,460	68	24,307	24	22,770	44
ORIENTALS	20,005	1,087	20,222	330	19,862	757
Under 35 years	16,230	210	18,162	60	15,364	150
35–49	20,613	676	20,378	206	20,761	470
50+	23,261	201	22,429	64	23,660	137

SOURCE: 1973 Survey of Doctoral Scientists and Engineers, National Research Council,
National Academy of Sciences.

rises with age, but the *relative* positions of blacks and whites are *reversed*
in the oldest and youngest age brackets. Young black doctorates—under
35—earn more than their white counterparts in either degree quality
category, but older blacks—over 50—earn *less* than their white counterparts in either degree quality category. These results hold up when the
sample is broken down into natural sciences and social sciences. It is
also consistent with a larger study by Professor Finis Welch of UCLA
which showed a much higher rate of return to education for younger
blacks than for older blacks—both absolutely and relative to their white
counterparts.[39] Two important factors are involved here: (1) the older
blacks were educated in an era when their public school education was
inferior not only by various quality measures but also in sheer quantity
(black schools had fewer days than white schools in their respective
school years),[40] and this poorer preparation could not help affecting later
capability, and (2) the level of job discrimination was also greater when
the older blacks began their careers, and this too could not help affecting

the later course of those careers, making it difficult for these blacks to exploit new opportunities as readily as the younger blacks just beginning their careers. A further implication of all this is that global comparisons of blacks and whites capture many existing effects of past discrimination, while an age-cohort breakdown of the same data permits a better look at the current results of current policies and the trends to expect in the future.

In summary, the salary differentials among these three racial or ethnic groups are small, both in the academic world and among holders of the doctorate in the social or natural sciences (academic and non-academic). With such variables as credentials, publications, and experience held constant, blacks equaled or surpassed whites in 1973—but they also equaled or surpassed whites with fields held constant in 1970, before affirmative action quotas. Without these variables held constant, the overall black-white differential was $62 per year in 1970 and $640 in 1973. Given that these are different samples, it is perhaps best to say that there were negligible overall differences among black and white academics in both years—that affirmative action has achieved nothing discernible in this regard. But if an arithmetic conclusion is insisted upon, then it must be said that there has been a negative effect of affirmative action, as far as black-white income differences are concerned.

Women

The classic study, *Academic Women* by Jessie Bernard, described women as "over-represented in college teaching." This was based on the fact that women were only 10 percent of the Ph.D.'s but constituted more than 20 percent of college and university faculties.[41] This was written in 1964—before affirmative action. Unlike HEW's crude "underutilization" measures, this study (by an academic woman) considered not only the number of women with the usual degree requirements, but also the high proportion of such women—as many as one-fourth of all female doctorates—who withdraw from work.[42] Withdrawal from the labor force is only one of many career characteristics which have a negative effect on the employment, pay, and promotion of academic women. Some others are:

1. Female academics hold a doctorate less frequently than male academics—20 percent as against 40 percent in 1972-73.[43]
2. Female academics publish only about half as many articles and books per person as do male academics,[44] and females are especially underrepresented among frequent publishers.[45]

3. Academic women are educated disproportionately in lower-paying fields of specialization, such as the humanities,[46] and they prefer teaching over research more so than academic men, not only in attitude surveys,[47] but also in their allocation of time[48] and in the kinds of institutions at which they work[49]—which are the low-paying teaching institutions more so than the top research universities with high salaries.

4. Academic women more frequently subordinate their careers to their spouses' careers, or to the general well-being of their families, than do academic men. This takes many forms, including quitting jobs they like because their husbands take jobs elsewhere,[50] interrupting their careers for domestic reasons,[51] withdrawing from the labor force (25 percent of women Ph.D.'s),[52] doing a disproportionate share of household and social chores compared to their husbands in the same occupations,[53] and a general attitude reported by women themselves of putting their homes and families ahead of their careers much more often then do male academics.[54] All this goes to the heart of the question of the actual *source* of sex differentiation—whether it is the home or the work place, and therefore whether "equal treatment" as required by the Constitution and envisioned by the Civil Rights Act would eliminate or ensure unequal results by sex.

None of these factors disproves the existence of sex discrimination, but they do mean that attempts to measure sex discrimination must be unusually careful in specifying the relevant variables which must be equal before remaining inequalities can be considered "discrimination." Unfortunately, such care is not evident in HEW pronouncements or in much of the literature supporting affirmative action. Even the comprehensive studies by Helen S. Astin and Alan E. Bayer make the fatal mistake of holding marital status constant in comparing male-female career differences.[55] But marriage has *opposite* effects on the careers of male and female academics, advancing the man professionally and retarding the woman's progress. Not only do the men and women themselves say so,[56] but the Astin-Bayer data (and other data) also show it.[57] Therefore, to treat as "discrimination" all residual differences for men and women of the "same" characteristics—including marriage—is completely invalid and misleading.

Marriage is a dominant—and negative—influence on academic women's careers. A study of academics who had received their Ph.D.'s many years earlier showed that 69 percent of the total—mostly men— had achieved the rank of full professor, as had 76 percent of the single women but only 56 percent of the married women.[58] In short, many of the statistical differences between the broad categories "men" and "women" are to a large extent simply differences between married women and all other persons. It is an open question how much of the residual disadvantages of single academic women is based upon employer fears of their becoming married academic women and acquiring the problems of that status. One indication of the difficulty of successfully combining academic careers with the demands of being a wife and mother is that academic women are married much less frequently than either academic men or women Ph.D.'s in nonacademic fields,[59] are divorced more frequently,[60] and have fewer children than other female Ph.D.'s.[61]

Much of the literature on women in the labor market denies that "all" women, "most" women, or the "typical" woman represent special problems of attrition, absenteeism, and other characteristics reflecting the special demands of home on women. For example, the "typical woman economist" has not given up her job to move because of her husband's move, but 30 percent of the women economists do, while only 5 percent of male economists accommodate their wives in this way.[62] Similarly, while most female Ph.D.'s in economics have not interrupted their careers, 24 percent had interrupted their careers prior to receiving the degree (compared to 2 percent of the men) and "another 20 percent" afterwards (compared to 1 percent of the men).[63] These are clearly substantial percentages of women and several-fold differentials between men and women.

The literature on women workers in general makes much of the fact that *most* women "work to support themselves or others," not just for incidental money.[64] However, this does not alter the facts (1) that women's labor force participation rates are substantially lower than men's[65] and (2) that married women's labor force participation declines as their husbands' incomes rise.[66] This is also true of academic women.[67]

In considering global male-female differences in career results, the question is not whether "most" women have certain negative career characteristics but whether a significant percentage do and whether that percentage is substantially different from that of men. Moreover, it is not merely the individual negative characteristics that matter but their cumulative effects on male-female differentials in employment, pay, and promotion. Nor can these differences in career characteristics be dismissed as subjective employer perceptions or aversions.[68] They represent in many cases *choices* made outside the work place which negatively affect women's career prospects. As one woman researcher in this area has observed: "One way of insuring that the academic husband's status will be higher than his academic wife's is to allow the husband's job opportunities to determine where the family lives."[69] But regardless of the wisdom or justice of such a situation, *it is not employer discrimination*, even though it may lead to statistical male-female differences between persons of equal ability.

One of the fertile sources of confusion in this area is the thoughtless extension of the "minority" paradigm to women. It makes sense to compare blacks and whites of the same educational levels because education has the same positive effect on black incomes and white incomes, though not necessarily to the same extent. It does *not* make sense to compare men and women of the same marital status because marital status has opposite effects on the careers of men and women. Minorities have serious problems of cultural disadvantages so that faculty members from such groups tend to have lower socioeconomic status and lower mental test scores than their white counterparts,[70] and black colleges and universities have never been comparable to the best white colleges and universities,[71] whereas female academics come from *higher* socioeconomic levels than male academics,[72] female Ph.D.'s have higher IQs than male Ph.D.'s in field after field,[73] and the best women's colleges have had status and student SAT levels comparable to those of the best male or coeducational institutions.

Women have been part of the cultural, informational, and social network for generations, while blacks and Jews have been largely excluded until the past generation. While minorities have been slowly rising in professional, technical, and other high-level positions over the past 100 years, women have declined in many such areas over the same period, even in colleges institutionally operated by women,[74] so that employer discrimination can hardly explain either the trend or the current level of "utilization" of women. Marriage and childbearing trends over time are highly correlated with trends of women's participation in high-level occupations, as well as being correlated with intragroup differences among women at a given time. In short, women are not another "minority," either statistically or culturally.

When male-female comparisons are broken down by marital status and other variables reflecting women's domestic responsibilities, some remarkable results appear. Although women in the economy as a whole earn less than half as much annually as men,[75] with this ratio *declining* from 1949 to 1969,[76] the sex differentials narrow to the vanishing point—and in some cases are even reversed—when successive corrections are made for marital status, full-time as against part-time employment, and continuous years of work. For example, in 1971 women's median annual earnings were only 40 percent of those of men, but when the comparison was restricted to year-around, full-time workers, the figure rose to 60 percent, and when the comparison was between single women and single men in the same age brackets (30 to 44) with continuous work experience, "single women who had worked every year since leaving school earned slightly more than single men."[77] These are government data for the economy as a whole.

The severe negative effect of marriage on the careers of women is not a peculiarity of the academic world. Other nationwide data on sex differences show single women's incomes ranging from 93 percent of single men's income at ages 25 to 34 to 106 percent in ages 55 to 64[78]— that is, after the danger of marriage and children are substantially past. For women already married, the percentages are both lower and decline with age—ranging from 55 percent of married men's incomes at ages 25 to 37 to only 34 percent at ages 55 to 64.[79] Apparently early damage to a woman's career is not completely recouped—at least not relative to men who have been moving up occupationally as they age while their wives' careers were interrupted by domestic responsibilities. In the early years of career development, single women's labor force participation rates are rising sharply, while those of married women are declining sharply.[80] Again, the data suggest that what are called "sex differences" are largely differences between married women and all others, and that the origin of these differences is in the division of responsibilities in the family rather than employer discrimination in the work place. The increasing proportion of married women in the work force over time[81] has been a major factor in the decline of the earnings of women relative to men.

Academic women show similar patterns. For example, the institutional employment of married women is "determined to a large extent" by the location of their husbands' jobs,[82] and this contributes to a lower institutional level for academic females than for male Ph.D.'s. Academic women apparently find it harder than other women of similar education to combine marriage and a career. One study of "biological scientists receiving their degrees during the same time period" found only 32 percent of such academic women married compared to 50 percent of the nonacademic counterparts, even though virtually identical percentages were married before receiving the Ph.D.[83] A more general survey of women holding doctorates found only 45 percent to be married and living with their husbands.[84] Although there were more married than single women among women doctorates in general,[85] in the academic world there were more single than married female doctorates.[86] Moreover, female academics had divorce rates several times higher than male academics.[87] Another study of college teachers found 83 percent of the men but only 46 percent of the women to be married.[88] Women in other high-level, high-pressure jobs requiring continuous full-time work show similarly low proportions married.[89]

Childbearing is also negatively associated with career prospects. Among Radcliffe Ph.D.'s, those working full-time had the fewest children, those working part-time next, those working intermittently next, and those not working at all had the most children.[90] Various surveys show that "female Ph.D.s who are married are twice as likely to be childless as women in the same age group in the general population" and even when they do have children, to have fewer of them.[91] The husband's prospects also have a negative effect on woman doctorates' careers: a woman married to a "highly educated man with a substantial income was less likely to work" or, if she did, was more likely to take a part-time job.[92] This parallels a negative correlation between married women's labor force participation and their husbands' incomes in the general economy.[93]

In research output, "the woman doctorate who is married and has children was less likely than the single woman doctorate or a childless married woman doctorate to have many scientific and scholarly articles to her credit."[94] It is not surprising that the married woman doctorate "tended to make a lower salary than the single women, even if she was working full time."[95] Unfortunately, studies of academic women have not simultaneously controlled for marital status, full-time *continuous* employment, publications, and degree level and quality.

The National Academy of Sciences data permit comparisons of the salaries of male and female doctorates who worked full-time both in 1960 and in 1973 and who responded to all the biennial surveys of the National Science Foundation from 1960 through 1973 (see Table 6).

This gives an approximation of full-time continuous employment, but does not show whether the respondent was employed full time in each of the years during which a survey was made or whether the respondent worked at all in the nonsurvey years. These data show female salaries at 83 percent of male salaries in 1970 (before affirmative action) and 84 percent in 1973 (after affirmative action)—a smaller proportion than in other data which controlled for other variables such as publications and degree quality. It also indicates no discernible effect of affirmative action programs.

A 1968 study of full-time academic doctorates found women's salaries ranging from 89 percent to 99 percent of men's salaries in the same field, with similar length of employment, and in broadly similar institutions (colleges versus universities).[96] These higher percentages—as compared with the results in Table 6—suggest that the distribution of

Table 6:   MALE-FEMALE SALARY RELATIONSHIPS (1970 AND 1973)
AMONG FULL-TIME DOCTORATES
INCLUDED IN ALL 1960–73 NSF SURVEYS

	AVERAGE ANNUAL SALARY	
FIELDS	1970	1973
NATURAL SCIENCES		
Men	$20,646	$24,854
Women	$17,061	$20,718
Ratio of women/men	.83	.83
SOCIAL SCIENCES		
Men	$21,442	$26,537
Women	$17,171	$21,027
Ratio of women/men	.80	.80
TOTAL*		
Men	$20,508	$24,851
Women	$17,073	$20,910
Ratio of women/men	.83	.84

*Includes miscellaneous fields as well as the natural sciences and the social sciences.
SOURCE: National Academy of Sciences.

women by institutional type and ranking and by years of employment explains a significant part of the male-female salary differences among academics. Moreover, since women academics with Ph.D.'s in this 1968 study earned 92.2 percent of the income of men academics with Ph.D.'s (even without controlling for publications), these figures indicate how small the sex differential was for even roughly similar individuals before affirmative action.

Even more revealing patterns appear in our tabulations of ACE data by marital status (Table 7). In 1969, academic women who never married earned slightly more than academic men who never married. This was true at top-rated institutions and at other institutions, for academics with publications and for academics without publications. The male salary advantage exists solely among married academics and among those who used to be married ("other" includes widowed, divorced, etc.).

The male advantage is greatest among those married and with dependent children. Being married with children is obviously the greatest inhibitor of a woman's career prospects and the greatest incentive to a man's. The salaries of women who never married were 104 percent of the salaries of their male counterparts at the top-rated institutions and 101

Table 7: ACADEMIC-YEAR SALARIES BY SEX AND MARITAL STATUS, 1968–69

Sex and Marital Status	Total				With Publications				Without Publications			
	Top Institutions		Other Institutions		Top Institutions		Other Institutions		Top Institutions		Other Institutions	
	Salary	Number	Salary	Number	Salary	Number	Salary	Number	Salary	Number	Salary	Number
Men												
Total	$13,704	26,493	$13,245	307,323	$13,697	26,033	$13,230	301,251	$14,075	459	$13,965	6,071
Presently married	13,562	23,623	13,175	280,637	13,549	23,209	13,159	275,248	14,323	413	13,969	5,389
With dependent children	14,180	15,996	13,636	200,570	14,179	15,728	13,623	196,640	14,242	267	14,273	3,929
Without dependent children	12,266	7,627	12,018	80,067	12,223	7,481	11,997	78,607	14,472	145	13,150	1,459
Never married	11,070	142	10,525	3,737	11,070	142	10,569	3,629	0	0	9,027	107
Other	15,065	2,727	14,548	22,947	15,120	2,681	14,540	22,373	11,838	45	14,856	573
Women												
Total	11,030	4,166	10,359	75,044	11,003	4,062	10,345	73,155	12,094	103	10,889	1,888
Presently married	10,264	2,839	10,021	60,484	10,213	2,753	10,012	59,016	11,875	86	10,403	1,467
With dependent children	9,727	1,255	9,645	17,246	9,626	1,207	9,640	16,734	12,255	48	9,809	511
Without dependent children	10,690	1,583	10,171	43,238	10,672	1,545	10,159	42,282	11,394	37	10,721	956
Never married	11,523	404	10,566	5,174	11,363	399	10,455	4,954	22,499	5	13,075	219
Other	13,176	921	12,419	9,384	13,236	909	12,427	9,184	8,633	11	12,045	200

NOTE: Data cover all races and all disciplines.
SOURCE: American Council on Education.

percent at other institutions. For women who were married but had no dependent children, the percentages fell to 88 and 84 percent, respectively. For married women with dependent children, the percentages fell still further, to 69 and 70 percent. For women and men without publications and in nonranked—essentially nonresearch—institutions, the "never married" women earned 145 percent of the "never married" men's incomes—confirming a general impression that women prefer teaching institutions, and therefore a higher proportion of top-quality women than of top-quality men end up at such places by choice. It also suggests that employers are not unwilling to recognize such quality differentials with salary differentials in favor of women.

In the literature on sex differentials and in the pronouncements of governmental agencies administering affirmative action programs, sinister and even conspiratorial theories have been advanced to explain very ordinary and readily understandable social phenomena: (1) academic individuals who are neither aiding nor aided by a spouse make very similar incomes, whether they are male or female, (2) academic individuals who are aided by a spouse (married males) make more than unaided individuals, and (3) academic individuals who aid a spouse (married females) make less for themselves than do the other categories of people. The social mores which lead women to sacrifice their careers for their husbands' careers may be questioned (as should the high personal price extracted from academic career women, as reflected in their lower marriage and higher divorce rates). But social mores are not the same as employer discrimination.

The fact that single academic women earned slightly higher salaries than single academic men suggests that employer discrimination by sex is not responsible for male-female income differences among academics. Moreover, even as regards social mores, it must be noted that academic women report themselves satisfied with their lives a higher percentage of the time than do academic men[97]—a phenomenon which some explain by saying that women do not put all their emotional eggs in one basket as often as men,[98] and which others explain by treating high research creativity as a somewhat pathological and compensatory activity of the personally unfulfilled.[99] The point here is that the evidence is not all one way, nor the logic overwhelming, even as regards apparently inequitable social mores.

On the basic policy issue of employer discrimination, such evidence as there is lends no support to this as an explanation of male-female career differences, and the slight but persistent advantage of single females over single males undermines the pervasive preconception that employers favor men when other things are equal.

NOTES

1. Michael R. Winston, "Through the Back Door: Academic Racism and the Negro Scholar in Historical Perspective," *Daedalus* 100, no. 3 (Summer 1971): 695.

2. Richard A. Lester, *Antibias Regulation of Universities* (New York: McGraw-Hill Company, 1974), pp. 3-4.

3. Ibid., pp. 62-63.

4. Ibid., p. 76.

5. Ibid.

6. Kent G. Mommsen, "Black Doctorates in American Higher Education: A Cohort Analysis," *Journal of Social and Behavioral Science*, Spring 1974, pp. 101-17.

7. Ibid., pp. 104, 107.

8. David Rafky, "The Black Academic in the Marketplace," *Change* 3, no. 6 (October 1971): 65. A sharp distinction must be made between personal experience of discrimination and general opinions that discrimination exists. Both minorities and women report very little personal experience of discrimination and, at the same time, a widespread impression that discrimination is pervasive. See "Discrimination: A Cautionary Note," *Law and Liberty* 1, no. 3, p. 11. Similar inconsistencies are found in opinion surveys of the general population. See Ben J. Wattenberg, *The Real America* (Garden City, N.Y.: Doubleday & Co., 1974), pp. 196, 198.

9. Kent G. Mommsen, "Black Ph.D.s in the Academic Marketplace," *Journal of Higher Education* 45, no. 4 (April 1974), p. 253.

10. Ibid., p. 256.

11. Ibid., p. 258.

12. Ibid., p. 262.

13. William Moore, Jr., and Lonnie H. Wagstaff, *Black Educators in White Colleges* (San Francisco: Jossey-Bass Publishers, 1970), pp. 64-65.

14. Daniel C. Thompson, *Private Black Colleges at the Crossroads* (Westport, Conn.: Greenwood Press, 1973), p. 155. See also Moore and Wagstaff, *Black Educators in White Colleges*, pp. 142-43.

15. For example, the "remarkable record of women's progress through the professional ranks of a hitherto rigid academic system" (*Change*, 7, no. 4 [May 1975]: back cover).

16. Jessie Bernard, *Academic Women* (University Park: Pennsylvania State University Press, 1964), p. 39.

17. John B. Parrish, "Professional Womanpower as a National Resource," *Quarterly Review of Economics and Business*, Spring 1961, pp. 58-59.

18. Bernard, *Academic Women*, p. 206.

19. Ibid., p. 74.

20. Ibid., pp. 2-3, 31-32, 38n-39n.

21. Christopher Jencks and David Riesman, "The American Negro College," *Harvard Educational Review* 37, no. 1 (Winter 1967): 3-60; Thomas Sowell, *Black Education: Myths and Tragedies* (New York: David McKay Co., 1972), pp. 255-59.

22. Lester, *Antibias Regulation*, p. 47.

23. Ibid., p. 42.

24. Juanita Kreps, *Sex in the Marketplace* (Baltimore: Johns Hopkins University Press, 1971), p. 52.

25. Rita James, et al., "The Woman Ph.D.: A Recent Profile," *Social Problems* 15, no. 2 (Fall 1967): 227-28.

26. National Academy of Sciences, *Doctoral Scientists and Engineers in the United States: 1973 Profile* (Washington, D.C.: National Academy of Sciences, 1974), p. 30.

27. Lester, *Antibias Regulation*, p. 50.

28. Mommsen, "Black Doctorates," pp. 103-4.

29. Mommsen, "Black Ph.D.s," p. 258.

30. David G. Brown, *The Market for College Teachers* (Chapel Hill: University of North Carolina Press, 1965), p. 83.

31. Lester, *Antibias Regulation*, p. 49.

32. Thompson, *Private Black Colleges at the Crossroads*, p. 155.

33. Mommsen, "Black Ph.D.s," pp. 258-59.

34. Ibid., p. 262.

35. Theodore Caplow and Reece J. McGee, *The Academic Marketplace* (New York: Basic Books, 1961), p. 41.

36. David G. Brown, *The Mobile Professors* (Washington, D.C.: American Council on Education, 1967), p. 26.

37. Lester, *Antibias Regulation*, p. 48.

38. Mommsen, "Black Ph.D.s," pp. 262, 259.

39. Finis Welch, "Black-White Differences in Returns to Schooling," *American Economic Review* 63, no. 5 (December 1973): 893-907.

40. Ibid., p. 894.

41. Bernard, *Academic Women*, p. 52.

42. Ibid., p. 66. See also Lester, *Antibias Regulation*, p. 42.

43. Alan E. Bayer, *Teaching Faculty in Academe, 1972-73* (Washington, D.C.: American Council on Education, 1973), p. 15.

44. Frank Clemente, "Early Career Determinants of Research Productivity," *American Journal of Sociology* 79, no. 2 (September 1973): 414; Lester, *Antibias Regulation*, p. 47. See also Brown, *Mobile Professors*, p. 78, and Bernard, *Academic Women*, p. 148.

45. Brown, *Mobile Professors*, pp. 76–78. See also Lester, *Antibias Regulation*, p. 42.

46. Bernard, *Academic Women*, p. 180; Brown, *Mobile Professors*, p. 81; Helen S. Astin and Alan E. Bayer, "Sex Discrimination in Academe," *Educational Record*, Spring 1972, p. 103; Helen S. Astin, *The Woman Doctorate in America* (New York: Russell Sage Foundation, 1970), pp. 20–21.

47. Bernard, *Academic Women*, pp. 141–42.

48. Astin, *The Woman Doctorate*, p. 73; Lester, *Antibias Regulation*, p. 42.

49. Brown, *Mobile Professors*, pp. 79–80.

50. Barbara B. Reagan, "Two Supply Curves for Economists? Implications of Mobility and Career Attachment of Women," *American Economic Review* 65, no. 2 (May 1975): 102–3. See also Astin, *The Woman Doctorate*, p. 102.

51. Reagan, "Two Supply Curves," p. 104.

52. Brown, *Mobile Professors*, p. 78.

53. Bernard, *Academic Women*, p. 221; Lester, *Antibias Regulation*, p. 39.

54. Reagan, "Two Supply Curves," p. 103. See also Bernard, *Academic Women*, pp. 151–52, 181–82; Astin, *The Woman Doctorate*, pp. 91–92.

55. "The regression weights of the predictor variables that emerged in the analysis of the men's sample were applied to the data for the women's sample to assess the predicted outcome when the criteria for men were used . . . . To award women the same salary as men of similar rank, background, achievements and work settings . . . would require a compensatory average *raise* of more than $1,000 . . ." (Astin and Bayer, "Sex Discrimination in Academe," p. 115).

56. Bernard, *Academic Women*, p. 217.

57. Astin and Bayer, "Sex Discrimination in Academe," p. 111; Lester, *Antibias Regulation*, pp. 36–37.

58. Helen S. Astin, "Career Profiles of Women Doctorates," in Alice S. Rossi and Ann Calderwood, eds., *Academic Women on the Move* (New York: Russell Sage Foundation, 1973), p. 153.

59. Lester, *Antibias Regulation*, p. 41.

60. Bernard, *Academic Women*, pp. 113, 206.

61. Ibid., p. 216.

62. Reagan, "Two Supply Curves," pp. 101–3.

63. Ibid., p. 104.

64. U.S. Department of Labor, *Under-utilization of Women Workers* (Washington, D.C.: U.S. Government Printing Office, n.d.), p. 1.

65. William G. Bowen and T. Aldrich Finegan, *The Economics of Labor Force Participation* (Princeton, N.J.: Princeton University Press, 1969), pp. 41, 101, 243.

66. Ibid., p. 132.

67. Astin, *The Woman Doctorate*, p. 60.

68. Jerolyn R. Lyle and Jane L. Ross, *Women in Industry* (Lexington, Mass.: D. C. Heath and Co., 1973), p. 13; Reagan, "Two Supply Curves," p. 104.

69. Quoted in Reagan, "Two Supply Curves," p. 102.

70. Horace Mann Bond, *A Study of the Factors Involved in the Identification and Encouragement of Unusual Academic Talent Among Underprivileged Populations* (U.S. Department of Health, Education, and Welfare, Project no. 5–0859, Contract no. SAE 8028, January 1967), p. 117.

71. Sowell, *Black Education*, pp. 255–59; Jencks and Riesman, "The American Negro College."

72. Bernard, *Academic Women*, pp. xx, 77–78; Alan E. Bayer, *College and University: A Statistical Description* (Washington, D.C.: American Council on Education, June 1970), p. 12; Astin, *The Woman Doctorate*, pp. 23, 25.

73. Bernard, *Academic Women*, p. 84.

74. Ibid., pp. 39–44.

75. James Gwartney and Richard Stroup, "Measurement of Employment Discrimination According to Sex," *Southern Economic Journal* 39, no. 4 (April 1973): 575–76; and "The Economic Role of Women," in the *Economic Report of the President, 1973* (Washington, D.C.: U.S. Government Printing Office, 1973), p. 103.

76. Gwartney and Stroup, "Employment Discrimination," p. 583.

77. "The Economic Role of Women," p. 105.

78. Gwartney and Stroup, "Employment Discrimination," p. 582.

79. Ibid.

80. Kreps, *Sex in the Marketplace*, p. 32.

81. Ibid., pp. 4, 19.

82. Bernard, *Academic Women*, p. 88.

83. Ibid., p. 113.

84. Astin, *The Woman Doctorate*, p. 27.

85. Ibid.

86. Ibid., p. 71.

87. Bernard, *Academic Women*, p. 216.

88. Ibid., p. 313.

89. Ibid., pp. 313–14.

90. Ibid., p. 241.

91. Lester, *Antibias Regulation*, p. 38.

92. Astin, *The Woman Doctorate*, p. 60.

93. Bowen and Finegan, *Labor Force Participation*, p. 132.

94. Astin, *The Woman Doctorate*, p. 82.

95. Ibid., p. 90.

96. Bayer and Astin, "Sex Differences in Academic Rank and Salary Among

Science Doctorates in Teaching," *Journal of Human Resources* 3, no. 2 (Spring 1968): 196. "Science" in the title includes the social sciences.

97. Bernard, *Academic Women*, p. 182.
98. Ibid., p. 152.
99. Ibid., p. 156.

Tuition Tax Credits: A Social Revolution

The Packwood-Moynihan tuition tax rebate legislation is, as Professor E. G. West aptly calls it, "a crucial event in the history of education."[1] Its "revolutionary potential for low-income groups"[2] has been missed by most other commentators and critics and deserves further exploration.

Why is this bill so important—and to whom? It is most important to those who are mentioned least: the poor, the working class, and all whose children are trapped in educationally deteriorating and physically dangerous public schools. Few groups have so much at stake in the fate of this bill as ghetto blacks. To upper-income families with children in college, the maximum $500 tax relief is hardly of decisive importance, when annual college costs range up to ten times that amount. The campaign of misrepresentation by the education establishment has depicted the affluent as the chief (or sole) beneficiaries, when in fact the opposite is nearer the truth. There are many times more students in elementary and secondary schools than in college, and among those children enrolled in pre-college private institutions, there are more whose parents earn from $5,000 to $10,000 a year than those whose parents are in *all* the brackets from $25,000 on up.

"Tuition Tax Credits: A Social Revolution," by Thomas Sowell is reprinted from *Policy Review*, Issue No. 4 (Spring 1978). *Policy Review* is a publication of The Heritage Foundation, 214 Massachusetts Avenue, N.E., Washington, D.C., 20002.

Even the current enrollees in private education are not primarily the affluent. The average family income of private elementary and secondary school children is about $15,000. But since the whole purpose or effect of the tuition tax rebate is to extend to others the opportunity for private education, the question is not so much who *now* goes to private school, but who *could* go after this legislation is in effect. No doubt those who went to college in past generations, before the G.I. Bill and other educational subsidies, were far more affluent than the general population, but to object to the G.I. Bill as aid to the affluent would be to miss the whole point—that it extended a privilege previously enjoyed by a few into an opportunity open to millions more. That is precisely what this bill does. That is precisely why it is being opposed and misrepresented by those whose jobs, pensions, and power derive from the public school bureaucracy.

PRIVATE SCHOOLS LESS EXPENSIVE THAN PUBLIC

While $500 does not begin to cover college costs, it does cover all or most of the cost of sending a child to many private day schools. Most of those private schools are not the expensive Andover or Exeter stereotypes, but rather schools costing a fraction of the tuition they charge— and having costs per pupil that are a half, a third, or a fifth of the per pupil cost in the public schools. It is not uncommon for Catholic parochial schools costing a few hundred dollars a year to have test scores higher than public schools in the same neighborhoods with per pupil costs well over a thousand dollars. One of the misrepresentations by opponents of the tuition tax rebate is that it would cost billions of dollars. They are talking about Treasury disbursements, which may be politically important. What is *economically* important is that a shift of students to lower-cost private schools can *save* billions of dollars for society as a whole.

Most of the private schools do not have the runaway pay scales or plush pensions that teachers' unions have extracted from politicians handing out the taxpayers' money. Few parochial schools are surrounded with tennis courts or contain many of the other expensive amenities or status symbols that add little to the education of children, but which have become part of the fringe benefits of public school administrators. Indeed, most private schools have far fewer administrators per hundred pupils, which is no small part of the reason for their lower costs or for the opposition of public school administrators to allowing parents a choice of where to send their children.

The crux of the controversy over this bill is *choice* and *power*. If parents are given a choice, public school officials will lose the monopoly power they now hold over a captive audience. That monopoly power is greatest over the poor, but it extends to all who cannot afford to simultaneously pay taxes for the public schools and tuition at a private school. Public schools in affluent neighborhoods where parents already have that option must pay some attention to those parents' wishes and be responsive. But parents in poorer neighborhoods and ghettos have no such leverage to use to get attention, response, or even common courtesy. The mere prospect of being able to remove their children to private schools changes all that. In other words, the benefits of the availability of tuition tax credit do not end with those who take advantage of it, but extend to those who keep their children in the public schools and never collect a dime from the Treasury—but whose children's needs now have to be taken seriously by public school officials no longer insulated or assured of a captive audience.

Much has been made of the fact that most of the enrollment in private elementary and secondary schools is in Catholic parochial schools. Like many other statements about the situation before this bill is passed, it is far from decisive in determining what the situation will be afterwards. The government is constantly overestimating the revenues to be gained from imposing a given tax by assuming that the pre-tax situation will continue unchanged except for the collection of the tax. In the same way, some are now assuming that the social, economic, and religious composition of families with children in private schools will remain unchanged after a subsidy that will put such education within reach of tens of millions of other people. Moreover, not all of the children enrolled in Catholic schools are Catholic. In urban ghettos, especially, it is not uncommon for many Protestant black families to send their children to Catholic schools as an escape from ineffective and dangerous public schools. About 10 percent of the ghetto youngsters in Chicago are in parochial schools. In some places, a majority of the enrollees in a Catholic school are non-Catholic. A parochial school can be a social service activity, like a denominational hospital that does not limit its medical care to co-religionists.

THE CONSTITUTIONAL ISSUE

The constitutional ban on government support for religious establishments raises legalistic issues for legislation whose initial impact may be more pronounced on Catholics. The First Amendment, as written, would not prohibit tax rebates for individuals to do with as they please and the G.I. Bill is used at Catholic colleges and universities, but the Supreme Court has sometimes drawn an arbitrary line between higher and pre-college education and made the Constitution more restrictive on the latter. However, the uncertain course of the Supreme Court in this area in recent years and some evidence of at least a pause in the trend toward judicial policymaking under the guise of interpretation leave reason to hope that extremist extensions of the "separation of church and state" doctrine will not nullify a bill that offers major benefits to all segments of the population. As things stand now, there is no Constitutional limitation on an individual's choice to donate money received from the government—whether as salary, tax refund, or Social Security benefits—to a religious organization. To say that the individual cannot choose to *buy* an educational service from the same religious organizations with money originating from the government seems inconsistent at best.

Another red flag to many is the possible effect of parental choice on racial integration. Visions of "segregation academies" are sometimes invoked (even though the tuition tax rebates cannot be used for any institution practicing racial discrimination). Quite the contrary is the case. In most of the nation's largest urban public school systems, there are not enough whites left to integrate, so any further racial integration in such places may be achievable only by the voluntary movement of black children into private schools. But even this is objected to by some "liberals," because blacks who take this opportunity to get ahead and leave the ghetto public schools would leave behind only the children of "the least educated, least ambitious, and least aware."[3] In other words, black parents who want to make a better future for their children must be stopped and their children held hostage in the public schools until such indefinite time as all other people in the ghetto share their outlook. Ethnic minorities in the past rose out of the slums layer by layer, but for blacks it must be all or none. This arrogant treatment of millions of other human beings as pawns or guinea pigs would be impossible when parents have individual choice. That is precisely why both the education establishment and the social tinkerers are opposed to it.

NOTES

1. E. G. West, "Tuition Tax Credit Proposals: An Economic Analysis of the 1978 Packwood/Moynihan Bill," *Policy Review*, Winter 1978, p. 62.

2. Ibid., p. 64.

3. "Kissing Off the Public Schools," *New Republic*, March 25, 1978, p. 6.

The "Need" for More
College "Education"

In the present climate of opinion, anyone who seriously questions the value of a college education is more likely to succeed in raising doubts about his own judgment than doubts about the American educational system. It has become a cliché that there is a flood of students at the college gates demanding an education, to which they have a "right" and for which society has a "need." The superficial indications—rising college enrollments and growing admissions pressures—seem to support this view. And yet one need not look very far below the surface to see how flimsy the case is for the great expansion of enrollments and facilities that is being constantly urged—significantly, more by politicians and college administrators than by professors.

Anyone who has taught in a typical American college is unlikely to be impressed by the urgency of student desires for more education. He may even be painfully aware of their resistance to, and evasion of, education. Of course it is still true that large numbers of people would like to be in college, for reasons which range from the sublime to the ridiculous. Most of them see college as a way to get ahead. What they do not say, but what is true nevertheless, is that it is a way to get ahead of those who have not been to college. A degree usually entitles the holder to a place in the employment line ahead of anyone without one. But from

Reprinted from *AAUP Bulletin*, Winter 1966; a publication of the American Association of University Professors.

the point of view of society as a whole, it can hardly be said that we are all going to get ahead of each other by all going to college.

No doubt everyone can benefit from college if it provides everyone with something valuable in itself, rather than simply a differential advantage in employment opportunities. But this is precisely what needs to be questioned rather than assumed. College obviously benefits *some* people both in terms of making them better human beings and more productive workers in their fields. The question is the *extent* to which this is true today, and the extent to which it is likely to remain true as the pressures of numbers force colleges to resort to expedients which undermine the educational process.

To criticize the drive for expanded college capacity is not to criticize the individuals who are pressing against the college gates. They are simply trying to cope with a world they never made. However, their desire to inhabit ivy-covered buildings for four years as a means of earning a higher income later on cannot be called a desire for more education, much less an objective need.

SUPPLY AND DEMAND

Before being willing to seriously question the value of American higher education, one may well ask: If that value is so much less than is claimed or commonly believed, why are college degrees so much in demand by employers? Surely practical businessmen do not continue to pay hard cash for something which proves to be of no value to them. Of course not. College graduates are in demand, for one reason, because a degree does indicate something, not necessarily about the education itself but about the person. It is a handy screening device. A degree shows that its owner had at least a certain staying power to continue pursuing his goal for four years. If his grades were good, it may indicate a certain diligence (or a judicious choice of courses), and if the school from which he came had decent entrance requirements, he probably has a reasonable amount of intelligence. None of this says anything about the actual value of the education itself.

Many businesses which are actively recruiting college graduates make no bones about their low opinion of what colleges teach. College men are preferred either because of certain qualities which degree requirements help screen in or out, or simply on the pragmatic ground that "college men seem to work out better in this job"—for whatever reason.

Similar reasoning often applies on a high school level as well. As a typical example, at the headquarters of a well-known corporation the elevator operators used to be grade school graduates. Now they have to be high school graduates. Veteran employees say that there has been no visible improvement in the elevator service as a result. However, this change of requirements may nevertheless have been necessary in order to maintain the original level of service. Despite the simplicity of the work, elevator operators must have certain qualifications: They must at least be depended upon to show up at the appointed time each day and be able to deal with the passengers with a minimum of friction. An educational requirement serves to eliminate job applicants without at least a certain amount of seriousness and level-headedness. At one time it took these qualities to finish grade school; now this has become so easy that the hurdle must be raised to the high school level to perform the same screening function. As for the education itself, no one imagines that it takes several years more schooling to push buttons on the new elevators than it took to turn a handle on the old. It is not the much-touted "technological revolution" which accounts for rising educational requirements on this job—or on many others like it.

These obvious facts would not need to be paraded at such length except that a vast literature has grown up in recent years, insistently arguing that money invested in meeting rising educational "needs" pays a big return to society. The basic method of determining the economic value to society of providing a college education to an individual has been to subtract the average lifetime earnings of those without a degree from the lifetime earnings of those with a degree. Graphs, equations, and other stage props have been employed in these studies, but despite their scientific aura, they have blithely disregarded the employment-screening function of a college degree. By the very same reasoning used in these studies, one could show that aristocratic birth was of great economic value to society in medieval times, since people with it earned considerably more than people without it.

This is not to say that a screening function is not a valuable function. It is just that the sheep could be separated from the goats without such staggering costs, if it did not involve the huge overhead expenses of classroom buildings, dormitories, football stadiums, and the like. As it is, an elaborate and costly charade is enacted on campuses across the country, with "education" being directed toward people who do not want it, but who go through the motions in order to qualify for jobs which do not need it.

An unfortunate fatalism pervades discussions of educational issues, as well as many other social issues. Current trends are regarded as being, if not inevitable from the outset, at least irreversible now. Frequently it is taken as "given" that employers demand a certain level of education, and the only question that is tolerated is how to produce that level for more people. But employer educational requirements cannot be independent of the average level of education currently available. Today, almost all employers demand a high school diploma because, like Everest, it is "there." Thirty years ago employers would not have dreamed of refusing to hire "dropouts" because that would have meant refusing to hire the bulk of the population. During World War II, employer hiring standards and union apprenticeship rules had to be widely disregarded because the men who met those requirements were away in uniform. Housewives with no experience outside the kitchen helped produce the greatest armada of planes, ships, and tanks that the world had ever seen. Other labor shortages in particular places since then have forced other require-ments to be reduced—and the work has gone on. It is simply not true that we must produce whatever level of formal schooling employers have grown accustomed to, and there is certainly no point in raising their expectations (at public expense) beyond what the work actually requires.

Increasing the supply of college degrees means increasing the de-mand for such degrees as a condition of employment. Far from being an anti-poverty measure, it would mean raising the barriers which a poor person must overcome in order to obtain an opportunity to demonstrate his ability to do a job. Poor people are likely to be helped very little by the expansion of college enrollments. They are almost certain to be harmed by the fencing off of still more jobs reserved exclusively for those with college degrees. It would be a tragic irony if the erection of more formida-ble obstacles to the advancement of the poor were accompanied by a chorus of self-congratulation over the democratizing of society.

Of course, the economic value of education is not its only aspect or necessarily the main consideration. However, the argument that is made on economic grounds must be answered on these grounds. The value of collegiate mass education is even more questionable as a means of developing the mind.

ELITES AND MASSES

The label "elitist" is widely used to dispose of people who oppose flinging the college gates open to all who knock. To say that college should be limited to those who are likely to gain something meaningful from it (without deteriorating the standards for others) is to invite not merely intellectual opposition but moral condemnation.

Sometimes the "democratic" approach to college education is accompanied by the mystique of the state university, where the poor kid from the wrong side of the tracks is supposed to get a start in life. The persistence of this belief shows the strength of myth in the face of fact, since most state schools are populated by students from above-average-income "middle-class" families. The really poor kid is better off in the Ivy League, where the richer schools can afford to subsidize him more adequately. Actually there is extremely little provision for the poor (or people of average income) in American colleges, despite much noble talk. What most of the tax support, scholarship contributions, etc., goes for is to allow middle-class families, who would have sent their children to college anyway, to do so with less strain. It may be a noble aim to prevent families with children in college from having to give up automatic transmission or a vacation at the beach, but it is not the same noble aim that is proclaimed in fund-raising appeals.

Poor people benefit very little from scholarships because most scholarships are too small to be of any practical use to anyone without considerable additional money of his own. Larger scholarships would enable people with lower incomes to go to college, but they would also mean fewer scholarships available out of a given amount of money—a fact not likely to be lost sight of by college administrators, politicians, or others who live by public relations.

Before becoming alarmed at the thought of an elitist snake being brought into our democratic garden, we should recognize the present educational situation for what it is. Rich people go to college at their own expense, middle-class people go with public subsidies, and most others do not go at all.

Concern for standards—for making college an intellectual experience for those who can absorb it rather than a four-year treadmill for all—has nothing undemocratic about it. On the contrary, it should lead to serious efforts to reach the still largely untapped reserves of talent among people unable to afford college. But making a higher education available to a wider range of people is not the same as increasing the number of students. More applicants allow greater selectivity. The waste in "mass education" is not merely the time, money, and effort thrown away on people who don't care. The waste includes the people who *do* care and who have the ability, but who wither in an educational system geared to the lowest common denominator.

A department chairman in a well-known state university once urged me to aim my teaching at the poorer students and suggested keeping the better students "busy" with additional assignments and the like. In other words, the students who really came to get an education and who were capable of doing so were to be treated as a problem; we were not organized to handle queer ducks like these. The chairman's attitude was by no means rare. Sometimes it is called being "practical" or simply dealing with the students "as they are." It could equally be called Gresham's Law.

Perhaps the best that can be hoped for is resistance to the clamor of politicians, college administrators, and those who thoughtlessly sentimentalize mass education. A more positive program might seek to broaden the social-economic base from which college students are drawn and select those who can actually utilize a real education. This has nothing to do with an "elitist" system in which the offspring of certain families are predestined from birth for education, leadership, and the good things of life. Education according to ability is further removed from this than is our present system.

EFFICIENCY IN EDUCATION

Along with the chorus of demands for more educational facilities has come a demand for more efficient use of existing facilities—a year-round academic year, maximum use of classroom and library space, introduction of teaching machines, etc. These suggestions are significant as indications of what people conceive of as "education." If education is the mere transmission of information from inside one head to inside another, then obviously one-third more of it can be done in a year than in nine months, and a professor lecturing to 150 students can do 10 times as much of it as one who teaches only 15. Since research, writing, and other such traditional academic pursuits take up time which could be used in the transmission of material to students, these activities are viewed with reservations, if not hostility. In line with this view of education are the sporadic outbursts of indignation over the fate of "good teachers" who have fallen victim to the publish-or-perish rule.

All of this changes drastically if education is thought of as the development of the mind, rather than the accumulation of information. The kind of individual attention which is required to untangle a student's thinking and develop his reasoning power is too time-consuming to be repeated for each member of a huge class. Yet this is a more lasting contribution than any "knowledge" which is crammed for exams and forgotten afterwards. Moreover, to develop disciplined analytical thinking in general or the particular species of it necessary in a particular subject matter obviously requires that the person teaching have it himself. This cannot be casually assumed. Moreover, it can be better judged by his peers around the country (or the world) than by the students in his classroom; the publish-or-perish doctrine is one consequence of this fact. Like any precept, it can be applied foolishly (writings may be counted rather than evaluated; flashy technique may be valued over sound reasoning, etc.), but the basic fact remains that it is necessary for the calibre of a man's mind to be judged by other trained minds in his discipline, not by untrained students.

This is not to say that students' opinions are worthless. Students are competent to judge cases of gross irresponsibility in the classroom—of which there are too many examples in even the best colleges—and perhaps even to judge pedagogical efficiency in the sense of percentage of successful transmission of material. What they are not competent to judge is precisely what is crucial: the *value* of what is presented—how well it prepares them for what will come later, either in more advanced study or in life.

A dedicated mediocrity may successfully transmit his inadequacies and confusions to generations of students, though his lectures may deserve an Oscar for gripping classroom entertainment, and his enforced departure may provoke student riots. Much sympathy has been poured out for a mythical creature called the brilliant-and-dedicated-teacher-who-has-just-not-published-anything. It is hard to imagine how, in a world of a million unanswered questions (and several million wrongly answered), a man who has mastered his field has nothing to contribute to it—or nothing that he would dare submit to the scrutiny of his peers! It is, of course, much easier to impress the sophomores three mornings a week.

Another type encountered often in discussion but seldom in practice is the great-mind-who-just-cannot-teach. There are sometimes thought to be a large number of such men, simply because of one's definition of "teach." If one implicitly accepts a mass education context and conceives of teaching as the ability to impress material on people who fundamentally don't care, then the classroom entertainer is obviously better for this sort of thing, and many a serious scholar has neither the talent nor the stomach for that role. But if the students are eager for understanding and the teacher has this understanding himself, then when the dust finally settles they will have it too. Men with very disorganized and unprepossessing classroom methods have frequently turned out superbly prepared students whose future performances were proof of the pudding.

Even the case of the top-flight professor who refuses to teach freshman (or undergraduate) courses is not one of such unmitigated sin as is sometimes supposed. Really first-rate minds are a rare resource, and they cannot be wasted frivolously. A Nobel Prize winner is better used addressing advanced students who can absorb and apply what he alone has to offer. There is no point in simply putting him on display in a large lecture class of freshmen who are there because they have a high school diploma and nothing better to do.

None of this is meant to deny that some universities are research factories where students are ignored. Some outstanding colleges may give better education than great universities because there is less of a research rat race—but such colleges are not staffed by men who do no writing at all. The problem must be seen in perspective. Research can distract from teaching, but so can golf, bridge, and a million other things. There is good, bad, and indifferent teaching going on at schools with little research, much research, and no research. There can be little doubt that the worst teaching of all goes on at nondescript schools whose faculties are incapable of any serious research.

EDUCATION VS. "EDUCATION"

Despite the absurdities of much that passes for education, there can be little doubt that real education makes a great contribution to society. It makes its contribution not only to those who directly acquire an education, but to those who come in contact with them, either personally or through various media of communication. This spreading influence of education makes it doubly important to be concerned with its quality. Admittedly, no one imbued with democratic ideals can be entirely satisfied with a situation where an intellectual elite does all the talking and the rest of us only listen. Obviously it would be better if everyone could participate as an equal in the marketplace of ideas. And yet if we insist that everyone be processed through a higher education institution—regardless of what this mass processing does to reduce these institutions to meaningless routine—then we are in fact concerned with appearances rather than with education.

Many mass educationists argue that a college education is bound to do *some* good for almost anyone; if it is less than ideal, we must still be "practical," accept half a loaf, etc. Few are bold enough to argue explicitly what is implied—that any benefit, however small, gained by additional students will balance any loss, however great, in the quality of education available to serious students.

Even the assumption that the additional students derive some net benefit from attending college is open to question. No doubt it is nearly impossible to go through four years of college without acquiring some miscellaneous bits and pieces of information. But as regards the real purpose of a college—to open the doors to the life of the mind—mass education frequently has the opposite effect of destroying whatever intellectual curiosity and concern the student may have had at the outset. For many it is the final confirmation of their suspicion that the intellectual aspect of life is all empty pretense. This kind of education does not open doors. It can close them for life. The idea of college-for-every-youngster ignores the simple fact that college is not the only place where the mind can develop, nor late adolescence the only time. But too often the empty formalism of tediously amassing credits for a degree is also the slow death of any intellectual interest.

Despite the unquestioned popularity of the idea, it is in fact a remarkable assumption that every seventeen- or eighteen-year-old is ready to begin four years of serious study and reflection. Yet the inertia of educational tradition is such that the question is almost never raised whether people of more mature years might not make better use of the facilities. Some professors refer nostalgically to the seriousness and interest of the World War II veterans who went to college on the G.I. Bill, but the experience of that period has been allowed to fade without leaving any impression on our national image of higher education. College is still widely viewed through a romantic haze as the last Paradise Lost of carefree youth.

In a field where self-delusions abound, none are more ludicrous than those which concern money. It is, for example, sometimes argued that low academic salaries are of minor importance because money is secondary for a really "dedicated" teacher, i.e., someone who is more interested in teaching other people's children than in supporting his own. The departure of able and conscientious men from teaching has shaken some people's faith in this convenient belief. Others, however, have been heartened by the fact that those who departed were readily "replaced," often with people whose talents do not subject them to the temptation of outside offers. Similarly, the popular approach to financing the education of talented students who cannot afford to pay their way is to give them a fraction of what is needed and try to have them make up the difference by washing cars or mowing lawns. This childish waste of valuable time and talent is even surrounded with the aura of the American Dream.

It would be naive to overlook the self-interest behind many of the glowing pleas for "expanded educational opportunity for youth." Since youth must compete against each other for jobs, more "opportunity" for tax-subsidized education of middle-class students means a continued escalation of degree requirements for jobs and corresponding restriction of opportunity for youths from poorer families. There will of course be greatly expanded opportunities for college administrators and politicians. The administrators will benefit from expansion of their little empires of buildings, students, and faculty. At the better colleges and universities there is a reluctance to pay the educational price which this statistical "achievement" would entail. But schools whose education is already a hollow routine have little to lose and it is not surprising to see them in the forefront of expansion.

The political benefits of expanding educational facilities promise to be even greater. Not only would politicians be able to sponsor legislation which helps numerous constituents, it would also be an opportunity to "do something" about the problem of unemployment. Since a disproportionate amount of unemployment exists among young people, a considerable statistical success can be scored by keeping them out of the labor force entirely for four years. Definitions being what they are, young people who waste their time around the house or on street corners are called "unemployed," while those who waste their time in classrooms are called "students." There are obvious possibilities here for using college as a sort of C.C.C. camp or W.P.A. project. Of course the W.P.A. never required expensive ivy-covered buildings as settings in which to while away time, or professors with long and costly educations to direct the "work."

The "Available"
University

One of the odd characters who appears from time to time in the comic strip "Li'l Abner" is "Available" Jones, an enterprising man whose time and talents can be rented for any purpose whatsoever. If you want to impress your girl friend by outdoing someone in sports or repartee, Available Jones can be hired to play the fall guy. Full of pent-up anger or frustration? Get it out of your system by giving Mr. Jones a good, hard kick in the behind, for a modest fee. The analogy with the modern university is all too apparent. But while Available Jones' occupation is seen as something of an oddity, it is often considered reasonable, if not inevitable, that universities alone of all institutions must serve the purposes of others. No one expects a gas station to cater to pedestrians, or churches to accommodate atheists, or a bar to make teetotalers feel at home. People go into one of these places precisely because they are in accord with its known purposes. But the university is expected to be "open" (to those unconcerned or contemptuous toward its goals), "relevant" (to the purposes of *other* institutions and movements), "involved" (in activities for which it has no special fitness), and "responsive" (to any demand whatsoever)—in short, available.

The apostles of Relevance argue as if the only alternative is a community of cloistered scholars talking only to each other while the suffer-

Reprinted from the *University of Chicago Magazine*, November–December 1970.

ing of the world goes on outside. This argument goes to the heart of the question whether a university has any intrinsic relevance or whether it must launch expeditions to go out and find relevance, and import it like some rare tropical plant. A look at the agony and progress of man over the centuries might suggest some value in the systematic development of the human mind and a continuing relevance of disciplined and informed thinking, in contrast to the kinds of visceral reactions, heady rhetoric, and grandiose visions which have spread so much blood and rubble across the pages of history. The tedious analytical dissection of ideas and problems, far from being a luxury of a leisure class, is a prime necessity for society's survival, much less its technical and social progress. Despite this vital function which lies at the heart of a university's role, it is clear that groups within the university, and sometimes whole universities, have lost their sense of purpose. Partly this is because the university's purpose has been obscured by an overgrowth of additional and often conflicting activities. The recognized importance of the university, which has caused it to be maintained for centuries by societies far poorer than today's, has made it a "hot property" in the hands of modern "operators," and its credentials an impressive backdrop for romantic posturing by adolescents of various ages, including faculty members and administrators.

The university, like every other institution of society, has never existed in a pure form designed to serve its ideal purpose. But it is nevertheless useful to note which of the alien features that have been grafted onto it have helped produce its current maladies. One of these has been the consuming desire to gain additional money, power, and prestige by serving outside interests—i.e., the pursuit of local and transient "relevance" rather than the general and permanent relevance inherent in the search for knowledge and understanding. Vocationalism, corrupt athletics, the establishment of "institutes" for some vested interest, "centers" for things currently making headlines, and "chairs" in some donor's pet idea are obvious examples. Another has been the acceptance of *bigger numbers* as an index of success—enrollments, buildings, faculty, news items, etc. The university has sold itself to the public as a veritable panacea for personal and social problems, playing on the credulous notion that processing everyone through ivy-covered buildings for four years was "education" and therefore "a good thing." Its pretensions have been greatly helped by the fact that even the worst education cannot prevent students from growing four years older in the course of four years, and that it is rare for a young adult not to acquire some elements of maturity and miscellaneous information over such a span of time. Moreover, the university is necessarily a testing ground of sorts—

of perseverance, if nothing else—so that employers find college degrees and records to be handy screening devices, regardless of what was actually taught. This in turn means that young people are forced to go to college in economic self-defense. In short, the colleges and universities have been in an ideal position to gain an ever-increasing captive audience. Now they are discovering that the audience can also hold them captive.

While there has been justifiable outrage at disruptions and violence on college campuses across the country and around the world, this feeling is no defense of university administrators, who have been far too clever for anyone's good, or of those faculty members who have abdicated responsibility for anything beyond personal ambitions and departmental log-rolling. The feeling of outrage is because, underneath all the cheap huckstering, the petty intrigues and casual betrayals, there is something vital to the life of the mind and the life of society which cannot be allowed to be destroyed.

The threat of destruction comes not from the actual physical assaults, disruptions, and turmoil on campus, for there is ultimately ample power to stop all of this, but from the ambivalence, expediency, guilt, and apathy in which it flourishes, and which is willing to buy it off at any price, provided only that convenient payments be arranged in easy (though perpetual) installments. It is symptomatic of the underlying values involved that the possibility of waking up some morning and finding a university building gutted by fire is the great fear; the prospect of waking up some day and finding the whole meaning of the university gutted does not arouse nearly as much concern.

The current struggle on college and university campuses is like some curious storybook battle in which one side has an overwhelming superiority in material resources but the other side possesses a few magic words that can spread confusion and paralysis among its opponents—in this case, "relevance," "black," "youth," and "idealism." While there is ample reason for the university's loss of confidence in its moral position, which is what makes such words effective, the real question is whether the guilty ambivalence of one side and the dogmatic self-righteousness of the other are the ingredients of an intelligent policy for the future.

RELEVANCE—TO WHAT?

So much of the loose talk about relevance assumes that it is something which can be determined *a priori* on the basis of the reactions of students while still studying a subject, rather than an empirical question to be settled after having tested its application in a variety of situations over a period of years. The great rush to be "relevant to the ghetto," for example, means in practice putting together courses and programs that will be favorably received by students from the ghetto or students interested in the ghetto. It does *not* mean an attempt to put together courses or programs whose *actual results* have proven to be beneficial in solving or ameliorating any major ghetto problem. The most relevant courses in the latter sense might turn out to be dry, tedious studies in medicine, accounting, or law—which is certainly not what the relevance people have in mind. They want to *talk about* the ghetto, or do studies that take them into the ghetto, satisfying their own emotional needs but doing little for the ghetto. If such talk and such studies had any significant value, there have already been enough of both to make the ghetto a paradise on earth. There isn't the slightest reason to expect the coincidence that those things which actually advance black people will simultaneously provide material for college courses which are any more exciting than the study of chemistry, physics, finance, and other dry studies which have helped advance other people.

If the world were in fact as direct and obvious as the relevance argument seems to assume, then of course the whole elaborate and dreary paraphernalia of systematic abstract reasoning would be unnecessary. There would be no need for all the graphs in economics and all the elaborate equations of probability in statistics. Our social problems could be solved by the same kind of direct common sense which told us, in the natural sciences, that the earth was flat and the sun moved around it. But the underlying assumption of all scholarship is that things look very different after systematic analysis than they do on the surface.

If a university is going to proceed on the basis of the spontaneous appeal of its offerings, then it is going to move in a non-intellectual (and often anti-intellectual) direction, much like the television industry which academics disdain—including some variant of the ratings (and consequent appeal to the lowest common denominator) and the other obtrusive features of television: flamboyant, irresponsible statements by people having something to sell, glitter rather than substance, and in general a presentation of a world of good guys and bad guys and show-downs and "action" as ways of explaining and dealing with the complexities of life. The search for villains—of whom there is never a shortage—can replace the analysis of causation, if exciting courses with instant appeal are the goal. But if being interesting and exciting is going to be the guiding star of higher education, we must face the fact that mass emotions and mass actions are always going to be more exciting than the lonely process of intellectual development. If we cannot convince students that they must do what is necessary rather than what turns them on, we owe it to everyone to at least make the effort. There is a sizable body of "sophisticated" opinion which operates on the theory that students cannot be reasoned with, but can only be "handled," meaning some judicious blend of partial concessions and fashionable talk. Conceivably they could be right, but to date this clever approach has not been notably successful either.

No sane person wants education to be irrelevant or believes that current educational practices are the ultimate perfection. The real question is—relevant to what? To what the student wants as he sits in the classroom, or to what he will discover he needs, years later, after he has gone and probably cannot return? Is building a general intellectual capability irrelevant because it is not *exclusively* relevant to the current headlines and slogans? Is a method of asking questions and testing answers less relevant than a course on how to promote a preconceived goal? In the sloppy language of today, opposition to any particular pattern of change is denounced as opposition to change, as such, and extravagant statements are made about the rigidity of the academic curriculum. Actually the opposite charge would have more substance: that American education, down through the years, has spent so much time getting on and off bandwagons that it has had little time for anything else.

If universities in their venality had not tried to appeal to wealthy donors by depicting their role as that of turning out pillars of the status quo—"well-rounded" young men in some YMCA or Junior Chamber of Commerce sense—then perhaps it would not be so easy for others to think of it as a staging area for revolution. Many young people actually believe that their teachers are trying to fit them into the existing social "system" or "machine," not realizing that most teachers find it hard enough to get them to understand their subject, and perhaps grasp something of the nature of intellectual inquiry in general, without trying to plan their lives and the destiny of society as well.

CAMPUS REVOLUTIONARIES

The Grand Illusion of campus revolutionaries is that the university is a microcosm of society at large, and that their victories there foreshadow their coming success in overthrowing the hated Establishment. The university is in fact unique in a number of ways which explain the revolutionaries' success there, despite their political insignificance nationally (except as a boon to people like Reagan, Yorty, George Wallace, and Spiro Agnew). Universities get most of their wealth from outside.

College officials can buy peace with other people's money. Professors can buy peace and popularity by eroding standards, at the expense of those conscientious students whose degrees will be devalued, but at no cost to themselves. Success in gaining concessions under these conditions is no indication of what to expect when it comes to more direct and fundamental challenges in society at large.

Campus revolutionaries sometimes engage in a kind of heads-I-win-tails-you-lose reasoning by which they argue that the very uproar against them shows the fear which they inspire in the Establishment and, by implication, the realism of their plans for revolution. What it really shows is that (1) the news media find that they make a colorful story, and (2) John Q. Public finds them repulsive, doesn't mind saying so, and votes for politicians who say so (a fact not lost on the politicians). The corporations, banks, etc., have no reason to lose a moment's sleep over them. The only kind of revolution student militants can produce in this country is a right-wing revolution, and they would have to get a lot stronger than they are to provoke that.

In the university environment, student revolutionary leaders are far more realistic than most faculty members about what is really involved in campus struggles. They understand that the name of the game is *power*. "Issues" are a means of mobilizing support and immobilizing opposition. The various sacred "causes" to which student revolutionaries are "committed" are usually not too sacred to be ditched at the earliest convenient moment after a campaign has gotten under way, and completely new demands substituted—demands which go for the jugular of power. As many times as this old melodrama has been played, it might be expected that everyone would begin to follow the plot by now. But words have a heady fascination, especially for those faculty members who cannot be bothered to analyze or who cannot muster the moral courage for making choices.

The usual apology for campus revolutionaries has been that they have "legitimate grievances" and that all other methods have failed. It must be recognized that (1) all unhappy situations are not grievances, that (2) even legitimate grievances do not excuse all acts, and that (3) to say that any institution can be brought to a halt as long as there are legitimate grievances—that is, as long as they are run by human beings— is to say that there can be no institutions. Moreover, rational methods have not "failed" because one party or faction did not get what it wanted. Given that there are always numerous contending groups demanding opposite things, every historical or conceivable system must "fail" by this standard.

None of this denies the need for changes, or even for sweeping changes, in universities. I would suggest, as a start, the abolition of academic tenure, prohibition of consulting fees, the destruction of the teaching assistant system, elimination of varsity athletics, and drastic cutbacks in enrollments. Any academic is bound to have his own list. What is crucial is to recognize that no reforms are so desirable as to be achieved "at all cost," because beyond some point the methods used may not leave anything worth reforming.

A university is an intangible structure of reciprocal commitments and obligations, a hierarchy of skills (which no democratic rhetoric can change), and an atmosphere of learning. It is very easy to cripple or even destroy the intangible reality of education, even though the physical plant remains unscathed and the bureaucratic machine keeps turning undisturbed. This process of destruction is already well under way at a number of institutions and is likely to become general unless university faculties are prepared to abandon their old parlor game of equally deploring this and that, and recognize that we live in a world where choices have to be made, priorities assigned, and responsibility taken.

One of the popular *non sequiturs* of the day is that universities must be peculiarly bad institutions since they are peculiarly beset with violent protests. The fact that violent protests are peculiarly *acceptable* on university campuses is seldom considered as a factor. If the average factory worker could lock his boss in the office and denounce the foreman as a "fascist pig" with impunity, we might discover that universities have no more grievances than many other institutions. But of course no one expects to grant to ordinary working people the kind of immunity from legal retribution for their actions which is common for college students. It is ironic that this socially and economically privileged group should now be demanding legal privileges (amnesty) as well, in the name of democracy and the masses. That they can put their own boredom with the university in the same category with the sufferings of the poor is a tribute to their gall, but that the rest of us take this seriously is no tribute to us at all.

BLACK EDUCATION

Race taps the depths of man's irrationality as few things can. In this area, intelligent and knowledgeable men say and do things whose illogic and self-defeating consequences would be apparent to them in any other aspect of life. There are no experts in this field, and those who imagine that they have found The Truth are the most untrustworthy guides of all.

Whether black students are brought to the university as part of the general recruitment and admissions procedures or in special programs, there is almost never a clear-cut definition of priorities beyond a nebulous desire to do good, make amends, or improve public relations. There are serious and lasting consequences to not thinking through at the outset whether the goal is to give direct benefits to needy individuals or to invest in individuals in ways designed to maximize the return to the black community and society at large. If the university is trying to make the intellectual investment for which it is peculiarly qualified, it will select the most able black students it can possibly find as its vehicles; if it is trying to play Lady Bountiful, its bias will be toward those who "need help" most, rather than those who can use it best. The second is the dominant approach, not only in universities but in social programs supported by the government and the foundations. They do not try to cultivate the most fertile land, but to make the desert bloom. This is often hotly denied by officials who insist that they are looking for the best black people available—subject, it will usually turn out, to a series of constraints or special emphases which make the original statement meaningless.

Most people are unaware of the extent to which the severe educational problems of black college students are functions of the manner in which they are recruited and selected, rather than simply being the inevitable result of "cultural deprivation." There is no question that the overwhelming bulk of black youth have been given grossly inadequate preparation in the public schools. However, the overwhelming bulk of black youth do not go on to college, and while the *proportion* of these youth who are educationally well prepared for college is very low, in *absolute numbers* there are literally tens of thousands of them who are, by all the usual indices—far too many for the top universities to be *forced* to have as many inadequately prepared black students as they do.

The claim that standardized examinations may be less reliable for ethnic minorities than for others has been used as a blanket excuse for recruiting and selecting black students on all sorts of non-intellectual criteria, from the ideological to the whimsical. Programs for black people tend to attract more than their fair share of vague humanitarians and socio-political doctrinaires seeking to implement some special vision. Not all are as obtuse as the special admissions committee for black students at one Ivy League university who objected to admitting three black applicants with College Board verbal scores in the 700s on grounds that they were probably—God forbid—middle class, and that there were other blacks applying who were more "interesting" cases—but this general kind of thinking is by no means rare. One consequence of this is that, despite the buzz of recruiting activity, there are many black students who belong in the best colleges in the country who have not been reached with the information and financial aid offers that would bring them there, and are languishing at some of the worst colleges in the country. At the same time other black students are in over their heads at the top colleges, struggling—or being maneuvered—toward a degree.

Faculty members are by no means exempt from the paternalism found in recruiting and admissions policies. Some professors grade black students more leniently than they would grade other students, and many hesitate to flunk them, either out of humanitarianism or a desire to avoid "trouble." One cynic said of his black students, "I give 'em all A's and B's; to hell with them." At least he understood the consequences of what he was doing. The double standard of grades and degrees is an open secret on many campuses, and it is only a matter of time before it is an open secret among employers as well. The market can be ruthless in devaluing degrees that do not mean what they say. It should also be apparent to anyone not blinded by his own nobility that it also devalues the student in his own eyes.

The greatest tragedy of the black man in America, after slavery itself, has been the simple fact that his own ability has always been far less important than how he happened to fit in with white people's preconceptions and emotional needs. What specific kind of black person would be fashionable with white people has of course varied considerably over the years, and between different groups of white people at a given time. But today's crop of white liberal and radical patrons of the mystique of "blackness" are in no fundamental way different from the old-time white Southerner who would accept any level of irresponsibility and incompetence from a Negro who met his preconceptions (who "knew his place"), and had only suspicion or resentment for a black man with competence, self-discipline, and capacity for hard work. At the height of the most blatant racial oppression, white Southerners were full of the same romantic notions about the special spiritual qualities and insights of black people which are currently in vogue among the more "enlightened" intellectuals. Nor has this been an exclusively American phenomenon. It was the most unabashed apostle of British imperialism who said, "You're a better man than I am, Gunga Din." The more things change, the more they remain the same.

"Black studies" is one of the signs of our times. After years of history being written as if blacks did not exist, suddenly their role was recognized, usually after a university building was seized. Suddenly, hastily constructed black studies programs began springing up all over the landscape, like intellectual shantytowns. Few things are more revealing than seeing white faculty members rationalizing and romanticizing the black studies programs on a campus where the black students are staying away from it in droves.

CONCLUSIONS

The university created a Frankenstein when it cast itself in the role of panacea for personal and social ills. A feeling has developed that anything worth doing at all is worth doing at a university. Even our revolutionaries believe that you must go to college in order to make a revolution. Some people want to see the university itself go off like a knight on a white horse to slay the dragons of social injustice. A more apt analogy would be a man charging into hell with a pitcher of ice water. The university's resources for direct social action are grossly inadequate to make a dent in the problem. Its greatest contribution would be to turn out people who are intellectually equipped to deal with social problems in ways that produce tangible results rather than symbolic acts. If a university is going to make a real contribution, it must make it *as a university*, not as a general fix-it shop. A proliferation of Quixotic endeavors may produce more glowing feelings and more good publicity, but it is a waste of specialized resources that can do more in the uses for which they were meant than anywhere else.

Practically every campus has a contingent of faculty members who are not above misappropriating the money, facilities, and good name of their institution for purposes of making themselves feel noble. The more activist and doctrinaire of these faculty members are absolutely impervious to logic and are prepared to explain away any facts. They cannot be persuaded; they can only be counteracted—and this can happen only if the great bulk of the faculty are prepared to come out of their laboratories and studies and sit on admissions committees, meet black students as individuals, and constantly monitor the decisions of administrators who are preoccupied with getting immediate problems off their necks without worrying about long-run consequences (the long run being any time after next week). It is a shame that highly trained people must devote precious time to miscellaneous campus activities, but the alternative is to leave gut decisions up to the operators and the doctrinaires, and we have seen how that has turned out.

The Intellect
of the Intellectuals

One of the most disturbing developments of the 1960s was the rise of anti-intellectualism among intellectuals. "Relevant" and "irrelevant" became magic words that superseded logic or facts. "Social" was another incantation that put various schemes ("innovations") above discussion and made objections or questions about them seem petty, mean, or dirty.

"Socially relevant" was a double whammy. One would as soon stand in the path of an express train as oppose something that was "socially relevant"—whether or not there was *any* evidence that it did any good, or considerable evidence that it did harm, or violated basic principles of logic. Questions of fact became questions of intent. Even the most devastating facts could be countered by asking where you were coming from.

Was this phenomenon a phase, like adolescent acne, or is it a permanent disfiguration—or perhaps even a growing cancer on the intellectual life in general and the academic world in particular? The trends are by no means clear as yet. There are signs that sanity is attempting a comeback, but comebacks by ex-champs do not always end well, and it is too early to tell if the 1960s are decisively over in academe. Indeed, there is a question of whether the decade of the 1960s was as unique as it liked to imagine itself, or whether what happened then was an eruption of trends

and forces long associated with intellectuals and therefore likely to
continue to be with us for a long time.

The very world "intellectual" is ambiguous. It refers to a certain kind
of process, revolving around logical deduction, systematic testing of
ideas, and a complex weighing of evidence. But the word also refers to
the flesh-and-blood people who make such activity their careers—and,
as people, they are not just the embodiment of those abstract principles.
Intellectuals are also subject to other powerful forces, rooted in emotions and reflecting the position of the intellectual class as a special-
interest group with its own aspirations, biases, and blind spots. These
other forces can easily cause the social group called "intellectuals" to
violate that set of procedures called "intellectual" principles.

Academic intellectuals are especially subject to emotional enthusi-
asms and especially insulated from the chilling effects of objective
reality. It is not merely that professors have never had to meet a payroll;
they have also never had to meet a scoreboard—or any other crucial
experiment whose outcome would determine their fate, by testing how
closely their ideas fit the actual reality. Academics are protected not only
by tenure but also by their own ability to rationalize, complicate, and
mystify. They do not like objective processes whose results cannot be
talked away.

In short, the very people whose work is based on the relationship
between ideas and reality are exempted from having to demonstrate
such a relationship—while merchants, athletes, policemen, and others
looked down upon by academics are regularly forced to demonstrate
such a relationship and to pay heavily for discrepancies. For academics,
the only test is whether what they say sounds plausible to enough
people, or to the right people.

INSULATED OCCUPATIONS

Tenure, "academic freedom," and other insulations are intended to
free the intellectual process from political and quasi-political pressures,
but they end up freeing the intellectual from a need to respect the
intellectual process, or to recognize any objective reality beyond his
fancies or the fashions of his fellow academicians.

Worse, like other insulated occupations (the civil service, for example), academic life attracts more than its share of those fearful of personal risks and ready to exchange individual responsibility for an assured
future. For such academics there is even a safety valve of being able to

aim defiant rhetoric at "the establishment," provided it is the kind of defiant rhetoric approved by their peers, and in tune with changing fashions.

SANCTIMONIOUS POMPOSITY

Finally, in spite of all the sanctimonious pomposity that is as much a hallmark of academic life as the cap and gown, academics are a special-interest group. Their special interest is to get their production costs paid for by other people (notably the taxpayers) and to give their product a good image so that it will sell. Whether their product actually helps the consumer afterwards is secondary, at best.

We understand these simple facts of life when it comes to soup manufacturers, used-car dealers, and circus barkers. But when the president of a university goes on television to claim that his product will cure a range of ills previously covered only by snake oil, he is regarded as a statesman-like lover of mankind, and his message is considered a public service announcement rather than advertising.

The academic world is one of the most effective special-interest groups precisely because it does not think of itself in those terms. Its words have the ring of sincerity when it turns every form of social malaise into a reason why its members should receive more money and power. Racial strife becomes a reason for academics to conduct a thousand social experiments leading to a million articles, reports, Ph.D. theses, etc.—costing billions of tax dollars. Poverty in general is a gold mine for intellectuals. Crime and violence provide another ready market for "expertise" (the quotes because nothing has actually worked). Academe has even mass-produced and mass-marketed its own parochial viewpoint, which looks for "solutions" to social "problems"—like answers in the back of a textbook. *Have notebook, will travel.* Academics will research anything—except the effectiveness of their own schemes growing out of previous research.

The Plight of
Black College Students

Black education at the college level expanded rapidly in the 1960s. In 1960, there were 200,000 black students attending college; by 1970 that number had more than doubled.[1] More importantly, the social composition and institutional destinations of these students changed drastically as well. Many predominantly white colleges and universities began seeking not only black students, but lower-class black students.[2] Whereas until the 1960s the majority of black students went to the predominantly Negro colleges and universities, an increasing majority now went to white institutions of higher learning.[3] Several factors in this situation led to severe problems.

The leading colleges and universities have been under special pressure to increase their minority enrollment, both because of their general visibility and because of a need to maintain their educational "leadership." Government funds and foundation grants to support special programs for black students were channeled disproportionately into these leading institutions, just as they are for other purposes. At the same time, the academic preparation of most black students was wholly inadequate to meet the usual standards of these schools. The average College Board scores of black students were often well below the median

Reprinted by permission of *Daedalus*, Journal of the American Academy of Arts and Sciences, "Slavery, Colonialism, and Racism," vol. 103, no. 2 (Spring 1974), Boston, MA.

scores at the high-quality schools they attended. In short, a demand was created for black students at precisely those institutions least fitted to the students' educational preparation. Moreover, the incomes of many of the students dictated that they go where large scholarship funds were available. Therefore, many black students moved into education institutions at the top in terms of research prestige, social class, and academic prerequisites, whether or not these were the schools best equipped to teach them.

When black students who would normally qualify for a state college are drained away by Ivy League colleges and universities, then state colleges have little choice but to recruit black students who would normally qualify for still lower level institutions—and so the process continues down the line. The net result is that in a country with 3,000 widely differing colleges and universities capable of accommodating every conceivable level of educational preparation and intellectual development, there is a widespread problem of "underprepared" black students at many institutional levels, even though black students' capabilities span the whole range by any standard used.

The problem is not one of absolute ability level, but rather of widespread mismatching of individuals with institutions. The problem is seldom seen for what it is, for it has *not* been approached in terms of the optimum distribution of black students in the light of their preparation and interests, but rather in terms of how Harvard, Berkeley, or Antioch can do its part, maintain its leadership, or fill its quota.

The schools which have most rapidly increased their enrollments of black students are those where the great majority of white American students could not qualify. However, since such schools typically do not admit underqualified white students, they have no "white problem" corresponding to the problem posed for them by underqualified black students. This problem must also be seen in perspective: the College Board scores and other academic indicators for black students in prestige colleges and universities are typically *above the national average* for white Americans. Special tutoring, reduced course loads, and other special accommodations and expedients for minority students are necessitated by programs geared to a student body which is not only above the national average, but in the top *1 or 2 percent* of all American students. The problem created by black students who do not meet the institutional standards may be grim or even desperate for both the students and the institution. Yet it does not arise because students are incapable of absorbing a college education. They may be incapable of absorbing an M.I.T. education, for example, but so is virtually everyone else.

The literature on black college students centers almost exclusively on what the white prestige institution ought to do. This is true whether the individual writing is black or white, whether he "militantly" favors or "traditionally" opposes such things as black studies and special admissions standards. Among black academicians, minority programs like black studies, and other special modifications of academic standards and practices, are demanded by so-called "militants" and bitterly opposed by so-called "moderates." Both groups, however, argue in terms of what the given white prestige institution should do to accommodate an increase in black enrollments. This perspective is as plain in moderates like Martin Kilson and Kenneth Clark as it is in militants like Allen Ballard.[4] They share the unspoken assumption of white academicians that students get a better education at a "better" institution. It is, however, well worth considering in what ways prestige institutions are "better."

Prestige universities achieve their standing almost exclusively through the quality of their research output. This has been decried in some quarters and denied in others, but the plain fact is that the ranking of leading departments in any academic discipline closely follows their ranking on quality and quantity of research output.[5] However valuable this special function may be for society in general, there is nothing about outstanding research performance which equips either the institution or the individual faculty member for teaching undergraduates in general, much less those with special educational and psychological needs. Indeed, many of the leading scholars who create a university's prestige have little or nothing to do with undergraduates. Even prestige colleges which emphasize their teaching role are geared to students with test scores in the top 1 to 5 percent. This is true not only of such well-known colleges as Amherst, Swarthmore, and Vassar, but also of lesser-known quality institutions like Davidson, Wells, and Hamilton.

Much of the current literature attempts to convince prestige institutions that they should adapt to serve students who do not meet their highly specialized academic requirements—students, in other words, more like those served by the vast majority of American colleges and universities. The possibility of distributing black students in institutions whose normal standards they already meet has been almost totally ignored. Worse, many institutions have set up special programs specifically and explicitly to do the *opposite* of this, to accommodate black students who do *not* meet the normal standards of the respective institutions. Under such programs, financial aid is not available to black students who meet the normal standards of these institutions, even when such students are very much in need of financial aid.

Policies of this sort are followed not only in programs established by individual institutions, but also in nationwide programs under both private and government auspices. The best-known program for placing and financing black students in law schools places an upper limit on the test scores students can achieve and still be eligible,[6] a limit well below the average test score in the law schools where they are placed. Many government scholarships for minority undergraduates require academically substandard performances as well as lower socioeconomic status. In some cases, such policies are explicitly defined legally; in others they simply exist in practice. Whatever the rationale for them in terms of retrospective justice, what they reward is a low performance level, whether or not a student is capable of more. Black high school students themselves have said that they refuse to perform at their best for fear of reducing their chances of getting the financial aid they need to go to college.[7] Although a number of critics have declared it "bizarre" to deny financial aid to academically qualified black students while favoring weaker ones,[8] their view does not necessarily prevail among academic administrators.

There is some evidence that able black students are often missed by the recruiting and admissions procedures of the leading colleges and universities, or else deliberately passed over. A more grave possibility, however, is that blacks at all levels of ability are systematically mismatched upward, so that good students go where outstanding students should be going and outstanding students go where only a handful of peak performers can survive. The net effect of this "pervasive shifting effect"[9] is to place students where they do not learn as much as they would in schools geared to students of their own educational preparation.[10]

Much of what has happened to black American college students at white institutions was foreshadowed in the earlier experience of African students in white institutions, not only in the United States and other Western countries, but also in the Soviet Union and the Eastern bloc of nations. In the case of visiting African students in the early 1960s, as in the case of American Negroes in the late 1960s, the primary emphasis was on getting their physical presence on campus in significant numbers. This was accomplished not only by special recruiting efforts but also by special financial aid policies and special academic standards, including, in some cases, a virtual absence of standards.[11]

The results were also very similar to what has emerged with black American students. Both black and white students bitterly resented these arrangements, and the resentment was directed at each other as well as at the administrations responsible for them. An observer of the pattern among African students in the early 1960s commented: "Many

African students are uneasily aware that they are kept men. Often they take refuge from this reality in defiantly revolutionary verbiage."[12]

It was observed that African students who studied in the United States tended to become anti-American, while those who studied in the Soviet Union tended to become anti-Soviet. A similar anger at their apparent benefactors became commonplace among American Negro students in the late 1960s. The African students' experiences differed, however, from those of black American students in several important respects. The Africans had neither sufficient numbers nor sufficient cultural homogeneity or ideological unity to mount sustained campaigns against college administrators, and therefore produced far fewer dramatic episodes such as mass demonstrations or disruptions. Also, African students were not granted concessions like special black studies departments.

It is against this background that the literature has discussed such issues as "open admissions," black studies, and faculty quotas. Several arguments have emerged for preferential admissions standards for black students. One is simply that "the number of Blacks qualified for admission to white colleges under traditional criteria is small" so that admitting "large numbers" of Negro students is synonymous with "a lowering of entrance requirements."[13] Here the focus is implicitly the institution and its guilt, atonement, or responsibility. Much rarer in the literature is the position that high costs are incurred "whenever a student is admitted to a school whose normal standards he does not meet, even though he does meet the normal standards of other schools."[14] Here there is recognition that black students, with all their educational handicaps, are not underqualified in an absolute sense, but only relative to the standards of particular institutions.

The costs incurred by current policies include not only the financial costs of remedial programs and special courses, but also "the intense anxiety and threat to the student's self-esteem." Some indication of this psychic cost is the high *voluntary* dropout rate among black students admitted under programs which do not allow them to be flunked out for some specified number of years. Personal accounts by students and observations by teachers reinforce the picture of black students under great pressure in unfamiliar settings.[15]

A leading proponent and architect of "open admissions" policies at the City College of New York boasts of the fact that 30 to 35 percent of the students admitted under those policies graduate[16]—in other words, the dropout rate is "only" 65 to 70 percent. The national dropout rate in the United States is about 50 percent, but this includes students with financial problems (unlike the open admissions students whose expenses are taken care of), students with attractive alternatives, and students who can return later at their parents' expense. Moreover, the white dropout is not laboring under the stereotype of mental incompetence which crushingly reinforces the black's sense of personal failure.

One of the most insistent arguments for special admissions criteria for black students is that the standard mental tests are culturally biased, and thus do not correctly measure a black student's ability and/or predict his college performance. There is indeed some evidence that tests underestimate the mental ability of lower-income people in general, as well as blacks in particular. Ironically, some of this evidence is from studies by Arthur R. Jensen, who is better known for his theory of innate racial differences in mental abilities.[17]

However, the question of predicting college performance is quite different from the question of innate ability or even of cultural bias. Tests may systematically underestimate a group's natural or potential intelligence and yet not underestimate their success in college, which requires many characteristics besides native ability. The predictive validity of a test is an empirical question, ultimately a matter of statistics rather than philosophy, and a variety of tests given in a variety of settings indicate that mental tests generally do *not* underestimate the future performance of lower-income people, including blacks, and in fact have a slight tendency to predict a better academic performance than that actually achieved.[18] In short, standardized mental tests tend to underestimate ability among blacks but to overestimate performance.

This is not nearly as paradoxical as it may seem. A college education presupposes not only raw intelligence but also years of mental habits which cannot be rapidly synthesized in remedial programs. The lack of a given reading speed or mathematical facility may endanger a person's academic survival in a particular institution. And, if blacks are maldistributed, they may run into trouble in most of the institutions they attend.

Another factor in the difficulties encountered by disadvantaged students is that the college itself is often as subject to cultural bias as the admissions tests. To some extent this may be a simple social class bias in lifestyles which creates needless disorientation among students from different social or racial backgrounds. However, insofar as the intellectual process has inherent requirements, there may be little that can be done in the short run to improve the disadvantaged student's chances of academic success at a particular institution, even if he has the same innate potential as everyone else and if all class bias is removed from the collegiate social scene.

It is misleading to depict opposing views on the admission of black students to college as due solely to different assumptions or theories which logically lead to different conclusions. In fact, many of the arguments are opaque moral imperatives: Help should go to those who "really" need it; it is not the black student's "fault" that he does not meet academic standards; compensation is due for past injustices, etc. Such arguments can be met only by shifting the whole basis of the discussion: Efficiency requires that help go to those who can best use it, not those who most need it; admission is not a morally based individual benefit but a socially based investment decision; compensation to individual A for what has been done to individual B is not a compensation, and may not even prove to be a benefit. These answers do not meet the original arguments on their own ground, but claim instead that different grounds are preferable.

In one way or another, the question of academic standards is central to both proponents and opponents of special treatment for black students. The extent to which black students actually receive special treatment at white colleges and universities is, however, a matter of heated controversy. Clearly "remedial" or "compensatory" courses and reduced course loads are special treatment, but straightforward and above board. Controversy centers around allegations that there are double standards in grading, credits given for courses with little content and no real demands, "incomplete" grades awarded for failing work, and failing dropouts disguised as temporary withdrawals.[19]

No one has stepped forth to defend such practices, but many argue that reports concerning them are exaggerated,[20] and some argue that black students need courses which cover, at a slower pace, the same material as regular courses at the same college.[21] Why black students should be channeled to fast-paced colleges to get slower-paced courses is a question that does not arise within a framework designed to produce a given demographic profile by institution. As for the prevalence of dishonest and clandestine double standards, its nature is such that it can only be estimated impressionistically. My interviews with academics from coast to coast convince me that double standards are a fact of life on virtually every campus, but not necessarily in a majority of courses. This situation may in fact present the maximum academic danger to the black student: enough double standards courses to give him a false sense of security and enough rigid standards courses to produce academic disasters.

Black academics tend to be especially severe in their criticisms of double standards for black students. The "benevolent paternalism" and "seemingly sympathetic" double standards of white faculty members, they say, tend to "generate feelings of inferiority in the students' hearts and minds in a way unlikely ever to be undone."[22] For some black students it promotes a "hustler mentality."[23] At the same time "it robs those black students who have done well from receiving real credit and the boost in confidence that their accomplishments merit."[24] Often this boost in confidence is very much needed as well as merited. The "lack of feedback," which double-standard grading implies, denies black students clear signals as to their progress and prospects[25]—signals they need in order to plan their lives rationally, both in college and after graduation.

Not all critics speak in terms of the harm double standards do to black students. Some argue from the more general perspective that "discrimination in favor of X is automatic discrimination against Y."[26] Moreover, in terms of the general racial atmosphere of the country in future years, it is argued that academic mismatching of black and white students in the same institution promotes a white sense of superiority and a black sense of inferiority and thus tends to "perpetuate the very ideas and prejudices it is designed to combat."[27] Finally, it is argued that academically outclassed students will turn to nonacademic means to "achieve recognition and self-expression,"[28] participating not only in "aggressive behavior" but also in attempts to change academic standards and practices in ways detrimental to education in general.[29]

Among the defenses or exculpations of double standards is the argument that various nonblack student subgroups have long concentrated on easy courses or easy graders—varsity athletes and fraternity members being prominent examples. There are problems with this approach, however. First, the least reputable of white academic practices is held up as a norm for blacks. Second, the whole purpose of athletes and fraternity members in attempting to reduce their academic responsibilities is to free their time for essentially nonintellectual purposes. And why should this be the goal of blacks trying to emerge from poverty?

Special recruitment of black faculty and the existence of faculty quotas, whatever they may be called, invoke many of the same arguments as those over special (lower) admissions standards for black students, and a number of others as well. Sometimes the existing black students on campus are cited as a major reason for seeking black faculty; it is argued that they can "relate" better to black faculty members because they tend to be either more sympathetic to the students' problems or more willing and able to impose tough standards, or both. A further argument is often made that a racially integrated faculty is beneficial to *white* students. By seeing Negroes in high-status intellectual roles, white students will supposedly carry forth into the world an image of blacks different from the degrading stereotypes of the past, and therefore set the stage for better racial attitudes and actions in the future. Finally, there is the moral argument that black faculty quotas compensate for past unjust discrimination in hiring and, by making blacks part of "the system," provide some built-in protection against future discrimination.

The argument that black faculty "relate" better to black students is not one readily testable by scientific methods. It is clear, impressionistically, that in some cases this is true, but a generalization of this sort requires either much more empirical evidence or much more logical analysis than a general consonance with currently popular racial beliefs. And it is not clear what the intellectual content or consequences of "relating" may be, where it does in fact occur. Some black faculty brought in under lower academic standards have been described as "better examples of continuing disadvantage than of its diminution."[30] The point here is not to claim that this is *typical* of black faculty members, but to suggest the possibility that although "disadvantaged" faculty members may indeed more readily establish rapport with disadvantaged students, there is not necessarily any intellectual benefit. It would be very useful to determine empirically whether black faculty members with high intellectual credentials (however measured) have more black students in their classes than they would by random chance. My impression is that they do not. However, the important thing is to find out, and it may be significant that no real effort has been made to check this key assumption of those who seek black faculty quotas.

The effect on the racial attitudes of white students, and through them on society as a whole, also turns crucially on the quality of the black faculty hired to fill the quotas. Proponents of quotas (including "targets," "goals," and "preferences") typically state that "of course" they want the black faculty members to be of as high a quality as white faculty members—but this crucial point cannot be "of-coursed" aside. If blacks performing capably in high-status, high-visibility roles can have a positive effect on future racial attitudes, then blacks giving substandard performances in such roles can have a negative effect—one, indeed, which builds on, and may appear to confirm, a whole history of racist beliefs. At almost any institution, of course, there will be black individuals of both kinds, just as there are white individuals of both kinds. The question is, what is the general impression likely to be created by faculty hired to fill quotas?

The past is a great unchangeable fact. That past, for black America, has included very few persons trained to be academic scholars. Moreover, many years of academic education are required for anyone, regardless of race, to qualify, even minimally, as a faculty member, much less as a mature scholar. In short, there are relatively few black scholars in existence, and the number cannot be greatly increased in the immediate future. And it is in this context that faculty quotas must be considered. Any "goal," "target," or "affirmative action" designed to make the percentage of blacks on faculties approximate that in the general population can only mean reducing quality standards. Disputes over reducing the quality of faculty members tend to center on its effect in reducing educational standards, an effect which is minimized by the tendency of good students to avoid or be steered around incompetent faculty members. Not so easily minimized is the effect of substandard faculty members on the racial attitudes of both black and white students.

With faculty quotas as with student quotas, the most prestigious institutions have the greatest incentives to maximize body count. In the case of faculty hiring, they respond not only to the public relations need to maintain visible institutional leadership, but also to the legal need to meet "affirmative action" goals as a precondition for receiving the federal money which is indispensable for maintaining their standing in research competition.

Much has been made of the fact that the government's "affirmative action" programs do not specify exact numbers to be hired from a given race. The government requires each college and university to submit some quota scheme if it wants federal money, but allows it to work out its own numbers and mechanics subject to federal approval. All numerical targets, however, need not be rigidly met. This allows the government to use financial pressure to force a certain kind of action, while retaining the option, should it become politically necessary, of repudiating the particular way the action is carried out. In particular, the government can deny that it required lower standards or any form of racial favoritism. It merely created a situation in which certain numerical results would insure the continued flow of government money, while others would threaten that flow and/or subject academic administrations to continuing demands on their time and resources to meet sweeping and repeated investigations. In short, the government has imposed race and sex quotas without accepting responsibility for them, while, in fact, carefully preserving its "deniability."

The importance of federal money for research activity obviously varies according to the importance of research activity in a given institution's scheme of things. This is obviously greatest at the prestige universities receiving the most federal support. Again, as in the case of black students, a great demand for black faculty is created at the top, and the same shifting effect on quality is at work. Faculty members, like students, are neither high nor low quality absolutely, but only relative to the particular institutions in which they operate. A faculty member who would be a respected scholar at a state college may be a second-class academic citizen at a prestige university. In terms of the supposed benefits of quota hiring, a black faculty member who could contribute toward racial respect at a good college may reinforce racism at a top research institution.

Although in some fields the salaries of black professors are marginally higher than those of their white counterparts,[31] a fact which may reflect the demand for additional "affirmative action" professors, there is little evidence that significantly more black faculty members have actually been hired since "affirmative action" policies emerged. Past discrimination in the white academic world is readily documented,[32] but the era chosen for comparison is crucial. *Immediately* before affirmative action, there was little evidence that blacks of a given level of academic preparation and performance averaged less than their white counterparts; a study in 1969 found that less than 10 percent of the black academicians at white universities believed that they had encountered employment discrimination.[33]

Moreover, some of the gains under affirmative action quotas are illusory. The actual hiring of minority faculty members (or women) is only one way of coping with "affirmative action" quotas; another is to generate recruiting activity and practices designed to show "good faith" *attempts* to comply. From the point of view of the black faculty member, this means that the number of *apparent* job opportunities is inflated beyond what is really available to him. Institutions seek to increase their black body counts not only in hiring, but also at the stages of sending recruiting letters or conducting interviews, whether or not they have any intention of proceeding beyond these preliminary stages.

The logic of quotas often extends beyond the hiring process. Faculty committees may also reflect the pervasive desire for minority representation. But to say that blacks must be "represented" in some fixed proportion, where this proportion is greater than the proportion of black faculty members, is to say that black faculty members must serve on more committees than white faculty members. To the individual black faculty member, this is hardly a benefit, and the more interested he is in the intellectual purposes which his position involves, the more of an imposition it is.

To the extent that "black" becomes synonymous with "substandard," the ability of the best black scholars to influence either black or white students is reduced. Indeed, substandard black faculty members have every incentive to undermine competent black faculty members. It is not at all uncommon for officials of black studies departments to acquire a voice or even a veto in the selection of black faculty members in other departments, and to use it against "conventional"—competent—black academics.[34] It could hardly be otherwise, given the threat that able black scholars represent to the less scholarly black academic's personal standing, value orientation, and influence with black students—factors on which his job may depend.

BLACK INSTITUTIONS

Most of today's predominantly black American colleges and universities began with predominantly or exclusively white faculties, administrators, and trustees. They were, in short, white-run institutions for black students. The evolution of black colleges and universities can hardly be understood without taking this fact into account. From the earliest times, this raised questions over which was more important, academic quality or black representation in positions of authority and prestige. There were literally only a handful of college-trained Negroes in the United States when most of the Negro colleges were founded after the Civil War, so white domination was inevitable at the outset. As time went on, a small but growing number of blacks began to acquire some higher education, even if it did not fully match that of the whites in the black colleges. By the 1880s, the question of black representation had become a live issue. A black leader declared in 1885 that the "intellects of our young people are being educated at the expense of their manhood," because in their classrooms "they see only white professors."[35] Other blacks—notably the parents of black students—insisted that quality education for black students took precedence over black representation among the faculty or administrators. "We should not allow a mistaken race pride to cause us to impose upon [the students] inferior teachers,"[36] they argued, and their view prevailed—for a time.

The issue did not die, but, despite the sporadic outbursts of rhetoric about black representation,[37] high-performance whites or whites with good public relations remained secure in their jobs. Even in the absence of any explicit or dramatic change in policy, however, increasing numbers of educated blacks led to increasing numbers of black scholars and administrators in the Negro colleges and universities. By the time of World War I, about half the faculty and administrators of the Negro colleges and universities were black.[38] The postwar "new Negro" and "black renaissance" era of the 1920s had an academic counterpart in a renewed and more insistent demand for black control of black academic institutions. An accelerated substitution of blacks for whites put these institutions firmly in black control by the end of the decade. Contemporary black observers chronicled a decline in academic standards in the wake of this rapid change. The celebrated Negro intellectual and dean of Howard University, Kelly Miller, described it as "a misfortune barely short of a calamity," and E. Franklin Frazier also depicted it as a setback for black education.[39]

The effects of this sudden change in academic personnel were not limited to the immediate period in which it occurred. Black faculty members and administrators had few alternative occupations open. This meant that black administrators clung tenaciously to their jobs and black faculty dared not oppose them or seem in any way to threaten them. Black administrators not only remained in office for extremely long periods of time, but exercised extreme power during their tenure. Academic freedom was one casualty of this situation. The tyranny at black colleges has been bitterly portrayed by black scholars and intellectuals, ranging from W. E. B. DuBois' essays[40] and E. Franklin Frazier's sociological studies[41] to Ralph Ellison's fictional classic, *The Invisible Man*.[42] Phrases such as "authoritarian," "autocratic," "paternalistic," and "domineering" abound in the literature.[43]

Another casualty was academic quality. It was not merely that initially there were not enough good black scholars to replace the departing whites, but also that the first generation of substandard scholars largely determined the atmosphere in which subsequent generations of black scholars would function or fail to function. The young E. Franklin Frazier was admonished for being too bookish at Tuskegee Institute. W. E. B. DuBois encountered hostility on more than one black campus. A list of Negro scholars alienated from the successive administrations at Howard University over the years would read like a Who's Who of black academic scholarship. While the intellectual achievements of these scholars could not be completely stifled, their voice in university affairs was minimized, and the shaping of institutions was largely in the hands of more tractable, but less able, men.

The administrators' need for men who would not "rock the boat" was particularly acute in view of the fact that the black administration was typically responsible to white trustees, white foundations, and/or white state legislatures. Since most Negro colleges and universities are located in the South, administrators had to suppress ideas and movements which were unacceptable to Southern white concepts about race relations or the intellectual capacity of the Negro. In short, the black administrators were virtual dictators over black faculty and students, and at the same time clearly clients of white power figures. More importantly, each generation of black administrators chose a succeeding generation after its own image, thereby driving the more intellectual and independent elements to the periphery of institutional affairs, or beyond. Thus the choice of black representation over academic quality had lasting negative consequences, even after large numbers of qualified black scholars and administrators had emerged.

The classic controversy in the black colleges was that between the conservative, vocationally oriented training program advocated by Booker T. Washington and the liberal education, with clear overtones of restructured race relations, advocated by W. E. B. DuBois. Neither the rhetorical differences nor the personal bitterness between the two men, however, should obscure the large overlap in their respective educational philosophies. Washington repeatedly recognized the need for higher intellectual work[44] and DuBois argued for vocational competence and work discipline.[45] Although their conflict arose partly from a difference in emphasis and partly from a difference in their choice of roles, it was, to a very large extent, a personality clash, exacerbated by the sociopolitical tendencies of the time. Booker T. Washington was accepted by white Americans as *the* spokesmen for black Americans, and in that role he was consulted and often held veto power on the advancement of other blacks in important positions in a variety of fields.[46] W. E. B. DuBois had a much smaller base of support, among blacks or whites, and aroused much more resentment and opposition among whites in positions of power.

It should be noted that during the period of the Washington-DuBois controversies in the early years of the twentieth century, DuBois was a liberal—a moderate by present-day standards—not yet the Marxist he was to become in his later years. One indication of DuBois' moderation during this period is that he was among those who congratulated Booker T. Washington on his famous Atlanta Exposition speech.[47] It was only after Washington's rise to power in the wake of that speech that DuBois turned against him. Even then, DuBois' opposition was directed against particular points on which he thought Washington was mistaken, and against the whites who gave Washington a power which DuBois considered dangerous for anyone.[48]

DuBois did not question Washington's desire to promote the advancement of black people; he did not accuse him of a "sell-out," although he did assert that his methods were counterproductive. Washington, as a man with a dominant power position to defend, was much more actively engaged in trying to undercut DuBois' smaller but growing influence.[49] Recent scholarship, however, has brought out Washington's extensive clandestine efforts in behalf of civil rights and political awareness for blacks,[50] so his real differences with DuBois were even less substantial than they might appear from contemporary writings and were, in considerable part, differences in tactics rather than in principle. Perhaps more basically, there were personal power differences and social differences. Washington was "up from slavery" while DuBois was descended from Negroes who had been free for generations—an important distinction in their time.

Both vocational and liberal arts education continued at black institutions, but with a historical trend toward the latter, except insofar as teacher education can be classified as vocational. To that extent, history has followed DuBois rather than Washington. However, the social and political conservatism and accommodation to white Southern racial "realities" which Washington espoused and practiced remained the hallmark of black college administrators for many decades. The fact that many of the leading academics were far more liberal or militant than their college administrators created another source of friction.

Even the best black colleges and universities do not approach the standards of quality of respectable national institutions. Although some black schools are often praised for high quality, hard data provide no support whatever for claims of high quality by any Negro college or university. None has a department ranking among the leading graduate departments in any of the 29 fields surveyed by the American Council of Education.[51] None ranks among the "selective" institutions with regard to student admissions.[52] None has a student body whose College Board scores are within 100 points of any school in the Ivy League. None has a library with even one-third as many volumes as the library of the University of Texas, much less the much larger libraries at such schools as Harvard, Yale, or Princeton. Many black schools are so small that a number of predominantly white institutions graduate more black students annually than they do. A study by two white scholars has found black colleges and universities as deficient in spirit as they are in academic matters, and while cries of "racism" have been raised against these men, they have said nothing which was not said earlier and more bitterly by black intellectuals.

Within the past decade, black colleges and universities have been losing their best-qualified faculty and their best potential students to white institutions. The period of integrationist philosophies raised questions as to whether or why they should continue in existence. The more recent period of black awareness has reduced this sort of pressure but has led to more scathing indictments of their policies. Black colleges have been defended on the grounds that (1) they were the only institutions realistically available to the majority of black students[53] during most of the history of black Americans, (2) the social need for black institutions for students who could not feel sufficiently at home in white institutions to realize their intellectual potential,[54] (3) black awareness, pride, and/or ideology can flourish in an all-black setting,[55] and (4) many black students are unable to meet the standards of white institutions.[56] The tone of both defenders and critics has been acerbic to the point of bitterness.

None of these arguments, however, is as strong as it once was. The historical argument for black colleges loses its relevance as the proportion of blacks who attend other institutions rises from a majority to an overwhelming majority. Similarly, the argument concerning the social needs of black students for the companionship and support of other black students is less compelling now that there are large numbers of black students on predominantly white campuses. Wayne State University, for example, graduates more black students than Fisk University.[57] Likewise, the need for black awareness, pride, and/or ideology, however defined or justified, does not logically entail the continuance of all existing black institutions. Finally, the inability of black students to meet white standards is exaggerated by the tendency of circumstances to concentrate black students in institutions where the majority of white students could not meet the standards either. None of this is an argument for the continuation of the deliberate policy of racial integration, which was once central to black organizations. Continued existence of all-black institutions is less urgent than its defenders imply. There is no *a priori* reason why they must be either deliberately destroyed or sustained at all costs.

In a sense, black studies have existed for generations. Booker T. Washington urged that such black leaders as Frederick Douglass[58] be studied and revered, and himself wrote a two-volume history of the American Negro.[59] W. E. B. DuBois wrote the landmark study of *The Philadelphia Negro* in 1899, and followed it with a long series of monographs on various aspects of black American life, as well as more personal sketches and essays. In the 1920s, Carter G. Woodson pioneered scholarly black history and, in the 1930s, Sterling Brown studied and expounded black literature and music. E. Franklin Frazier became the foremost scholar on the sociology of black Americans, with works ranging from narrowly focused academic studies of black residents and family patterns to a wide-ranging critique of the black middle class. White scholars, notably Gunnar Myrdal, have also contributed to the study of black Americans.

Much of the white scholarship on black Americans, however, has been permeated by presuppositions of black inferiority, as are, for example, the historical writings of U. B. Phillips,[60] the sociological writings of Edward B. Reuter on mulatto superiority among Negroes,[61] and innumerable psychological works attempting to prove the intellectual and/or emotional inferiority of blacks. Such writings were particularly dominant during the period of Social Darwinism in American social thought and coincided with an outpouring of scholarship designed to show the inferiority of southern European and Jewish immigrant groups. In sheer volume of material, the writings attempting to prove the inferiority of European immigrant groups may have exceeded that on blacks, if only because of the long controversy preceding the exclusionary immigration laws of the 1920s which are applied to Europeans but not to Negroes, and because the presumption among whites of black inferiority required less "scientific" support.

Black scholars struggled against the myths and misconceptions about American Negroes and, aided by such studies as Myrdal's classic, *An American Dilemma*, slowly changed the interpretation of Negro life reflected in textbooks and popular literature. The civil rights movements of the 1960s created still more interest in the "hidden" history of black involvement in, and contributions to, many aspects of American life. In one sense, the demand for black studies in the university was the culmination of this long trend.

However, the *sudden* and *simultaneous* demands all across the country in the late 1960s cannot be explained in this way. The kinds of black studies demanded reflected far more immediate circumstances—notably the desperate academic condition of black students at white colleges and universities. It is significant that demands for black studies were most insistent at white institutions, particularly at the most academically demanding ones. The demands for black studies differed from demands for other forms of new academic studies in that they (1) had a strong racial exclusionary tendency with regard to students and/or faculty; (2) restricted the philosophical and political positions acceptable, even from black scholars in such programs; (3) demanded larger areas of autonomy than other academic departments or programs; and (4) often sought a voice or veto on the admissions of black students and the hiring of black faculty in the institution as a whole. In short, black studies advocates sought a withdrawal of blacks from academic competition with whites and rejected traditional academic standards, whether exemplified by white or black scholars.

In their justifications for the particular constellation of features they demand, black studies advocates shift at crucial points in their arguments from logical or empirical development to assertions as to the perceptions of black students. For example, the "exploitative aspects of graduate school" are asserted to be different "in kind, not only in degree" for the black student, but when it comes to specifics it is stated:

> While the objective situation might be the same for both, the subjective state is actually quite different for Black and white students.[62]

Questions of academic qualifications are dismissed rather than discussed. Quality standards are equated with being "white-like."[63] Such arguments are typically long on colorful characterizations—"academic colonizers," "institutional racism," "house niggers"—and short on specific systematic empirical tests of specific hypotheses. Indeed these very processes of hypotheses-testing are rejected. These rejections are often characterized as "methodological" differences, when in fact they are differences in social-political preconceptions. The very tools of intellectual inquiry are declared to be "conservative tools," and the black intellectual is said to have to add "something extra."[64] But what this something might be is left undefined: "Writing at the beginning of the development of Black Social Science, one can say only what it might become."[65] The black scholar must use "his sense of Black consciousness as the cutting edge to redefine reality,"[66] and the black community must "intervene" to prevent any research on blacks that it does not like.[67] The basis for these decisions is left unspecified, and the basis for conclusions already reached is also dealt with summarily: That "racism in America is endemic to capitalism" was "settled long ago" by a writer who listed racism as one of the features of capitalism.[68] That the mass media oppresses blacks is "starkly evident."[69]

Such black studies advocates assume the bad faith of all—black and white—who have a different argument and the only question they give serious attention and space is how to characterize or explain this dishonorable behavior. Essentially, whites are dismissed as racists and blacks are dismissed either as dupes or opportunists "who pant after professional elevation."[70] This literature leaves no place for honest disagreements based on personal differences in the weighing of complex information or different estimates of uncertain future prospects, much less for different interpretations of the elaborate mosaic of the past.

Critics of black studies programs have argued (1) the educational disadvantages of black isolation, (2) the self-defeating nature of the lower standards of these courses, (3) the self-delusions involved in the content of such programs and in their related political activities, and (4) the need for alternative courses as a means of acquiring the skills necessary to better the students' own condition and that of black people in general. The classic criticism of black studies programs, by a distinguished black scholar, asserts that "the way to the top" is through other channels. This needlessly ties the criticisms of black studies to a philosophy of integration and personal advancement, both of which are suspect in the eyes of many black students. In fact, the hard skills needed for personal advancement in a racially integrated setting are even more urgently needed for "nation building" on a separatist model. Any form of black self-sufficiency would require blacks to gain proficiency in a much wider range of scientific and technical skills than they need in a society where they can readily purchase the fruits of such skills from members of other racial groups.

CONCLUSION

The economic and social progress of black people has proceeded in spite of a failure to solve all these problems or even to resolve all differences within the black community. The prospects of a definitive solution to the problems of black education are as remote today as ever, but the continued progress of black people seems solidly based in spite of this. Much of the bitterness among black intellectuals, academic and nonacademic, reflects the special problems of a particular set of black people with a peculiar personal and social history. They are, in many cases, products of the cultural and/or physical assimilation process which is now held to be generally shameful and which, in particular aspects, has been and still is indisputably shameful. Their need for expiation or atonement is not conceptually identical with the black population's needs, and in practice the symbolic purifying acts of the intellectuals, including students, may be counterproductive in terms of the economic or other advancement of the black population as a whole. For example, the fields in which black students and faculty members specialize (sociology, political science, etc.) are not the same as the areas in which the black population has expressed its priorities—for medicine, business, and other technical skills.

Despite bitter antagonism among various schools of black intellectuals, there are important areas of agreement. All agree that black faculty and students feel enormous pressures at white institutions—pressures to perform by traditional academic standards and at the same time to be "relevant" to the problems of black people. The pressures to meet standards can only be exacerbated by continuance or acceleration of policies which lead to a systematic mismatching of students and faculty with their respective institutions. The pressures on students could be eased, however, by assigning financial aid to the selected students, and allowing each one to use the aid at whatever institution he chose. This would lead to a distribution of black students in accordance with their own assessments of their preparation and interests, not in accordance with any institution's need for a given demographic profile. For black faculty members, better matching of institutions and individuals could be achieved by a vigorous enforcement of nondiscriminatory hiring policies. This would force institutions to justify their decisions by professional criteria rather than racial percentages. Over a period of time this could lead to a distribution of black scholars to institutions where they could command the most respect rather than a distribution reflecting the institutional needs of white colleges and universities to safeguard their federal money.

Another point on which black intellectuals of widely differing views agree is that education is highly respected in the black community. Historically, education has been the main escape route for those black Americans who have advanced socially and economically. Many understand this who understand neither the educational superstructure nor intellectual prerequisites or traditions. The repudiation of educational and/or intellectual standards by some black intellectuals is more in keeping with the attitudes of some middle-class whites than with the views of the black population in whose name this repudiation is often made. The naive hopes produced among black Americans, as among Americans generally, will undoubtedly be modified by experience to something more realistic, but the central role of education seems more likely to be strengthened than weakened in the long run.

NOTES

1. Allen B. Ballard, *The Education of Black Folk* (New York: Harper & Row, 1973), p. 65.

2. Thomas Sowell, *Black Education: Myths and Tragedies* (New York: David McKay Co., 1972), chap. 6.

3. Ballard, op. cit.

4. Martin Kilson, "The Black Experience at Harvard," *New York Times Magazine*, September 2, 1973, p. 37; Ballard, op. cit., *passim*.

5. Kenneth D. Roose and Charles J. Andersen, *A Rating of Graduate Programs* (Washington, D.C.: American Council on Education, 1970), *passim*.

6. Nancy Fulop, "The 1969 CLEO Summer Institute Reports: A Summary," *University of Toledo Law Review*, Spring–Summer 1970, p. 648.

7. Solveig Eggerz, "Accentuate the Negative," *Call: The Newspaper of Capitol Hill*, July 26, 1973; Sowell, op. cit., p. 136.

8. Fulop, op. cit., p. 649.

9. Clyde W. Summers, "Preferential Admissions: An Unreal Solution to a Real Problem," *University of Toledo Law Review*, Spring–Summer 1970, p. 384.

10. Ibid., pp. 392–93.

11. David Hapgood, "The Competition for Africa's Students," *The Reporter*, September 12, 1963, p. 42.

12. Ibid.

13. Ballard, op. cit., p. 83.

14. Summers, op. cit., p. 385.

15. James Alan McPherson, "The Black Law Student," *Atlantic*, April 1970, p. 99.

16. Ballard, op. cit., p. 96.

17. Arthur R. Jensen, "How Much Can We Boost IQ and Scholastic Achievement?" *Harvard Educational Review*, Winter 1969, p. 100.

18. Arthur R. Jensen, "Selection of Minority Students in Higher Education," *University of Toledo Law Review*, Spring–Summer 1970, pp. 440, 443; Donald A. Rock, "Motivation, Moderators, and Test Bias," ibid., pp. 536, 537; "Studies of superior Negro high school and college students seem to indicate that they differ somewhat from white students insofar as their achievement is not as high as that of white groups of comparable abilities," E. G. Rodgers, op. cit., p. 22; Ronald L. Flaugher, *Testing Practices, Minority Groups and Higher Education: A Review and Discussion of the Research* (Princeton: Educational Testing Service, 1970), p. 11.

19. Sowell, op. cit., pp. 131–32, 210–13.

20. Ballard, op. cit., pp. 84–90.

21. Ibid., p. 97.

22. Derrick A. Bell, "Black Students in White Law Schools: The Ordeal and the Opportunity," *University of Toledo Law Review*, Spring–Summer 1970, p. 552.

23. Ibid., p. 553.

24. Ibid., p. 552.

25. Ibid., p. 551.

26. Macklin Fleming, "The Black Quota at Yale Law School," *The Public Interest*, Spring 1970, p. 47.

27. Ibid.

28. Ibid., p. 46.

29. Ibid.

30. Gordon D. Morgan, *The Ghetto College Student* (Iowa City: The American College Testing Program), p. 29n.

31. Unpublished Ph.D. thesis by Kent Mommsen.

32. Michael R. Winston, "Through the Back Door: Academic Ransom and the

Negro Scholar in Historical Perspective," *Daedalus*, Summer 1971, p. 695; James Allen Moss, "Negro Teachers in Predominantly White Colleges," *Journal of Negro Education*, Fall 1958, pp. 451–62.

33. "Of 554 black faculty members, eight percent stated that difficulty in finding their present job was caused by discrimination," David M. Rafky, "The Black Academic on the Marketplace," *Change*, October 1971, p. 65.

34. Sowell, op. cit., pp. 214–15.

35. James M. McPherson, "White Liberals and Black Power in Negro Education, 1865–1915," *American Historical Review*, June 1970, p. 1362.

36. Ibid.

37. Ibid., pp. 1364–66.

38. Ibid., p. 1370.

39. Ibid., p. 1378.

40. W. E. B. DuBois, *The Education of Black People*, ed. Herbert Aptheker (Amherst: University of Massachusetts Press, 1973), pp. 46–48, 52–56.

41. E. Franklin Frazier, *Black Bourgeoisie* (New York: Collier Books, 1962), p. 71.

42. Ralph Ellison, *The Invisible Man* (New York: Signet Books, 1952), chaps. 2–6.

43. Tobe Johnson, "The Black College as a System," *Daedalus*, Summer 1971, pp. 801, 804. See also St. Clair Drake, "The Black University in the American Social Order," ibid., p. 845; Winston, op. cit., pp. 702, 707.

44. " . . . some have gotten the idea that industrial development was opposed to the Negro's higher mental development. . . . I would say to the black boy what I would say to the white boy, Get all the mental development that your time and pocket-book will allow of,—the more, the better. . . . " Booker T. Washington, *The Future of the American Negro* (New York: The New American Library, Inc., 1969), pp. 79–80; " . . . no one understanding the real needs of the race would advocate that industrial education should be given to every Negro to the exclusion of the professions and other branches of learning. . . . There is, then, a place and an increasing need for the Negro college as well as the industrial institute. . . . " Booker T. Washington, "Educational Philosophy," *Great Lives Observed: Booker T. Washington*, ed. E. L. Thornbrough (Englewood Cliffs: Prentice-Hall, 1969), p. 41.

45. DuBois, op. cit., pp. 68–69. See also Myrdal, op. cit., p. 889n.

46. Louis R. Harlan, *Booker T. Washington: The Making of a Black Leader, 1856–1910* (New York: Oxford University Press, 1972), pp. 258–59; Gilbert Osofsky, *Harlem: The Making of a Ghetto* (New York: Harper & Row, 1968), pp. 164–65; Louis R. Harlan, "Booker T. Washington in Biographical Perspective," *American Historical Review*, October 1970, pp. 1584–85.

47. Harlan, *Booker T. Washington*, p. 225. See also ibid., p. 265.

48. W. E. B. DuBois, "The Souls of Black Folk," *Three Negro Classics* (New York: Avon Books, 1965), p. 243.

49. Harlan, *Booker T. Washington*, p. 303; Harlan, "Booker T. Washington in Biographic Perspective," op. cit., p. 1586; Louis R. Harlan, "The Secret Life of Booker T. Washington," *Journal of Southern History*, August 1971, pp. 407-9.

50. August Meier, "Toward a Reinterpretation of Booker T. Washington," in August Meier and Elliott Rudwick, eds., *The Making of Black America* (New York: Atheneum, 1969), 2:126-27, 130; Harlan, "The Secret Life of Booker T. Washington," op. cit., pp. 396-98, 399, 400, 401, 402.

51. Roose and Andersen, op. cit., *passim*.

52. James Cass and Max Birnbaum, *Comparative Guide to American Colleges*, 5th ed. (New York: Harper & Row, 1972), pp. 761-66.

53. C. Eric Lincoln, "The Negro Colleges and Cultural Change," *Daedalus*, Summer 1971, p. 624.

54. Ballard, op. cit., p. 151.

55. St. Clair Drake, op. cit., p. 877; Henry Allen Bullock, "The Black College and the New Black Awareness," *Daedalus*, Summer 1971, pp. 594-95.

56. Christopher Jencks and David Riesman, "The American Negro College," *Harvard Educational Review*, Winter 1967, p. 42.

57. Ibid., p. 31.

58. "I think we should be ashamed of the coloured man or woman who would not venerate the name of Frederick Douglass," Booker T. Washington, *The Future of the American Negro*, p. 180.

59. Booker T. Washington, *The Story of the Negro* (New York: Negro Universities Press, 1969) [originally published by Doubleday, Page & Co., 1909].

60. Ulrich Bonnell Phillips, *American Negro Slavery* (Baton Rouge: Louisiana State University Press, 1969) [originally published by Appleton-Century-Crofts, Inc., 1918]; *Life and Labor in the Old South* (Boston: Little, Brown, 1929).

61. Edward Byron Reuter, *The Mulatto in the United States* (Boston: Richard G. Badger, 1918).

62. Nathan Hare, "The Challenge of a Black Scholar," in Joyce A. Ladner, ed., *The Death of White Sociology* (New York: Vintage Books, 1973), p. 74.

63. Douglas Davidson, "The Furious Passage of the Black Graduate Student," in Ladner, ed., op. cit., p. 30.

64. Ronald W. Walters, "Toward a Definition of Black Social Science," in Ladner, ed., op. cit., p. 323.

65. Walters, op. cit., pp. 192-93.

66. Ibid., p. 199.

67. Ibid., p. 207.

68. Ibid., p. 196.

69. Ibid., p. 200.

70. Hare, op. cit., p. 70.

Social Science and General Education

Every field must have both descriptive information and analytical principles, and within each field some point is reached where analysis supersedes description. I would argue that this point is largely determined by how spontaneously interesting the purely descriptive material may be. Clearly, a mere description of the inanimate physical world has little interest; neither does a bare synopsis of events in a novel or a poem. Such areas must be analytical or reflective, almost from the outset, if they are to hold anyone's interest. But the social sciences focus on people, and people have a certain spontaneous interest for other people. Many aspects of human life remain interesting when merely described, or when the accompanying analysis consists only of surmises, suggestions, or even a dialogue or visceral opinions. This enables the social sciences to get away with a lower intellectual level of discourse than could be tolerated in the physical sciences or, to a lesser extent, the humanities. Moreover, the sheer volume of background information necessary for dealing with social-science complexities provides a legitimate reason for remaining at the descriptive level for a considerable time. In the natural sciences, the corresponding complexities are summarized in mathe-

Reprinted from *The Philosophy of the Curriculum*, ed. by Sidney Hook, Paul Kurtz, and Miro Todorovich (Prometheus Books, Buffalo, N.Y., 1975), pp. 165–68.

matical and statistical formulations that make it unnecessary for molecules or chromosomes to become a central preoccupation. In the more structured humanities, elaborate traditions of long standing limit current subjective input, much as mathematical-statistical formulas reduce it in the natural sciences.

Economics, as the "exceptional" social science, confirms this pattern. People are the subject matter of economics to a much lesser extent than in the other social sciences. *Things* are the proximate subject matter of economics—though ultimately it is in their relationship with people. The balance of payments, the interest rate, and the Gross National Product are not things that cause adrenalin to flow spontaneously. They can become interesting only within some intellectual framework, in the light of various hypotheses, and with some systematic procedure for analysis. Even introductory economics must introduce analysis or risk annihilation.

The comparisons of the various disciplines have thus far been in terms of a static picture as of a given time. But the disciplines differ enormously in age: mathematics, the natural sciences, and the humanities are many centuries older than the social sciences. Economics again is somewhat different from the other social sciences. It is more than two centuries old, or more than double the age of sociology. It may be that the disciplines will approach a similar pattern over time as the need for structural analysis increasingly permeates the thinking of the professions—and ultimately the lay public.

How does this relate to general education? The problems of the social sciences—notably diffuseness and dilettantism—are even more pronounced in "general education," as that is usually conceived and practiced. General-education courses in social science largely purvey information (including misinformation) and make minimal demands in the form of disciplined analysis, even if such courses do tax memory or patience. The avoidance of such courses by distinguished scholars in the social sciences may be more to their credit than a cause for blame or dismay. Even the so-called leading lights of the social sciences cannot possibly provide a sweeping "general understanding of society and the place of the individual in it." One of the ways in which the natural sciences are more mature is that they do not pretend to offer courses on "organic and inorganic matter in space and time." If such a course were somehow forced into the catalogue, it should not be a source of consternation if leading chemists, physicists, and biologists left it to be taught by the more reckless assistant professors.

When discussing general education, there is a tendency to pour out our fondest hopes and indeed to put forth a list of demands that would shame student radicals. These demands are often individually sound, and their goals urgently in need of realization, but collectively they are often impossible in the context of a four-year college and a 24-hour day. There is no question that there will be compromise—whether rationally devised or forced upon us by intractable constraints. What can be sacrificed without sacrificing the essential goals?

If the history of social-science education has any lesson, it is that analytical methods are essential intellectually and—in the long run—are even required to maintain student interest and respect. These methods of course differ by field so that the natural sciences, the social sciences, and the humanities should all be represented in general education. What will have to give then? The breadth we would like to see in each field will have to be sacrificed. It is undoubtedly desirable that a student know philosophy as it has evolved from Socrates to Camus, but it is ultimately more important that he know something about the analytical methods of philosophy. Even if these analytical methods are taught historically, a course devoted solely to William James has more chance of success than a course that sweeps across the centuries in a semester. Merely trying to understand one thinker is an education in the process of interpretation and criticism, usually beginning with initial misconceptions, which are virtually inevitable, and proceeding through uncritical acceptance, followed by the devastating criticisms of various opponents and the burden of empirical evidence. It may not be worth it to go through all this just to understand William James (or any other thinker or subject), but it is worth it to understand, first, what is meant by understanding, and second, to exercise discipline and judgment in evaluation. To me, that is what general education is all about—not breadth of subject matter but depth of analytical methods and breadth of applicability.

This kind of general education—in-depth studies in a wide range of subject areas—need not be adversely affected by the problem of faculty specialization or the problem of student choice of courses. It is precisely the specialist who can best lead a student through the intellectual labyrinths of his field to a narrowly circumscribed goal. A series of narrowly focused general-education courses in scattered fields can also allow the student to "do his own thing" *without doing it in his own way.* If he is charged up to study imperialism, then this visceral energy can be usefully employed to get him through a series of demanding theoretical and empirical investigations, beginning with a dissection of the theories of imperialism in Marx, Lenin, J. A. Hobson, and others, and proceeding to hypothesis testing with statistics. If racism is his interest, then he can get into the complexities of the IQ controversy or wrestle with the economics of discrimination. Some of these things can be done by an entering freshman, while others require special skills. This means only that general education cannot be localized in a particular span of time and regarded as a phase that passes, never to return. So much the better. This approach also means that general-education courses should not concentrate on "covering" a particular subject area, but rather on *uncovering* the complexities that lie beneath many apparently simple questions.

Testimony Before Congressional Subcommittee*

Thomas Sowell: There is a very serious problem at the supply stage of minority and female individuals in mathematics, the natural sciences, and engineering. In fact, this is part of a more general problem which extends well beyond those fields. Inadequate mathematical and scientific preparation severely limits career choices, even within the social sciences, and can affect job prospects in clerical and other fields not normally thought of as requiring any scientific background.

For example, minority and female faculty members are not only concentrated disproportionately in fields requiring little or no mathematical preparation—such as the humanities, education, the social sciences, and so forth—but also within a given field, such as economics, they are concentrated in the more nontechnical subspecialties—that is, consumer economics rather than econometrics.

The less technical, the less demanding fields are almost invariably the less well-paid fields. In the general labor market, even clerical jobs which require passing tests—such as civil service examinations—contain questions that can be answered easier or faster by someone with a facility in mathematics, so that even here an inadquate scientific background is a competitive handicap in the job market, though the job itself may have nothing to do with science.

The question is: How is this very real problem being met by the

*House Subcommittee on Science, Research, and Technology, February 23, 1977

legislation under consideration here? The approach taken by Senate bill S. 3202 and the corresponding House bill H.R. 12566 is an approach which has already been tried repeatedly in other fields, especially during the 1960s, and which has failed repeatedly, and at tragic personal cost to many of the minority students, quite aside from the money wasted.

The crucial need is for upgraded skills for individuals, not for a larger body count of particular kinds of people at particular institutions.

Yet, the basic approach of this proposed legislation is for larger body counts in various institutions. Skills are indeed mentioned, but only in assumptions and pious hopes. When it comes to hard cash, money is to be paid for body count—that is, in the language of the bill—for having "substantial minority student enrollment," for being "geographically located near minority population centers," or for countering "under-representation."

This emphasis on body count rather than on skill development is a familiar pattern from the 1960s, and it is worth noting some of the personal and institutional disasters produced by this approach.

Youngsters with insufficient skills were drawn into programs which ruthlessly sacrificed them to the pursuit of federal and foundation money on campus after campus. For example, one-half of the black students at Cornell University in the late 1960s were on some form of academic probation, a fact by no means unrelated to the guns-on-campus tragedy at that institution. The same proportion were on academic probation at the University of Chicago. And more than 90 percent were "not in good standing" at Wayne State Law School. Things like this happened at colleges and universities across the country, though some were able to keep the exact figures under lock and key, while they issued inspiring statements to the public.

The proposed legislation, like the ill-conceived programs of the 1960s, requires no monitoring of actual skill development by independent testing organizations—of which there are many, such as the Educational Testing Service in Princeton, which administers the nationwide College Board examinations.

The bottom line of the proposed legislation is money to be paid for physical presence—body count—not educational results. The approach of the proposed legislation is for institutional subsidies for going through certain motions, not individual support for achieving educational results. The direct beneficiaries are to be colleges, universities, and proposed "centers."

By contrast, consider the GI bill, which supported individuals pursuing their educational goals wherever they chose to pursue them, provided that they continued in good academic standing at some accredited institution. This did away with any need for either legislators or other government officials to decide whether certain institutions are "inspiring" for students, as claimed in S. 3202, or have been a lot less than inspiring, as reported by a number of scholars who have studied these same institutions—for example, E. Franklin Frazier, Ralph Ellison, Jencks and Riesman, etc. It did away with any need for chancy forecasts or blithe assumptions as to how the improvement of scientific skills today would translate into "representation" in specific occupations tomorrow. It was enough that the Government supported and rewarded the upgrading of skills.

A similar approach now would do much to bring much-needed skills to minority, female, and other disadvantaged youngsters, so that they could advance and compete on the basis of ability. If the more mathematically and scientifically prepared minority youth choose to become economists rather than engineers or geneticists rather than mathematicians, that is a personal matter and is certainly no misuse of the skills, whatever its impact on the numbers and percents which are a constant preoccupation of the proposed legislation.

The proposal to create minority graduate centers is a proposal to create campus ghettos, which would be especially inexcusable in mathematics and the natural sciences, which are among the most universal of human activities. There is no black mathematics or Hispanic engineering.

Moreover, the emphasis on graduate scientific education puts the emphasis at precisely the wrong end of the educational experience. Mathematical and scientific skills build on previous mathematical and scientific skills, so that the effort needs to be concentrated in the early school years where the battle for scientific literacy is won or lost.

The NSF bill is not a way to educate minority youngsters; it is "pork barrel" legislation for academics, and it is not surprising to find those who stand to gain by it already on record in favor of it. The bias of this bill is further indicated by its proposal to staff various NSF committees with people chosen for their activism in a political sense, rather than for their scientific or educational achievements.

Not only must minorities be a majority of a key board, according to the original Senate bill these are not to be minority individuals chosen for their scientific standing but because they are members of organizations which have a record of favoring the body count approach.

In summary, the educational needs of minority youngsters are too important, both for them and for the country, to be sacrificed to institutional interests and fashions.

What matters is not the rhetoric of the bill, but the financial incentives it creates. If the final legislation pays for body count, it is going to produce body count—at whatever cost in human terms. If this money is to be paid only for demonstrated skill development, then that is what it will produce. And that is what we need.

Thank you.

Mr. Harkin: Thank you very much, Dr. Sowell.

That brings up the question I asked earlier about the "push and pull" or the "pull upward" type, where emphasis ought to be placed. From my own experience and my own background—I went to law school, but I do have a basic science background also—I remember when I went to law school there was a program for black students that they brought from various colleges in the South—I went to law school at Washington—and gave them an intensive summer program of training, and put them into law school. Many of them didn't do well in law school as such, at the beginning, but later they did. And a couple of them were very close friends of mine and have become very successful lawyers.

Do you perceive some kind of a difference between that—I think you allude to that in your testimony—is there a difference between, let's say, the study of law or social science and the types of science and engineering that we're talking about here? In other words, can you leap-frog in one, but you can't in another?

Dr. Sowell: I think that would be one difference. I must say that, even in the social sciences and in the law, when you judge these programs, they all turn out some successful individuals. By the same token, there are people without education at all who are successful in business without a higher education. I understand, for example, that the two richest men in the world haven't finished high school.

But, aside from that, when I've looked at these programs as a whole, I haven't found that level of success in them. One of the things that happens in many of these programs—I'm talking generally, not the scientific program—at first is that you draw people into a certain level of institution which is inappropriate for their educational background. That is, you have someone at Harvard who would have been an excellent student at Rutgers, and he may be a failure at Harvard. The guy who succeeds at Harvard by some sort of superhuman effort might have succeeded with less of a superhuman effort, might have succeeded more, someplace else, in a less highly competitive environment.

Now, if I can use the example of Cornell again, in the sixties (1960s) I looked into the College Board scores of the black students at Cornell. Those students scored in the 75th percentile on a national level; that is, they were better than three-quarters of all American college students.

The reason they were on probation was that they were at Cornell, where the students at that time ranked somewhere in the top 1 percent on a national level of college students—so that those same students distributed differently in society would undoubtedly have been on the dean's list, in good standing, and so on, around the country.

To get more specifically back to the question that you asked, about the scientific area, I think it's even harder in the scientific area to do this because one thing does build on another. For example, in the state of California, a study has been done in San Francisco of black students who in the 10th grade averaged 6.6th grade level on various standardized tests. What that does, quite aside from the question of whether those tests are culturally biased and so on, it keeps them from taking the first course in algebra in high school, which in turn keeps them from taking the first course in calculus in college, which in turn puts a great number of occupations off limits before they even set foot on the campus.

The same thing is true of female students. Someone mentioned the University of California. The University of California, Los Angeles, and Berkeley, pick about the top 12.5 percent of the students in California. Even from this select group of students, 43 percent of the men—that is, men in general, not minority students—and 92 percent of the women did not have enough math when they came to the University of California at Berkeley to take the standard introductory calculus course. And so for all those students, all these areas we're talking about were just off limits from the beginning.

So there is a tremendous problem for minorities and equally for women, which you can follow through their careers, in terms of what fields they can go into, how well they can do in those fields, and so on.

Mr. Harkin: Your statement about Cornell and that Cornell experience, does this have the opposite effect? Would that then lend credence to the argument there ought to be an establishment of minority centers—

Dr. Sowell: No.

Mr. Harkin: —rather than going to traditional . . .

Dr. Sowell: No. I think that's saying that some third party ought to decide that minority students should be in white schools, or saying that some third party ought to decide that minority students ought to be in black schools.

I think the minority students, like the people who received the GI bill, should distribute themselves where they see fit, into such schools as they can get into.

Mr. Harkin: In other words, if I understand you correctly, what you're saying is if we put $36 million in this program in 1 year—that's the upper limit, let's say—do you think that money would be better spent by individual grants rather than going to institutional types of grants, more like the GI bill type of thing?

Dr. Sowell: I would say that, and I would say the distribution I would favor would be one that would put much more emphasis further back in the educational process, to make sure that people have not put whole fields of the academic world off limits to themselves by the time they're in high school.

Mr. Harkin: But as I understand the testimony of Dr. Jackson, the centers would be more or less like the hub of a wheel, with spokes going out to the various high schools and grade schools, providing the basis of support for science education and teaching in the schools.

Dr. Sowell: That is one of the things I had in mind when I spoke of pious hopes. There's nothing in the bill that says the money is contingent on that.

Mr. Harkin: That's true. But that is basically the concept of how it would operate, but it's not written—

Dr. Sowell: I don't know why one would think—for what reason one would think that people who are teaching in a graduate science and engineering program would be the best people to teach at the very low level of math in the elementary and high schools. In fact, if I were to make a wild guess, my guess would be that the people who are at that high level probably have a much more difficult time understanding the math difficulties of a teenage kid—one that was having trouble with the math—than someone who was, let's say, a teacher of math or something for that age level.

I can't believe that just because one is a scientist that one can teach at that low level of math. In fact, I would think, if anything, it would make it much more difficult.

I don't have the view, for example, that the introductory math courses, introductory calculus course, let's say, would be better taught at a major university with a tremendous number of high-prestige scientists. I just don't believe that.

Mr. Harkin: How do you get those grade school and high school students with all of the various institutional barriers they have to getting into science, whether it's teachers they have in the school, the lack of role models they can see to give them the desire, how do you start breaking this—

Dr. Sowell: I think role models will not be a substitute for math. I think if the students have the background they will go on in that. George Washington Carver did not have role models; he was raised by a German couple. So I don't think that's necessary—I think that can be overdone very easily.

I wouldn't want to get into a debate on amateur psychology. But certainly, in terms of skills, what we do know is that the skills are absolutely necessary. We can speculate about role models all we want, visibility, all that sort of thing.

Mr. Harkin: Again, I perceive a difference between engineering and science and things like law. A person with an eighth grade education could become a very good lawyer.

Dr. Sowell: Yes.

Mr. Harkin: You don't need that high school and college education. In fact, you used to be able to read for the law, and things like that.

When you get into math, if you miss a basic math course, you can't go on to algebra or calculus.

Dr. Sowell: That's right.

Mr. Harkin: Or in chemistry, if you're missing basic chemistry courses then you can't go on to the advanced chemistry courses, and one has to be built on the other. I'm concerned that maybe in the social sciences you can leap-frog, as I call it.

Dr. Sowell: You can do it less and less. In economics, if you don't have calculus, for example, you're not allowed to major in economics at UCLA. It's just that simple. It's becoming more so in the other fields, psychology, even sociology. The other areas normally thought of as softer sciences are becoming less soft; they're requiring more statistics. The statistics themselves require more math.

Mr. Harkin: Again, if in establishing these minority centers we do break the cycle and somehow get the people back into the lower levels, the primary and secondary school levels who have a good background in science, to instill in young people—I can't remember who it was who mentioned it; maybe it was Dr. Jackson. But he had one teacher that really instilled in him the desire for chemistry. All of us I think can point to that kind of experience we had in our own educational background.

Perhaps these centers then would develop that kind of a person, to go back and instill in people, especially black people, a desire to stay in math or economics or chemistry or engineering.

Dr. Sowell: I expect if the Government were to make money available to schools contingent upon their ability to raise the mathematical level of their students in general, that you would find them raising the mathematical level of the students in general. I think if you're going to pay them for going through certain motions, they will go through those motions and collect the money.

Mr. Harkin: Dr. Sowell, you have reaffirmed my belief that scientists are about as difficult to agree with one another as farmers. [Laughter.]

Chairman Thornton: Thank you, Mr. Chairman.

Well, the postulation of the issues and the differences of opinion is readily apparent, and the testimony is most valuable in highlighting a full range of differences. That's what we're called upon to do, is to have issues presented, articulated well, and then to see if there are some areas which then emerge which lead to a course of action.

I'd like to explore for just a moment whether there are some areas where there might be agreement.

Dr. Sowell: Yes.

Chairman Thornton: Starting with the statistics of the small proportion of the cadre of outstanding scientists, engineers, professionals, who are drawn from minorities, is it reasonable to assume that there is something deficient in our institutions which leads to, or has not solved a problem of wide participation in these professions?

Dr. Sowell: I'd incline that way, though I wouldn't lean very heavily on that because I don't share the assumption that in the absence of some kind of institutional barriers or arrangements, people would be randomly distributed.

I think what I know of a number of areas would suggest to me that that's the case. If I look at activities totally within the control of the individual, what programs he watches on television, what games he plays, and musical instruments, I don't find that normal or random distribution. That's one reason for my hesitation.

I'm inclined to believe, though, for other reasons, that the institutions are deficient, that they simply don't put the emphasis that they should on subjects like math, and that by not doing so they then bar people, inadvertently as it may be, from many occupations they otherwise might enter and where they might have a lot to contribute.

Chairman Thornton: At least the variation from the results which you would expect from a random sampling though is evidence—it might not be conclusive evidence—that there is something wrong with the institutions. In other words, we're on a proper subject of inquiry here as to—

Dr. Sowell: Yes. I think what's wrong with the institution, though, is likely to be that it doesn't provide enough of certain skills, rather than the people who have the skills don't use them in a certain way because they're not inspired, and so forth.

For example, take the female case such as we have the data for. If only 8 percent of the women who enter college are capable of taking a first-year course in calculus, then we needn't talk about anything else as regards why there are fewer women, for example, in the sciences. That is sufficient unto itself. And no amount of role models is going to do very much for the other 92 percent. I don't have the corresponding data for blacks at the college level, but clearly it would be something approaching that order.

Chairman Thornton: Now, if you do make that first threshold step, that the failure of getting a statistically proportional representation of women, of minorities, in these professions shows a possible deficiency in the utilization of human resources, and skills—

Dr. Sowell: It's a failure to develop the skills.

Chairman Thornton: Yes. If it does then, that calls for some innovative ideas to how to address that problem. I'm trying to see how far we can go in agreement here.

Not between you and me, but between you and the other witnesses.

Dr. Sowell: Sure. The word "innovative" bothers me, aside from the fact it's become fashionable.

Chairman Thornton: Yes.

Dr. Sowell: The schools—I've studied some black schools that have had some very different kinds of results, much better results. I don't find them innovative. I find them just doing things that other schools that get good results also do with their other students.

I'm not willing to say if there's a problem, a serious problem, then we must do something sort of unprecedented, or follow someone's inspired idea. Clearly one must do something, but whether that something would fall under the category of innovative is another matter entirely.

Chairman Thornton: Something different. It's not certainly—innovation is not a new idea. Francis Bacon said in "Novum Organon" that it would be unsound and contradictory to suppose that that which has never been accomplished cannot be accomplished except by means which have not yet been tried.

I think that is as true today as when he said it.

What we are trying to search for here is whether there are things that we can do in adjusting our institutions, and what things we might be able to do, in order to address a problem which I think you and all other witnesses do agree does exist in this area.

Dr. Sowell: Yes. I think that if one is, for example, prepared to put more money at the elementary school level, with the continued flow of money being contingent upon demonstrable results as judged by some independent third party, then I think you can do a great deal.

I think if you're going to have the usual situation where educational programs judge themselves, then where they judge themselves they have an unbroken record of success despite the fact that we find more and more kids in college who can't write, who can't figure, and so on—so I think the crucial thing is whether or not you're going to have any continuous monitoring, either by having independent organizations test for results or by allowing students to have a choice under the sort of GI bill arrangement whereby they decide whether the school's inspiring or not.

We needn't decide in advance once and for all whether the schools are inspiring. The students themselves are perfectly capable of deciding just how inspiring those schools are as compared to other alternatives available to them.

Chairman Thornton: I'm inclined to agree with your suggestion that the success or failure of programs is going to depend upon the degree to which you are able to motivate individual skills and individual development, and that it is not always correct by modeling a program and attempting to put people into that program that you do allow this kind of individual development.

At the same time, I wonder if you might agree with the thrust or not of the testimony previously given by Dr. Jackson that a useful purpose institutionally could be achieved by targeting supportive environments and giving them added capacity to develop this kind of individual skill.

Dr. Sowell: I frankly don't know what that means.

Chairman Thornton: Well, that was what I drew from what his testimony was, that he was seeking to address the problem of targeting supportive environments of existing institutions which did tend to promote intellectual curiosity and development of skills, and to add to those institutions some added capacity for bringing out the kind of individual responses that he believed should—

Dr. Sowell: If those words refer to hopes, I share those hopes. If they refer to any process, they don't refer to any process that I can identify.

Chairman Thornton: OK. I think you've done an outstanding job of focusing upon some of the real intellectual and philosophical problems with which we are grappling here, and there is a need to distinguish between hopes and aspirations and institutions and solutions. I want to thank you for your testimony.

Dr. Sowell: Thank you.

Chairman Thornton: Thank you, Mr. Chairman.

Mr. Harkin: Thank you, Mr. Chairman.
Just one final follow-up question.

Dr. Sowell: Yes.

Mr. Harkin: The chairman's question brought this to my mind. And that is there are various things that will compel a student to take up certain courses or proceed in a certain discipline, and I'm just wondering if because of the affirmative action programs that we have today will that be enough of an economic incentive to inspire minority centers to get into these areas, especially in affirmative action programs that are now developing in engineering and the sciences?
What kind of an impact, economic impact, will that tend to have? Will that tend to solve a great part of this problem?

Dr. Sowell: Well, I must say first that I have never perceived the problem myself, in my own experience, as being one of inspiring minority students to want to go into these fields. I've seen many minority students who do want to go into those fields. Some of them go into those fields and find it very different from what they expected. And certainly they differ from what their previous education has prepared them to cope with.
So I don't think the problem is one of the numbers of inputs. It's a problem of getting survival and success in those fields.
Secondly, as to affirmative action, I'm not sure whether you're referring to hiring or you're referring to educational programs. By affirmative action do you mean affirmative action hiring programs?

Mr. Harkin: Yes.

Dr. Sowell: Or affirmative action education programs?

Mr. Harkin: Affirmative action hiring programs.

Dr. Sowell: That would depend upon the actual impact of those programs. I've done a little research on this myself. The impact seems virtually nil for the period for which I've studied it.

Mr. Harkin: I guess I'm looking at it from an economic standpoint, the supply and demand. What about the demand for minority—

Dr. Sowell: Well, if there were a lack of demand then I would expect to find some unemployment level that would reflect that, and I don't find anything like that.

When I studied, for example, minority faculty as compared to general population faculty, I don't find that minority faculty with given credentials, given publication records, did significantly worse. That is—and also holding the fields constant—that they did significantly worse, or did significantly worse before or after affirmative action than majority faculties with exactly the same credentials.

The big problem is that the minority faculty are distributed rather differently in those fields. They're much more heavily concentrated in the lower-paying fields and had very different credentials. That is, they have a Ph.D. less often, have it from a top institution less often, and so on, for very obvious historical and economic reasons—and that explains the variation that you get.

But, for example, in the study I did, there was something like $600 a year difference between black faculty and white faculty, and yet when you broke that down by fields and you broke that down by these various qualifications, blacks did at least as well as whites in most of the fields. The problem was that blacks were distributed differently.

The same thing is true of women. The major part of the difference between men and women is that men and women are working at different jobs, and that too reflects their educational preparation and what that means in terms of future opportunities.

Mr. Harkin: Mr. Wells, do you have any questions?

Mr. Wells: No, Mr. Chairman.

Mr. Harkin: Mr. Sowell, thank you very much.

Dr. Sowell: Thank you.

[Additional information was submitted in a letter, which follows:]

Center for Advanced Study in the Behavioral Sciences
Stanford, Calif., February 24, 1977

Hon. Ray Thornton

Chairman, Subcommittee on Science, Research and Technology
U.S. House of Representatives, Rayburn House Office Building
Washington, D.C.

Dear Mr. Thornton:

In my testimony before your subcommittee on February 23, and particularly in my reply to your question, I may have left an important point insufficiently clear, and would like to clarify it somewhat now, if I may. You referred to "innovative" methods for teaching black young people the skills needed for mathematical and scientific careers, and pointed out that what has never been accomplished is unlikely to be accomplished, except by methods that have never been tried. The latter proposition is of course correct in itself, but it seems tragic for policymaking that so little has been generally known about educational methods which have been successful in teaching generations of black youngsters the skills they need—and most of these methods have been "traditional" rather than "innovative." The schools in which this has been accomplished have been run by blacks, by whites, by clergy, by public school officials, etc.—in short, by all kinds of "role models." Within walking distance of where we were talking, there was a school which for 85 years (1870–1955) continuously turned out highly trained black youngsters who (1) as a group scored above the national average on IQ tests more than thirty years ago, (2) who were graduating with honors from Ivy League colleges more than half a century ago, (3) who have produced a disproportionate share of all the black pioneers in the whole country, in fields ranging from the military to the academic to the United States Senate. There are similar black schools in New Orleans, in Brooklyn, and in Atlanta, and—unlike the one in Washington—they continue to be successful institutions till this day. After all this, it is by no means a foregone conclusion that either educational "innovations" or amateur psychology are necessary to teach black kids math and science, much less that some particular colleges and universities have the inside track on performing this feat.

A second point that deserves emphasis is the use of "representation" data as a basis for inferences. Implicit in this is the assumption that there would be some approximation of randomness in the distribution of people, in the absence of institutional barriers or social problems, and that such data provide a valid measure of progress in these respects. I happen to believe that there are institutional barriers and social problems for entirely different reasons, but the "representation" data is wholly unpersuasive as evidence, and potentially disastrous as an index for monitoring policy effects. People are not randomly or proportionally distributed, even in activities wholly within their own individual control, such as their choice of card games or television programs. For example, bid whist players are not a random sample of the American population, or even of the black population, within which they are concentrated today, for reasons that go far back into social history. Almost everything that people do depends on a whole mosaic of values and traditions, which differs with the groups to which they belong. Equal opportunities must be created, and that is still a large, unfinished task. But neither logic nor evidence leads to an expectation of statistical proportionality, and reliance on the "body count" approach to policy has great potential for harm, both at the stage of implementing policy and judging the results.

I am taking the liberty of enclosing Xerox copies of some material that bears on the issues in the pending legislation. Both are from my book *Black Education: Myths and Tragedies*. The material from pages 130–31 deals with the pitfalls in special programs for black students on white campuses, and pages 256–59 deal with the black institutions, whose quality and inspiration were promoted at the hearings. My purpose is not to try to convert you to my conclusion on these matters, but to point out why it is hazardous to allow anyone to build his assumptions into the structure of financial incentives, and why individual college students should be supported, so that they can choose their own best options among the educational institutions for which they qualify. This may not be feasible for pre-college education—which is where the problem is concentrated, for mathematical inadequacies here eliminate the bulk of minority and female individuals from scientific fields before they ever set foot on a college campus. The problem is not trying to inspire the 10 percent who still have such an option at that point, but in trying to create such an option for some of the other 90 percent. Some form of results monitoring is clearly needed if the money spent is to lead to educational skills, and math and science are areas where such monitoring should be most feasible, given the standardized content of basic courses and the possibility of objective testing.

On one point I would like to agree with the other witnesses. There is not enough money being proposed to do the full job that needs doing, though it is clearly too much money to let go to waste, or to pay out in exchange for rhetoric and hopes. But the real issue is not whether the proposed sum for planning grants may be wasted, but whether an opportunity will be wasted to confront the very real educational problems of minorities, female and others in scientific areas, and the corresponding waste of the nation's human resources.

Sincerely,

Thomas Sowell

Enclosures (From *Black Education: Myths and Tragedies*)

(first enclosure, pp. 130–31)

Official reports on special programs for black students not only do not tell the whole story, they are themselves a major camouflage effort in many cases. Almost invariably, they are written by people who are involved in the very programs they are evaluating. At the same colleges where official reports paint a glowing picture of success, private discussions among faculty members and administrators often paint a picture of desperate efforts to prevent widespread failure from becoming total disaster. For example, Cornell's special program has been a great success according to its administrators and according to well-planted stories in the press, but a statistical study showed that *one-half* of the black students in it had grade averages so low as to be on some form of academic probation. An *internal* memorandum of this program in January 1971 refers to the "phenomenal attrition rate" among students and proposed a number of substantial changes to cope with it. Similarly, a statistical study at the University of Chicago also found that one-half of the black undergraduates were on some form of academic probation. At the Wayne State University Law School 90 percent of the entering black students either failed or were "not in good standing" at the end of their first year. At most institutions college officials manage to keep such data under lock and key, and confine their public statements on the subject to inspiring generalities.

Does this mean that top quality schools of this sort cannot find black young people who are capable of handling their demanding work? No. That is the primary myth that needs to be exposed. The tragic irony is that current recruiting and admission practices overlook, bypass, and even reject outright very capable black students in favor of less-qualified black students who fit a more fashionable stereotype. It is this policy and philosophy which leads to the educational failures which are either covered up or attributed to "cultural deprivation."

There are many ways in which academic failures can be disguised: (1) students may be steered away from tough courses, instructors, or majors, to easy courses, instructors, or majors; (2) "incompletes" may be handed out instead of failing grades; and/or (3) a student who would otherwise be flunked out of college may be given "another chance." He may even be allowed to "voluntarily" take a leave of absence from the school "temporarily" and never return. In this way, official attrition rates are kept low on paper, regardless of how many students waste years of their lives and leave with lasting scars. At one Big Ten university, a black graduate student was "passed" on his doctoral exams with the "understanding" that he would leave the graduate school and never attempt to write a dissertation for the degree.

(second enclosure, pp. 256–59)

Myth No. 1—There are "good" Negro colleges at the same level as various nationally respected white colleges.

The absence of any objective indices might permit this assertion to sneak by, but using such indices as exist: (1) there is not one black college in which the students' College Board scores average within 100 points of the average at Lehigh, Harpur, Hobart, Manhattanville, or Drew—deliberately picking schools that are not in the Harvard-Yale-MIT category, where scores would average at least 200 points above those at any black college; (2) there is not a black college or university in the country whose library contains one-third as many volumes as the library at Wisconsin, Virginia, NYU, or Texas, or one-tenth as many as at Harvard; (3) there is not a black economics department whose entire staff publishes as many scholarly articles in a year as outstanding individuals publish each year in a number of good departments; (4) there is not one black department anywhere in the country which is ranked among the top twenty in anthropology, biology, chemistry, economics, engineering, English, history, mathematics, physics, political science, psychology, sociology, or zoology. The two black medical schools (Meharry and Howard) have been found to be "among the worst in the nation" and most of the black law schools are "only one jump ahead of the accrediting agencies," while the graduate programs in the arts and sciences at the Negro universities are not even "adequate" by national standards.

There is simply no point talking nonsense about the quality of Negro colleges. None of them ranks with a decent state university, and it is a farce to talk of them in the same breath with any of the schools we normally think of as among the leading academic institutions. No pious phrases from the Carnegie Commission about the "high academic standards" at some Negro colleges or unctuous characterizations of "able and heroic teachers and administrators" by the United Negro College Fund can change the brutal facts. These facts themselves need to be changed—not described in pretty words.

> *Myth No. 2*—The educational shortcomings of the black colleges are an inevitable consequence of the academic deficiencies of their entering black students.

This myth is widely accepted even by many who see right through the first myth. Since it is undeniable that most students in the black colleges have substandard educational backgrounds, this carefully cultivated myth enables colleges to excuse all their own errors, misdirected and counter-productive practices. Despite low proportions of academically capable students, many black colleges have substantial absolute numbers of such students—and do a miserable job of developing their potential. The Jencks and Riesman study found what any informed observer knows, that the black colleges "fail to challenge their ablest students." Often it is precisely these top-level students who are most likely to have a mutually antagonistic relationship with the faculty and the administration—in some cases, even flunking out or dropping out of school. Anyone familiar with the black colleges will have examples come immediately to mind. The bright students are a threat to the whole stultifying process of rote learning, textbook memorization, and similar features of inferior education, and their desire to analyze, criticize, or explore further is a very direct threat to the inadequate faculty members typically found in such institutions. Such students are repeatedly silenced by faculty members unable to cope with their inquiries and insights—too often permanently silenced, as far as intellectual development is concerned. It would be a very worthwhile project to trace the academic fate of black entering freshmen with outstanding qualifications as a test of the apologetic theory that the poor end-product is due to poor raw material. It is significant that this apology has been repeated for generations without ever being tested. In part it is a consequence of the remoteness of white trustees, donors, and legislators from the realities of the black colleges. Nor are these schools simply concentrating their efforts on the less able students. The study by Jencks and Riesman concluded that "these colleges do even less than comparable white colleges to remedy their students' academic inadequacies." In short, they fail both the inadequately prepared and the adequately prepared.

Myth No. 3—The shortcomings of the faculty members at Negro colleges are an inevitable consequence of inadequate financial resources to attract better-qualified scholars.

Here again the attempt is made to blame failure on factors beyond the college's control, rather than on things very clearly within their control. The real failure of the black colleges is not a failure to attract good people, but a failure to keep good people. The faculty turnover rate is phenomenal in the black colleges—with the best-trained and most conscientious teachers often being precisely the ones most likely to leave after one or two years. When people accept a faculty appointment, they know in advance what the salary will be, what the teaching load will be, whether there are research facilities or not, etc. In short, those things which are beyond the college's control are already known and are accepted. What is not known in advance are precisely those things which are within the college's control—the authoritarian administration, the lack of standards, and the demoralizing atmosphere of petty intrigue and favoritism. None of these things is unique to black colleges. But the degree to which they exist there is more than many good people will accept.

Veblen's
Higher Learning
After Fifty Years

Thorstein Veblen told friends that he planned to use the subtitle, "A Study in Total Depravity," for his book *The Higher Learning in America.* Presumably they dissuaded him, for although this phrase appeared in the text[1] when this minor classic was published in 1918, another subtitle was substituted which was only slightly less inflammatory: "A Memorandum on the Conduct of Universities by Business Men." While it shared the elaborate indirection and subtle irony of Veblen's other writings, *The Higher Learning in America* showed less of the witty rapier and more of the angry broad axe. The cool detachment associated with Veblen repeatedly gave way to indignation and even exhortation. Here clearly was something about which he felt deeply, not merely because of his lifetime of work in the university, but because of his commitment to the values and ideals which it was supposed to represent.

THE UNIVERSITY IN THEORY AND PRACTICE

Veblen had a strong sense of the purpose of a university, which in turn reflected his conception of the role of ideas. He opposed the pragmatic view of his contemporaries William James and John Dewey that ideas were primarily instrumental means of achieving some external

Reprinted from the *Journal of Economic Issues* by special permission of the copyright holder, the Association for Evolutionary Economics.

goal. For Veblen "the idle curiosity" was the driving force of intellectual activity. It was this "impulsive proclivity to master the logic of facts" which "urges men to the pursuit of knowledge...."[2] According to Veblen, "a knowledge of things is sought, apart from any ulterior use of the knowledge so gained."[3] This was particularly true of the kind of knowledge developed in and entrusted to the university. He regarded it as the conviction of modern society at large that "'the increase and diffusion of knowledge among men' is indefeasibly right and good."[4] To Veblen, university men were "keepers of the sacred flame"[5] involved in "the quest for truth"[6]—the kind of heady phrases which he would have used only ironically in other contexts. The irksome paraphernalia of the university he characterized as "all this skillfully devised death of the spirit."[7]

Education as an economic investment—a notion which had appeared in Adam Smith and Sismondi long before the modern concern with it[8]—was foreign to Veblen's conception:

> The place of disinterested knowledge in modern civilization is neither that of a means to private gain, nor that of an intermediate step in "the roundabout process of the production of goods."[9]

All those branches of the university which developed skills for personal or social gain were "interlopers" in a field where "irresponsible science and scholarship" should reign. He had no use for "technical and professional schools" whose "animus" was "worldly wisdom" in contrast to the "idle curiosity" of "scientists and scholars."[10] Yet he also opposed the merely decorative acquisition of dead languages and Homeric lore, where these were used as leisure class symbols.[11] Veblen did not deny the social value of training in applied areas; he simply insisted that its "place is not in the university."[12] A university was established for "intangible, immaterial uses,"[13] though he recognized that in practice the typical American university had come to resemble a "department store"[14] with something for everyone. To explain why and how the university had departed from its initial and still avowed goal was a major purpose of *The Higher Learning in America*.

Veblen rejected not only the pragmatic view of instrumental knowledge but the whole rationalistic conception of man on which it was based. Here Veblen was more in the tradition of Burke, Adam Smith, and Sismondi, who argued that man operates on feelings, traditions, and prejudices, whose useful effects—if any—are largely unintended by-products. The idle curiosity produces knowledge and insights which can be turned to good use—indeed, it is more fruitful in this regard than the pragmatic approach[15]—but that is not its driving spirit. In his special field of economics Veblen rejected the dominant conception of a rationalistic economic man responding logically to objective circumstances.[16] Human behavior was based on "conventional, habitual elements"[17] and was sometimes "quasi-tropismatic...."[18] This did not mean that it was chaotic or unpredictable. On the contrary, Veblen saw the pattern of men's thinking as deriving systematically (though unconsciously) from the kind of work they did.[19] In a larger socio-historical context this led to an eventual clash of technically-trained and business-minded men, from which a new social order would emerge.[20] But as regard contemporary trends in higher education, Veblen saw the habitual and largely thoughtless American faith in "businesslike" operation of organizations extended to universities with tragic consequences.

By making the university "a faithful travesty"[21] of business, foreign elements of competition, advertising, serving the customer's tastes, and concern for the current volume and future expansion were intruded into the scholarly enterprise. It was "bad business" to produce a higher level of product than the student customer wanted,[22] and good business to produce complementary products which would please him—sports, fraternities, pageants—as well as to push expansion into related lines of output which would appeal to a wider public, such as watered-down extension courses and dispensing "erudition by mail order...."[23] As a large and expanding multi-product firm, the university had to be concerned with its relations with a large lay public, and to emphasize those features of itself which could be readily understood by those who had no conception of its intellectual mission:

> To the laity a "university" has come to mean, in the first place and indispensably, an aggregation of buildings and other improved real estate. This material equipment strikes the lay attention directly and convincingly; while the pursuit of learning is a relatively obscure matter, the motions of which can not well be followed by the unlettered, even with the help of the newspapers and the circular literature that issues from the university's publicity bureau.[24]

In this context "the exigencies of competitive business" impose a policy of "decorative real-estate, spectacular pageantry, bureaucratic magnificence, elusive statistics, vocational training, genteel solemnities and sweat-shop instruction...."[25] The university, however, never becomes completely and wholeheartedly businesslike. There remains "something of an amiably inefficient and optimistic solicitude for the advancement of learning at large, in some unspecified manner and bearing, some time, but not to interfere with the business at hand."[26]

This is justified by the claims of practicality, by the belief that "in order to serve God in the end, we must all be ready to serve the devil in the meantime."[27] Yet despite a "competitive need of formidable statistics"[28] and "costly stage properties,"[29] much of this activity is simply a result of the university administrators' own "gross ambition for magnitude"[30] and an "unreflecting propensity to make much of all things that bear the signature of the 'practical.'"[31] It is not even a perversion of purpose but a loss of purpose: "Worldly wisdom . . . has become a wisdom of ways and means that lead to nothing beyond further ways and means."[32]

There is, for example, a drive for an "increase of the enrollment and the obtaining of funds by use of which to achieve a further increase."[33] It is not economic pressure but an "aimless utilitarian" outlook[34] that drives schools down this path. The well-endowed institutions follow a policy which "differs in no sensible degree from that pursued by the needier establishments."[35] Even the "potentially independent" institutions engage in the "pathetic clamour for popular renown," for "increased enrollment," and the "race for funds."[36]

The "boyish imitation" of big business[37] is due partly to the general atmosphere of the country and partly to the fact that businessmen dominate boards of trustees who pick presidents after their own image.[38] The "executive heads of these competitive universities" are not of a scholarly bent but are rather "peculiarly open to the appeal of parade and ephemeral celebrity, and peculiarly heedless of the substance of their performance."[39] The office shapes and limits the incumbent. Its conflicting pressures make ambiguity the "dominant note of his official life"[40]; it is an office which will not abide an "ingenuous incumbent."[41] He becomes "an itinerant dispensary of salutary verbiage" at "gatherings of the well-to-do. . . ."[42] At the university he is likely to be preoccupied with "petty intrigue"[43] and with "much fine-spun strategy to be taken care of under cover of night and cloud."[44] The president "must be a man of scrupulous integrity, so far as may conduce to his success, but with a shrewd eye to the limits within which honesty is the best policy. . . ."[45]

Veblen's view of college presidents was paralleled by his opinion of "those chiefs of clerical bureaus called 'deans.'"[46] While high administrative officials "will commonly occupy an advanced academic rank and so will take a high (putative) rank as scholars and scientists," this indicates neither their qualification for office nor the traits which they are likely to exhibit in their work: "They will be selected on the same general grounds of fitness as their chief—administrative facility, plausibility, proficiency as public speakers and parliamentarians, ready versatility of convictions, and a staunch loyalty to their bread."[47]

Part of the problem of the university lay in its thoughtless acceptance of inappropriate business standards, and part in the intrinsic deficiencies of these standards even in their own field. According to Veblen, "the spirit of American business is a spirit of quietism, caution, compromise, collusion and chicane."[48] Universities as "competitors for the traffic in merchantable instruction"[49] follow similar policies. There is need for a "large turnover and quick returns" which eclipses "the uneventful scholastic life that counts toward the higher learning in the long run"[50]; rival universities "bid against one another" for graduate students with fellowships[51] whose stipends are "small and numerous" to produce "a more advantageous net statistical result than a smaller number of more adequate stipends" for "carefully selected men" who might reflect more credit on the institution in the long run.[52] This activity was as futile as it was false. Public relations strategy as "an engine of competition" was a means of achieving "differential gains" between institutions but "has no aggregate effect."[53]

Veblen also noted the defensive side of this public relations activity in avoiding offense to socio-political orthodoxy[54] and concern over "such domestic infelicities" of the faculty members "as might become subject of remark."[55] Political orthodoxy was maintained through faculty selection rather than pressure: "there need be no shadow of constraint during their incumbency."[56]

Against the businesslike pressures of the university is the countervailing fact that "the presence of scholars and scientists of accepted standing is indispensable to the university, as a means of keeping up its prestige." Veblen added:

> The need of them may be a need of their countenance rather than of their work, but they are indispensable, and they bring with them the defects of their qualities. When a man achieves such notoriety for scientific attainments as to give him a high value as an article of parade, the chances are that he is endowed with some share of the scientific animus, and he is likely to have fallen into the habit of rating the triumphs of science above those of the market place. Such a person will almost unavoidably affect the spirit of any academic corps into which he is intruded. He will also, in a measure, bend the forces of the establishment to a long-term efficiency in the pursuit of knowledge, rather than to the pursuit of a reputable notoriety from day to day. To the enterprising captain of erudition he is likely to prove costly and inconvenient, but he is unavoidable.[57]

Thus in the university "the principles of competitive publicity carry with them a partial neutralization of their own tendency."[58]

TEACHING AND SCHOLARSHIP

Veblen saw no conflict between teaching and research, but unlike others of this persuasion who regard scholarship as a prerequisite for good teaching, Veblen saw teaching as a necessary stimulus to good scholarship—which was to him the primary function of a university. Teaching "belongs in a university only because and insofar as it incites and facilitates the university man's work of inquiry. . . . "[59] A professor "cannot without detriment to his work as scientist or scholar serve as a taskmaster or a vehicle of indoctrination."[60] Veblen had no use for the inspirational teacher concept:

> The student who comes up to the university for the pursuit of knowl-
> edge is expected to know what he wants and to want it, without compul-
> sion. If he falls short in these respects, if he has not the requisite interest
> and initiative, it is his own misfortune, not the fault of his teacher.[61]

This approach was of course at the opposite pole from that of a business trying to please and increase its clientele. Veblen's view of that clientele was also at the opposite pole from those who wished to have the schools follow his interests. The fallacy of being guided by the clientele in an enterprise whose *raison d'être* is to change the clientele's thinking would seem to be obvious, but it was missed by such eminent men as John Dewey among Veblen's contemporaries and Adam Smith among his predecessors. Smith, for example, had argued that the deficiencies of universities were due to the professors' not having to compete for students.[62] Veblen argued that the terms of such a competition were likely to reflect the students' deficiencies:

> . . . sane competitive business practice insists on economy of cost as
> well as a large output of goods. It is "bad business" to offer a better grade
> of goods than the market demands, particularly to customers who do
> not know the difference, or to turn out goods at a higher cost than other
> competing concerns.[63]

The same competitive pressures which cause an increase in course output to maintain a creditable "statistical showing" lead also—through cost considerations—to making this output "meagre and threadbare" intellectually, as the faculty are required "to dispense a larger volume and a wider range of knowledge than they are in any intimate sense possessed of."[64] Instead of teaching those things which lie within the scope of "the special aptitudes of the departmental corps,"[65] the businesslike university must offer as full a line of merchandise as its competitors: "Competitive enterprise, reinforced with a sentimental penchant for large figures, demands a full schedule of instruction."[66] This in turn leads to "perfunctory labour" on the part of the faculty and to the students' looking upon academic credits as merely something "to be accumulated for honourable discharge" in four years.[67] These features are particularly present in undergraduate education, and the latter tends to dominate the university as the largest part of the business:

> What counts toward the advancement of learning and the scholarly character of the university is the graduate school, but what gives statistically formidable results in the way of a numerous enrollment, many degrees conferred, public exhibitions, courses of instruction—in short what rolls up a large showing of turnover and output—is the perfunctory work of the undergraduate department, as well as the array of vocational schools latterly subjoined as auxiliaries to this end.[68]

It is not merely that the undergraduate division of the university is likely to be statistically dominant, but because it is part of the same administrative machinery, its administrative methods—"the undergraduate scheme of credits, detailed accountancy, and mechanical segmentation of the work"—are "carried over into the university work proper."[69] This occurs more for psychological than rationalistic reasons:

> The businesslike order and system introduced into the universities, therefore, are designed primarily to meet the needs and exploit the possibilities of the undergraduate school; but, by force of habit, by a desire of uniformity, by a desire to control and exhibit the personnel and their work, by heedless imitation, or what not, it invariably happens that the same scheme of order and system is extended to cover the graduate work also.[70]

Not only the methods of work but the volume of work of the undergraduate college tend to be imitated by the graduate school. The kind of work, faculty, and students who cannot flourish under this arrangement "tend to be lost by disuse and neglect, as being selectively unfit to survive under that system."[71] The kind of student who can survive is the one who can "make the substantial pursuit of knowledge subordinate to the present pursuit of credits, to be attended to, if at all, in the scant interstitial intervals allowed by a strictly drawn accountancy."[72] The "grading or credit system," which "is subject to a ceaseless proliferation of ever more meticulous detail" is one which "progressively sterilizes" individual "initiative and ambition."[73]

The increasing attempts to control and direct the students are paralleled by attempts to control and direct the faculty. From a business point of view, the faculty are employees[74] though in reality a professor cannot be an employee "in respect of his scholarly and scientific work."[75] Academic freedom, for Veblen, was primarily freedom to pursue one's academic duties—"a free hand and a free margin of time and energy"[76]—rather than freedom of an academic individual from reprisal for his nonacademic activities. Even his caustic accounts of pressures for political orthodoxy[77] decry their effects on the quality of university personnel or on "the moral or social sciences"[78] as such, rather than claiming a special privilege for the academic person.

AN ASSESSMENT

Perhaps the most striking thing about *The Higher Learning in America* is its contemporary ring after half a century. It might easily have come off the presses this year. To what extent it appears as satire and to what extent as straight reporting probably depends more on how long the reader has taught, and where, than on the time which has elapsed since its publication. The trends it pointed out have not only continued but have been accentuated by developments since Veblen—the large government and foundation grants for which universities compete, the many "practical" activities on which academic people spend more time, and the clamor for universal higher education[79] which is heard on all sides.

But however prophetic Veblen may have been or however shrewdly he may have observed and characterized the academic world and its foibles, there are still questions as to his analyses of *causes*. Was he right for the wrong reasons, or did his analysis pinpoint the causes as tellingly as the effects?

The central theme of *The Higher Learning in America* is that the defects of the academic system are attributable, in the words of the subtitle, to "the conduct of universities by businessmen." Through their power to grant or withhold gifts, through their power as trustees to pick the university president and through the pervasiveness of business principles in the society at large, businessmen play a large role in American higher education and therefore share a large part of the blame for its shortcomings. Yet by Veblen's own admission the university has never become a wholly businesslike institution; and though he largely ignores differences between schools, there are nevertheless very important differences in the extent to which colleges and universities serve intellectual purposes rather than the idols of the tribe or the marketplace, as well as important differences in the relative influence of businessmen, state legislatures, and religious bodies on the conduct of universities. While pure types are hard to find for experimental purposes, the mixtures vary enough to test Veblen's hypothesis as to the effect of businessmen's influence, though Veblen himself characteristically overlooked the need to have any test for his theories other than intuitive plausibility.

For example, state universities, in which the influence of businessmen is relatively less and that of public opinion as expressed through the state legislature is relatively more, would permit some testing of his hypothesis. So too would church-related institutions in which ecclesiastical influence supplants that of the businessman, or military academies in which still another group has the dominant influence. Does the experience of state universities suggest that they are more or less concerned than others with maintaining an intellectual rather than a narrowly utilitarian view of education, more or less prone to the bureaucratic stultification which Veblen called a "skillfully devised death of the spirit," more or less inclined to be a department store, more or less given to mass production methods, more or less likely to treat the faculty as employees and the students as wards? Although state universities vary considerably among themselves, it seems fairly clear that on the whole they fall below their private counterparts at each level on most of these points. The same can be said in general for church-related schools or military academies. Indeed, the institutions which have come closest to embodying the intellectually liberal ideals which Veblen supported have been precisely those which have been privately endowed by wealthy businessmen and which have received continuing support from the same quarter.[80] No doubt each of them provides some examples of unhealthy influence by the holders of the purse strings, and yet as compared with alternatives of popular, political, military, or ecclesiastical influence, they refute the notion that businessmen are the main cause of the malaise of American education. Foreign commentators on the American scene from Tocqueville to Myrdal have commented on the pervasive American illusions about education which have led to the peculiar features which it exhibits.

The idea that alien "business principles" are too often intruded into the work of the academic world has stronger support, but again it is by no means clear that such principles are more influential in universities with greater businessmen's influence (as trustees, donors, etc.) than in state universities, church-related schools, or military academies. Indeed, the things Veblen found most objectionable are characteristic of *bureaucracies* in general rather than businesses specifically, except insofar as business has acquired bureaucratic dimensions and tendencies. The needless duplication and mutually canceling strategic moves by rival institutions which Veblen denounced in universities are characteristic of governmental, military, ecclesiastical, and other bureaucracies, and of business primarily as it tends to *depart* from the classical economic patterns of business.

The anti-establishment rhetoric of Veblen has been pressed into service by many who espouse educational causes and values completely at variance with his. Certainly the "New Left" demands for a greater student voice in educational policy and course content, for more "teaching" and less "research," for more concern about the "real world" rather than "theories," are all at opposite poles from Veblen. More than anything else, Veblen had a sense of the *purpose* of a university, that it should not prostitute itself for other purposes for which there were other institutions. This contrasts sharply with the unspoken premise of both the academic bureaucrats and their activist opponents that universities should be made to serve various "worthy" purposes, that anything worth doing at all is worth doing in a university.

Veblen's severity with the businessman, and his tendency to attribute the lion's share of academic ills to him, was paralleled by his leniency with the faculty and his tendency to make them merely pawns, accessories, or dupes at worst. Yet universities are influenced in important ways by the goals the faculty pursue—or by the faculty's failure to pursue any goal other than an easy life. That complete academic self-government might degenerate into a mutual tolerance of slipshod performance—the picture Adam Smith gave of the university faculties of his day[81]—was not even considered as a possibility in Veblen's call for abolition of college administrators and trustees.[82] Nor was it acknowledged that any part of administrative overseeing was an attempt—however future or dysfunctional—to make faculty members live up to their responsibilities.

The faculty was never considered by Veblen as a narrow self-interest group with goals different from those of scholarship or teaching. Yet it is obvious that faculty self-selection can mean an opportunity to surround oneself with colleagues who are congenial, rather than with colleagues who best serve the interests of the university, the students, or society. Narrow self-seeking is also evident in the faculty tendency to view academic freedom as a fringe benefit of theirs rather than a feature designed to promote scholarly undertakings, as Veblen viewed it. Thus, despite its name, academic freedom has in practice come to mean primarily freedom to engage in various *non*academic activities, rather than freedom to pursue specifically academic duties according to conscience and integrity[83]—as if freedom from retaliation on the job for one's life off the job were any less desirable for truck-drivers or musicians than for professors.

The Higher Learning in America takes on a special significance when viewed against the background of Veblen's own checkered academic career, his own "domestic infelicities" which were so often "the subject of remark," his early difficulties because he "did not sufficiently advertise the university,"[84] his forced migrations from school to school, and his unpopular courses with low enrollments—from which came a remarkable number of well-known economists. Yet it would be too facile to view his work simply as an apology for his own lack of academic success. Even if such motivation could be established, it would be irrelevant to the larger question of the validity of his arguments. If anything, the fact that the academic system selected out Veblen as unfit to survive should raise further grave suspicions about that system.

NOTES

1. Thorstein Veblen, *The Higher Learning in America* (New York: Sagamore Press, Inc., 1957), p. 192. Cf. Max Lerner, "Editor's Introduction," *The Portable Veblen*, ed. Max Lerner (New York: Viking Press, 1958), pp. 10–11.

2. Thorstein Veblen, ibid., p. 148.

3. Ibid., p. 4.

4. Thorstein Veblen, *The Place of Science in Modern Civilization* (New York: Russell & Russell, 1961), p. 3; Thorstein Veblen, *Essays in Our Changing Order*, ed. Leon Ardzrooni (New York: The Viking Press, 1954), p. 338.

5. Thorstein Veblen, *Essays in Our Changing Order*, p. 340.

6. Thorstein Veblen, *The Higher Learning in America*, p. 106.

7. Ibid., p. 94.

8. Adam Smith, *An Inquiry into the Nature and Causes of the Wealth of Nations* (New York: The Modern Library, 1937), p. 265; J. C. L. Simonde de Sismondi, *Nouveaux principes d'économie politique*, 3rd ed., ed. G. Sotiroff (Geneva and Paris: Edition Jeheber, 1953), 1:131, 254.

9. Thorstein Veblen, *The Higher Learning in America*, p. 146.

10. Ibid., pp. 17–18.

11. Thorstein Veblen, *The Theory of the Leisure Class* (New York: The Modern Library, 1934), pp. 392, 395–96.

12. Thorstein Veblen, *The Higher Learning in America*, p. 14.

13. Ibid., p. 59.

14. Ibid., p. 65.

15. Thorstein Veblen, *The Place of Science in Modern Civilization*, p. 9.
16. Ibid., pp. 73, 245, 251.
17. Ibid., p. 250.
18. Thorstein Veblen, *The Higher Learning in America*, p. 173.
19. Ibid., p. 4; Thorstein Veblen, *Essays in Our Changing Order*, p. 25; Thorstein Veblen, *The Vested Interests and the Common Man* (New York: The Viking Press, 1946), p. 9.
20. Cf. Thorstein Veblen, *The Engineers and the Price System* (New York: The Viking Press, 1954), *passim*.
21. Thorstein Veblen, *The Higher Learning in America*, p. 202.
22. Ibid., p. 85.
23. Ibid., p. 140.
24. Ibid., p. 101.
25. Ibid., p. 128.
26. Ibid., p. 195.
27. Ibid., p. 9.
28. Ibid., p. 141.
29. Ibid., p. 106.
30. Ibid., p. 17.
31. Ibid., p. 141.
32. Ibid., p. 44.
33. Ibid., p. 92.
34. Ibid., p. 176.
35. Ibid., p. 177.
36. Ibid.
37. Ibid., p. 141.
38. Ibid., p. 59.
39. Ibid., p. 178.
40. Ibid., p. 182.
41. Ibid., p. 197.
42. Ibid., p. 187.
43. Ibid., p. 42.
44. Ibid., p. 67.
45. Ibid., p. 66.
46. Ibid., p. 186.
47. Ibid., p. 69.
48. Ibid., p. 51.
49. Ibid., p. 65.
50. Ibid., p. 64.

51. Ibid., p. 95.

52. Ibid., p. 96.

53. Ibid., p. 169.

54. Ibid., pp. 132–37.

55. Ibid., p. 119.

56. Ibid., p. 137.

57. Ibid., p. 128.

58. Ibid., p. 129.

59. Ibid., p. 12.

60. Ibid., p. 14.

61. Ibid.

62. Adam Smith, *The Wealth of Nations*, pp. 717–19.

63. Thorstein Veblen, *The Higher Learning in America*, p. 85.

64. Ibid., p. 83.

65. Ibid., p. 81.

66. Ibid., p. 84.

67. Ibid., p. 75.

68. Ibid., p. 73.

69. Ibid., p. 79.

70. Ibid., p. 73.

71. Ibid., p. 93.

72. Ibid.

73. Ibid.

74. Ibid., p. 67.

75. Ibid., p. 63.

76. Ibid., p. 81.

77. Ibid., pp. 131–37.

78. Ibid., p. 131.

79. Cf. Thomas Sowell, "The 'Need' for More 'Education,'" *AAUP Bulletin*, Winter 1966, pp. 380–84.

80. Most of the outstanding radicals, including Veblen, have taught at precisely such schools.

81. Adam Smith, *The Wealth of Nations*, pp. 717–19.

82. Thorstein Veblen, *The Higher Learning in America*, p. 202.

83. So pervasive has this derivative notion become that in some universities there is far less danger from voicing the "wrong" political views than from giving low grades, teaching courses that are considered "too tough," etc. Pressures in these latter areas are far less likely to call forth instant and universal indignation over breaches of academic freedom.

84. Joseph Dorfman, *Thorstein Veblen and His America* (New York: The Viking Press, 1945), p. 174.

Academic Tenure*

One thing that troubles me about tenure is determining its rationale and purpose. Many of the good things that go on under a tenure system, and that such a system is supposed to encourage—for example, scholarly research and high-quality teaching—would, I presume, exist in the absence of tenure.

Tenure is essentially a differential privilege; that is what we are actually discussing today. The point about job security strikes me as totally without foundation. What tenure in fact accomplishes is a redistribution of insecurity. Those with it become more secure but those without become more insecure, as they must now absorb *all* changes in employment. And so the real question is: What are we trying to do with tenure aside from preserving it for those who have it? Is tenure in truth a fringe benefit like golf club membership or saunas for the faculty? Or is it something that is peculiar to the needs of this profession?

Although academic freedom is this famous, often-cited something, I am continually amazed at how seldom people define what they mean by the term. Does academic freedom mean freedom in your academic duties, freedom to carry out those duties according to your own professional discretion? I have found that the people who use this term rarely

*(Discussion at the University of San Diego Law School)

Reprinted from "Motivating the Law School Faculty in the Twenty-First Century: Is There Life After Tenure," *Journal of Legal Education* (1979).

apply it to this type of freedom. Instead they use it to mean *non-academic* freedom for academics—that is, freedom from reprisal for one's non-academic activities, whether political, social, or whatever. The term is most often used in this sense. Why then should this kind of freedom be available to teachers but not to truck drivers or chorus girls?

Insofar as there is merit in the academic freedom notion, it is a way of preserving diversity or fostering bold, creative thinking. Thus the correct question is: Does tenure accomplish these laudable goals? If we look at other occupations that do and that do not enjoy this kind of job security, do we find diversity and creativity? Think for a moment of the civil service!

As an economist, I am also interested in the cost-effectiveness of tenure. Undoubtedly good things result from tenure. But bad things also result. Therefore, what stikes me as strange are the categorical terms in which this system is usually discussed. Throughout life we employ incremental decisionmaking, but for some odd reason we have allowed an either-or process to be used in educational institutions. If tenure is denied, job security is minimal; if it is granted, job security is almost total. Only blatant misbehavior, gross incompetence, or death results in termination.

Now let us look at duplication, the most obvious cost of the tenure system. If a tenured faculty member does not teach well, an institution may be forced to hire someone else to teach that person's subjects— despite the fact that its supporters assert that tenure encourages careful selection processes.

One of the real problems of any group of people trying to rise out of poverty is that so many benefits have been created for incumbents that before anyone is hired, prospective employees have to demonstrate an extremely high probability of success. At one time a person who had just come off the boat, who did not even speak English, and who had no skills could walk into an employer, be hired, and go to work immediately under a piece-rate system. The employer really did not care if the new arrival produced half as much or twice as much as other employees, for earnings were based on the amount of production. We have now established so many benefits for incumbents that less willingness is manifested to hire people in the first place. In the end, all decisionmaking is biased in favor of incumbents; decisions are by definition made by incumbents. Therefore, what happens to a profession or to any subset of people over a long span of time is not important, for those who create institutions are those who are present at any given time.

What, if anything, makes tenure cost-effective? It is an untaxed, in-kind benefit. On the one hand, tenure is an advantage in that the institution may transfer this benefit to the individual without tax consequences. On the other hand, because tenure is an in-kind benefit, its value to each individual differs. People cannot adjust tenure to their particular tastes as they can adjust money. The crucial question here is: To whom is tenure of greater value? Obviously the more capable a person is, the less she or he needs tenure. To someone who, for example, has just received the Nobel Prize, tenure must have close to zero value. However, to someone who has achieved little distinction in his or her field, tenure is, of course, of great value. Thus it makes a great deal of difference what kind of person is involved.

If a person is a very bold person, the kind we want to promote, the kind who is supposed to add spice to the academic atmosphere, tenure has little value. For a very cautious or timid person, it has great value. In fact, I think that the answer to the question of why we do not find diverse, bold, or innovative people dominating the civil service in any country is that we have created a benefit attaching to civil service positions that is of enormous value precisely to timid, uncreative people. It is true that when some people are given protection, they become bolder. However, it is also true that making timid people bold is difficult. Once you have hired timid people, how do you make them bold? You do not accomplish this transformation by granting tenure, so you give them the other benefits—for example, pay raises, institutional support services for research, and peer approval. But all these are also benefits that may be lost—things a timid person may worry about losing. Thus you continue to pay a very high price for a very low return.

Book Reviews

Private Black Colleges at the Crossroads by Daniel C. Thompson. Westport, Conn.: Greenwood Press, Inc., 308 pages, $11.50.

Black Educators in White Colleges by William Moore, Jr., and Lonnie H. Wagstaff. San Francisco: Jossey-Bass, Inc., 226 pages, $8.75.

Both these books are hybrids. They combine the results of surveys with a considerable amount of editorializing. *Private Black Colleges at the Crossroads* is a quietly thoughtful book. *Black Educators in White Colleges* is more brassy, "relevant," and often reckless. Perhaps nowhere is it more reckless than when it says of itself, "this book should be required reading." However, it does contain enough substance to be worth a discriminating reading by those with the patience for continually separating wheat from chaff.

In *Private Black Colleges at the Crossroads*, Professor Daniel C. Thompson of Dillard University develops the theme that the private black colleges have made a unique contribution to the education of American Negroes, and indirectly to American society as a whole; have done this with grossly inadequate financial support while drawing upon

Reviews of *The Education of Black People: Ten Critiques, 1906–1960*, by W. E. B. DuBois (edited by Herbert Aptheker), and *The Education of Black Folk: The Afro-American Struggle for Knowledge in White America*, by Allen B. Ballard, are reprinted by permission from the *Journal of Higher Education*. Copyright ©1974 by the Ohio State University Press.

a pool of underprepared students from inferior Southern schools; are now faced with severe financial problems threatening their survival, largely as a result of increased competition from white institutions and from *public* black institutions; but still have an important role to play and need to redirect themselves and to receive additional funds in order to fulfill these new roles.

In the course of developing these arguments, Thompson explores at length the social backgrounds of both students and faculty at the private black colleges, their aspirations and behavior in the academic setting, the dominant educational theories and practices of these schools, the overwhelming power of administrators, and the background influence of the trustees. All in all, it is an informative analysis of the private black colleges—much of it applicable to black colleges and universities in general—and it should be viewed as such whether or not one accepts his plea for the continued existence of these institutions.

While Thompson argues for their survival and growth, he unflinchingly portrays the deficiencies, flaws, and perversities of the black colleges. They have "generally weak faculties, far below average student bodies, and inadequate, often sterile, academic programs. . . ." Their libraries are grossly substandard. Their campuses have "an unnaturally easy, relaxed, nonchalant academic atmosphere" in which even "their most capable and talented students make no sustained effort to succeed in college beyond the mere passing of a required program of courses." Even those students planning to go on to graduate school feel no urgency about being prepared, "because they believe that certain rules would simply be set aside for them."

The faculty suffer from poor qualifications (only 25 percent hold a doctorate, including suspect doctorates from foreign universities), low morale, and high turnover. A mere 4 percent have ever been published in scholarly journals. Far from welcoming progress, many faculty members are afraid of what would happen to them "if their colleges found enough funds to significantly improve the faculty." All real power is concentrated in the college president, who is typically "authoritarian," "arbitrary," and "capricious" and surrounds himself with weak and incompetent subordinates. The trustees also come in for criticism, both for being out of touch with education and social reality, and for failing to raise any substantial money for improvement.

Despite all this, Thompson struggles manfully to vindicate these colleges historically and to show why they should survive and flourish. In doing so he fights various straw men, pointing out that test scores are not everything, that Ph.D.'s are not everything, that publications are not everything—and elaborating the well-known reasons why the black colleges do not rate well by such measures. He blames much of the black colleges' troubles on their imitating something he calls "the Ivy League model" of education by fact memorization. This model may not ring a bell for those with personal experience in Ivy League education, though it certainly describes the educational approach of the black colleges. One of the most frequent arguments used by Thompson to justify the survival of black colleges is that these colleges educated the majority of black people who have a higher education today, including those who have achieved intellectual distinction. Such reasoning could as easily "justify" the continued existence of segregated and inferior public schools—for most educated Negroes, including the leading black intellectuals, came out of these kinds of institutions.

Thompson laments that black colleges "can't get essential help because they do not measure up—and they can't measure up without essential help." The implication is that money is the way out of this vicious cycle. Yet some heavily financed attempts to advance selected black institutions have led to little more than higher salaries and better surroundings for carrying on the same level of education. Thompson's own bleak picture of the intellectual isolation of scholars in black institutions gives one clue as to why money cannot attract either black or white academics in the numbers needed to make an impact. The authoritarian administration, the confused or belligerent students, and the general anti-intellectual atmosphere cannot be bought out with money.

Black Educators in White Colleges is a smaller and much simpler book, though jazzed up with rhetorical flourishes. Its theme is that black academics are unhappy about many things in white institutions; the things they want and don't have are the result of white racism; and wherever the numerical "representation" of blacks is low, it is due to racial discrimination, and any other explanation deserves only contempt. The logic of the numbers leads the authors to single out as especially discriminatory the two-year community colleges, and such places as Montana, South Dakota, Utah, and American Samoa. They note in passing that some black academics refuse to go for interviews in places where there are virtually no other blacks living already, but they miss the larger point: that minority individuals may *choose* to enter or not enter some situations, that it is not all a matter of other people's decisions, "exclusions," and "discrimination."

For example, black academics may *prefer* four-year colleges to two-year colleges, and this may be one significant reason why they are underrepresented in the latter, especially in places with virtually no black communities. To hold fast to the racial percentage test would require us to believe that among two-year colleges, those in Alabama and Mississippi are less discriminatory or "racist" than those in Montana and Utah. It is rare to find, in most aspects of life, that people are distributed by race, sex, etc., in proportion to their numbers in the general population. Tons of survey research tell us how participants in all kinds of voluntary activities differ by race, sex, income, education, and age. The idea that people are randomly distributed is a triumph of *a priori* ideas over common evidence.

The data presented by Moore and Wagstaff indicate another reason for the underrepresentation of black academics in white institutions: it is their generally less prolific rate of publication and their lesser academic credentials. According to Moore and Wagstaff's own survey, about two-thirds of the black academics in four-year colleges (and 83 percent of those in two-year colleges) "have not written a single article." More than three-quarters have never even *reviewed* a book, much less written one. More than 80 percent of the black academics in four-year colleges *lack* a Ph.D. Anyone familiar with the bitter history of black Americans will understand why so few have thus far acquired the tangible evidences of scholarship necessary for a viable academic career. But given the facts, "underrepresentation" is hardly a basis for the sweeping conclusions and shrill denunciations that dominate this book—and, indeed, dominate a large portion of the literature and underlie official government policy on affirmative action.

Moore and Wagstaff repeatedly denounce the academic emphasis on publications and credentials. Whatever the merits of the "irrelevance" claim, the call for new criteria is very different from showing that the old criteria are deliberate exclusions, particularly since they date from an era when there were virtually no black academics to be excluded. While Moore and Wagstaff are quite free in their use of words like "elitist," "racist," and "psychotic," they suddenly become squeamish about another blunt word, "quota." They invoke the recently popular notion that "quota" means absolutely rigid numerical requirements, so that if affirmative action policy allows any flexibility at all, a quota can be disclaimed. Yet far from being an obscure new technical term, "quota" is a very old, common word whose meaning was not a subject of controversy before and is still not a subject of controversy in any other area. The essence of a quota is that certain criteria are *numerical* rather than *qualitative*.

To say that "body count" reasoning does not establish racism is not to deny the existence of racism in the academic world or elsewhere. The tragic fact is that racism is still far more pervasive than most white Americans admit, and this book points out some of its patterns, as seen not only by the authors but by their thousands of survey respondents. These descriptive impressions and analyses are among the most useful parts of the book. There are also related problems faced by black academics: nonacceptance by colleagues, intellectual isolation, insubordination by whites on the staffs of black administrators (wittingly or unwittingly encouraged by the attitudes of higher white administrators), and the ever-nagging doubts of the black academic as to why he was hired. The tragedy is that none of these problems is likely to be helped by the kind of policies advocated by Moore and Wagstaff, and many will be aggravated.

The authors rightly point out that there are so few blacks with Ph.D.'s that if every such individual were hired by white colleges and universities—a 100 percent drain of black institutions, government, and the private sector—the net result would be only two or three blacks hired per white institution. The conclusion they draw is that resistance to affirmative action stems from white paranoia, since blacks could not displace many whites even under the most extreme conditions. But another interpretation is that academic institutions are being asked to undergo a convulsive change in procedures, criteria, and power distribution (faculty versus administration) in order to produce gains which can only be minuscule. Moore and Wagstaff themselves show how phony recruiting activity is generated to "keep the Feds off our back."

An even more grim prospect is that the present period of severe academic retrenchment under financial pressure—which is independent of minorities, women, or affirmative action—may lead the many white academics who *must* be refused jobs or promotions to blame the tiny fraction of black academics for their troubles. In their preface, the authors refer (in a different context) to "wounds that will take generations to heal." Quotas have the potential for creating such lasting bitterness.

Does this mean that nothing constructive can be done about the serious educational and social problems discussed in these books? It does not. The question is whether policies should be directed at symptoms or at underlying problems—and whether the policies shall represent prepackaged "solutions" or mechanisms which allow individuals to work out their own destinies. For example, academic financial aid could be vested in black students themselves, to be used at whatever institutions they chose, regardless of what their choices would mean in terms of body count at Harvard, Dillard, or anywhere else. As for black academics, not only are more young, black Ph.D.s coming along, they include some intellectually impressive individuals who can doubtless do much to change the grim statistics and the degrading stereotypes of today.

They deserve something better than a legacy that renders their competence suspect.

The Education of Black People: Ten Critiques, 1906–1960 by W. E. B. DuBois, Herbert Aptheker (ed.). Amherst: University of Massachusetts Press, 1973, xii + 171 pages, $10.00.

The Education of Black Folk: The Afro-American Struggle for Knowledge in White America by Allen B. Ballard. New York: Harper & Row, 1973, xii + 173 pages, $6.95.

It would be hard to imagine two more contrasting books on the same subject. W. E. B. DuBois' ten essays on black education span half a century; Allen Ballard's book is very contemporary, not only in content but in rhetoric. DuBois' essays are penetrating and passionate, and yet striving for balance and understanding of those whose philosophy differed from his own—including his historic adversary, Booker T. Washington. Ballard's writing, on the other hand, is dominated by the rhetorical style of the Left in the 1960s—substituting innuendoes for insight, self-righteousness for passion, and of course smearing all who disagree and twisting their words beyond recognition. Both books are highly critical of the role of whites in black education, but while DuBois' central focus is always on blacks, and what is educationally best for them, Ballard's preoccupation is with "Whitey's" sins, his obligations, and his vulnerabilities. DuBois was a great polemicist, in the service of various positive beliefs and schemes, rather than a point-scorer whose main concern is his adversary or the grandstands.

DuBois' early essays deal, obliquely or directly, with educational issues deriving from his general controversy with Booker T. Washington. These essays help to clarify somewhat the scope and substance of the differences between DuBois and Washington. Together with the recently published *Booker T. Washington Papers* (and Louis Harlan's biography), they paint a very different picture from the stereotype often presented of these two opposing giants. Both men understood and accepted the need for *both* vocational training and academic higher education. They differed in emphasis and tactics. The growing bitterness of their conflict cannot be explained by the differences in their philosophical positions. The earlier DuBois, at the time of his controversies with Washington, was relatively moderate as compared to the later, Marxist DuBois who is celebrated by today's militants. Moreover, as Washington's recently published papers reveal, his later conciliatory speeches and writings concealed major clandestine efforts by Booker T. Washington to secure the civil rights and political advancement of blacks. In short, the differences between the two men, at the time of their historic conflict, were not very large—certainly smaller than the differences between various leaders in other ethnic groups who managed to cooperate for common goals. Any full explanation of the depth of antagonism between DuBois and Washington must include these two men's personal, temperamental differences and the fact that DuBois was descended from the black elite who were free well before the Civil War, while Booker T. Washington was "up from slavery" and much more in touch with grassroots Negroes than the aristocratic DuBois could ever be.

DuBois' telling criticisms of the vocational education philosophy epitomized by Booker T. Washington and Tuskegee Institute included both their educational and their socio-political weaknesses. Educationally, vocational training meant in practice a training in methods which were rapidly becoming obsolete. The "practicality" emphasized by Washington was little more than glorified shortsightedness. Socially and politically, Washington's approach was much more acceptable to the white South and to conservatives generally. DuBois eloquently attacked this as selling the black birthright for a mess of porridge. He denounced those who would "teach black men only such things and by such methods as are momentarily popular," and declared that the purpose of education was "not to make men carpenters but to make carpenters men." DuBois recognized "a measure of truth" in the vocational education philosophy and himself preached many of the same homely virtues preached by Booker T. Washington: cleanliness, thrift, hard work, and technical knowledge. However, DuBois opposed "a philosophy of lying by word or deed for the sake of conciliation."

DuBois argued that black students came to college "with souls that have been hurt and crushed" by oppressive racial laws and practices, and therefore needed "inspiration and light." He said that American Negroes had "lost their own social heritage" and that Negro colleges should attempt to recapture it by approaching education from a racial perspective—but expanding from this beginning "toward the possession and the conquest of all knowledge." In his latter and more radical phase, DuBois called for "a re-examination of the old, of the European, and of the white," but even in this later period he rejected the idea of "teaching Negro science or merely Negro history or Negro mathematics."

These esays make it possible to follow the metamorphosis of DuBois from a defiant young liberal to an embittered Marxist in his old age. Throughout, his was a finely trained and subtle mind, even when most wrongheaded, and there is something to be learned from each essay. Critics and commentators have often contrasted the young DuBois who urged the education of the "talented tenth" of blacks and the later DuBois who spoke of "the masses." Yet, whatever his changing philosophical bent or rhetorical style, DuBois argued throughout his life that black colleges and universities should become centers for promulgating a social philosophy and a social blueprint, as well as developing intellectual disciplines. But, early and late, DuBois also warned against propaganda in the name of education and urged that all philosophies be examined. There was no attempt to reconcile this view with the view that education should inspire certain beliefs and promote certain lines of action. The indoctrination and activist role of higher education grew to central importance as DuBois became more Marxist in his later years—and with it the role of the college-trained elite in planning the lives of their fellow man grew even beyond what was envisioned for the "talented tenth." Elitism now called itself equality, but was more elitist than ever.

The tragedy of the DuBois-Washington conflict was not simply that one man was wrong on this point and the other was wrong on another point. That is inevitable among human beings. The tragedy was that one man—Booker T. Washington—was regarded by white America as "the" black spokesman, and all opposing ideas from other blacks, such as DuBois, were disregarded, deflected, or stamped out. The tragedy was not in the particular man who was chosen for this role, but that *any* man should have been chosen for such a role. In a more openly competitive situation, the best ideas of a whole range of thinkers could have been utilized, instead of putting on any one man the impossible burden of being right on the enormous range of complex issues involved.

To turn from DuBois' essays to Ballard's *The Education of Black Folk* is to move forward in time and backward intellectually. While Ballard's book has a few interesting statistics and occasional insights, it lacks the clear ring of passionate sincerity and honest advocacy which runs through DuBois' writings. Instead there are debater's tactics, including the labeling of opponents, shifting the bases of argument, simple *obiter dicta* on the "real" reason for this or that behind the "camouflage" or "smokescreen," and repeated assertions that "it is no accident" that this or that happened—the only choice apparently being between Ballard's special explanations and pure random chance.

Considerable space is devoted to defending "open admissions"—in which Ballard was deeply involved at C.C.N.Y.—largely on grounds of the guilt and atonement of white institutions. The distribution of black students is presented as a problem of how the leading institutions should maintain a certain body count of blacks rather than as a problem of how black students should best be distributed to maximize their own educational benefit. There is virtually no student of any color who cannot meet the normal standards at *some* school out of the great variety of institutions found among the 3,000 colleges and universities in the United States. Why students must be deliberately mismatched with institutions in order to present a certain statistical picture is a question never answered—or even faced—by Ballard. Given the *a priori* commitment to a given institutional demographic profile, Ballard proceeds to show ways in which high-pressure, research-oriented institutions can accommodate these demands by methods which amount to becoming something *other* than high-pressure, research-oriented institutions. The idea that there are different institutions for different purposes and different kinds of students is never dealt with.

DuBois' essays are enduring encounters with the great issues of black education. Ballard's book is a peculiarity of our time. Indeed it represents a fashion which reached its peak in the late 1960s and is now visibly receding, as its bitter consequences begin to overshadow its glittering words.

Index